HEART & SOUL

Higher Education Action Research Techniques & Strategies of University Leadership

by

Joseph Martin Stevenson, Debra A. Buchanan, Melissa Druckrey, Jeton McClinton & Karen Wilson-Stevenson

Joseph Martin Stevenson

Karen Wilson-Stevenson

HEART & SOUL

Higher Education Action Research Techniques & Strategies of University Leadership

by

Joseph Martin Stevenson, Debra A. Buchanan, Melissa Druckrey, Jeton McClinton & Karen Wilson-Stevenson

ACADEMICA PRESS
WASHINGTON~LONDON

Library of Congress Cataloging-in-Publication Data

Names: Stevenson, Joseph Martin, author. | Buchanan, Debra A., author. | Druckrey, Melissa, author. | McClinton, Jeton, author. | Wilson-Stevenson, Karen, author.
Title: Heart and soul : higher education action research techniques and strategies of university leadership /
Joseph Martin Stevenson, Debra A. Buchanan, Melissa Druckery, Jeton McClinton, Karen Wilson-Stevenson
Description: Washington : Academica Press, 2020. | Includes references and index.
Identifiers: LCCN 2020937880 | ISBN 9781680531688 (hardcover) | ISBN 9781680531695 (paperback)

Copyright 2020 Stevenson, Joseph /

DEDICATION

For the faculty, students and staff at all Historically Black Colleges and Universities (HBCUs), and other Minority Serving Colleges and Universities -- *"Still Making America Great"*

and

Dr. Richard A. Schmuck
Righteous-Reckoning Researcher
and Super Action Hero in Higher Education
-JMS

Chairs, Deans, and Vice Presidents,
Tuskegee University

Dr. Melva Williams and Dr. Herman Felton
Higher Education Leadership Foundation

and

Dr. George T. French
President
Clark Atlanta University

No action without research, no research without action.
Kurt Lewin (1948)

*"Mostly" (an adverb), we should put our hearts and
souls into administrative and academic decision-making for
measurable, corrective actions to support the fundamentals and
foundations of academic governance*
-JMS

CONTENTS

FIGURES ix
FOREWORD xi
SECTION A 1

1. BACKDROP FOR AMERICAN HISTORICALLY BLACK
UNIVERSITIES AND COLLEGES AND HIGHER EDUCATION 3

2. PREVIEW, OVERVIEW
AND HISTORY OF THE "AR" IN HEART 23

3. NEW PARADIGMS AND
PARAGONS FOR HIGHER EDUCATION LEADERS 33

4. DESCRIPTION OF SCOPE
AND SEQUENTIAL FRAMEWORKS FOR HEART 41

SECTION TWO 139

1. SELF REFLECTIONS AND CONTINUOUS IMPROVEMENT
FOR TEACHING -INSTRUCTION-CLASSROOM 141

2. ACTION RESEARCH METHODS FOR TEACHING-
INSTRUCTION-CLASSROOM 149

3. PROACTIVE AND RESPONSIVE ACTION RESEARCH
TEACHING- INSTRUCTION-CLASSROOM 169

4. COOPERATIVE AND COLLABORATIVE WORK-GROUP
PROCESSES FOR TEACHING-INSTRUCTION-CLASSROOM 193

5.
FINAL COMMENTS AND CAUTIONS FOR HEART 239
BIBLIOGRAPHY 243
APPENDICES 251
INDEX 263
ABOUT THE AUTHORS 267

FIGURES

Figure 1	Three, Days, Thirteen Steps, Twenty-Three	11
Figure 2	Oscillating from the NOW to the NEXT to the NEW	36
Figure 3	Force Field Analyses	145
Figure 4	Situation, Target, Path-Plan-Procedure-Project-Proposal Concepts	145
Figure 5	Potential One-on-One Collaborations	199
Figure 6	Typical Face-to-Face Workgroups	201
Figure 7	Campus-Wide Stakeholder Action Research	205
Figure 8	Faculty-Staff-Student-Stakeholder Taskforces	206
Figure 9	Questions for One-On-One Interviews	211
Figure 10	Themes in the Data	212
Figure 11	Changes for Charleston College	212
Figure 12	Special Survey of Charleston College Student Athletes	214
Figure 13	Greater Good Problems	220
Figure 14	Action Ideas at Greater Good College	221
Figure 15	Results from the Walker Advisory Board Working with the Expert	225
Figure 16	Hopes and Concerns of the Monterey Bayou Faculty	232
Figure 17	Ways Data are Collected from Monterey Bayou Faculty	232
Figure 18	Key Points to Refine On-line Instruction at Southeastern	234
Figure 19	Three Open-Ended Interview Questions	235
Figure 20	Taskforce Recommendations	236

FOREWORD

Higher education is undergoing profound change at an unprecedented pace in today's academic marketplace. From the perspectives of the writers, this accelerating and precipitating change has motivated us as passionate observers of academe to read well-chosen publications about meeting demands and responding to needs among our nation's historically Black universities and colleges (HBCUs). We have captured the essence of expediting the critical analysis processes needed to confront the challenges of academic administration, finance, student life, technology, and other areas in the academic enterprise. Today's administrators and academicians must be able to make balanced decisions based on a methodology that is compendious, laconic, unambiguous, clear, and credible. The authors have provided this methodology based on their collective experiences in perhaps the toughest sector of the academic marketplace – the HBCU sector.

The timing of this *savvy* book could not be better. Given the recent media coverage about controversial and debatable decision-making at institutions of higher learning, this book can serve as a resource for meeting institutional challenges, approaching them with sequential structure, getting key stakeholders involved in *analytics (patterns) & informatics (processes)* and formulating vetted recommendations for future arbitration. The action research process for making these tough decisions with **HEART & SOUL** provides a collaborative convergence to advance the process expeditiously, judiciously, and strategically from a collegial examination of facts and issues. This process supports the widespread advocacy in higher education for fostering organizational learning, leveraging human capital, institutionalizing human empowerment, and growing learning communities of practice for success.

The development of this desk guide is driven by a need to probe decision-making prisms that are often overshadowed by political expediency, personal agenda, power positioning, partial ideologies, personal comfort or convenience, and other institutional inhibitors that cloud decision-making centered from thought balance, data authentication, internal consistency, vetted validation, and verifiable collaboration -- in brief, "truth.". -- The Authors

SECTION A

1.
BACKDROP FOR AMERICAN HISTORICALLY BLACK UNIVERSITIES AND COLLEGES AND HIGHER EDUCATION

This book (desktop), primarily for stakeholders and audiences at historically Black universities and colleges (HBCUs), introduces the general concepts of diagnostic, prognostic and prescriptive action research for *data-driven decision-making* by college and university administrators who are constantly trying to make daily decisions to advance their campuses in a marketplace that has become penetrated with competitiveness and unprecedented with growing global demands and accelerating societal needs. We consider this book's content and context to be a work in progress as challenges in higher education emerge, manifest, evolve, and change in the academic marketplace and space. A unique feature of our book is the powerful use of verbs and adverbs to drive and vet collective leadership actions at America's treasured HBCUs. While adverbs such as: very, enough, really, instead, especially, exactly, soon, hopefully, essentially, obviously, significant, and merely are often used in academic language and lexicon, too often we do not capture them in clearly measurable context and content. This is essential for data-driven discourse within an academic institution with student learning at the center --- rightfully so. The Appendices of this publication are helpful in this regard.

All universities and colleges can leverage with and profit from this convenient desktop guide for day-to-day leadership challenges and management issues. Leadership is simply a matter of matching the right idea to the right problem at the right time in the correct way (Bolman and Deal, 1984). The search engine, *Questia* (2013) recently recognized that "higher education administration is the provision of instructional leadership and the day-to-day management of colleges and universities...most higher education administrators begin their careers as teachers and prepare for advancement into education administration." We have found that higher education faculty are not necessarily trained in administrative decision-making, yet their input, their involvement and their engagement is so important to academic governance. Section one of this desktop guide is organized by: (a) initially providing an environmental profile of a particular sector in higher education; (b) introducing some of the principles for diagnostic and data driven making for higher education action research; (c) giving an overview for the history of higher education action research; (d) suggesting new paradigms and paragons for higher education leadership; and (e) recommending administrative frameworks, processes and thirteen steps for higher education action research.

Our culminating thirteen steps in section one of the book provide a prototype for campus administrators to consider; however, we strongly encourage administrators of our book to design and develop their own prototype based on institutional capability, resources, capital, infrastructure, capacity, and environment. The hypothetical scenarios in our book are different but the specific suggested steps are similar. While section one of the book focuses on action research for administrative decision-making for solving problems, responding to concerns, resolving issues or addressing other institutional challenges, the second half of the book focuses on using action research for self-reflection, classroom intervention and other areas that contribute to the "professorial" development of the administrator. We recommend two additional books for the readers that should serve as complementary and companion information resources to this book. They are:

Given the perplexing, perpetuating and persistent challenges that are often specific to American minority-serving colleges and universities, we are strongly encouraging that these institutions, in particular, examine these above referenced books and our action research concepts for increasing student persistence toward degree completion and graduation; improving alumni and constituent relations; fundraising and external relationship building; fine-tuning and refining financial stewardship; enhancing media relationship building; improving athletic administration and academic compliance; implementing support services and infrastructure for student life; diversifying the campus culture and climate; and developing new academic program innovations on campus, online and in their targeted community market share. The *American Treasures* book uses current research data and interviews to present a cogent discussion of strategies and tactics needed to keep the HBCU community a healthy and vital component of American educational life. The threats and problems of intuitional life are not glossed over, rather they are discussed within the parameters of successful planning and implementation.

Our premise in this book is that to be an effective unit administrator, one must also be an effective academician in the classroom. Thus, section two will culminate with: (a) addressing self-reflection and continuous improvement for professional development; (b) reviewing the differences between traditional research and action research; (c) profiling methods for proactive and responsive action research for classroom purposes; (d) recommending some principles for cooperative research; (e) concluding with overall final comments about action research and forewarning our desktop guide users with some cautions and other considerations. In other words, the first half deals with institutional-action decision-making in the workplace from an ***administrative*** perspective and the second half deals more with academic decision-making in the classroom-action from a ***faculty*** perspective. Appendices A, B, and C (Livingston, 1980) of our desktop guide describe verbs that can be used in action research. The general concepts from this desktop guide grew out of the progressive initiation of "decision-making units," or "DMUs" later described in this desk guide, and the successful implementation of knowledge management and action research at a historically Black research-intensive university in the Deep South (Stevenson, 2003).

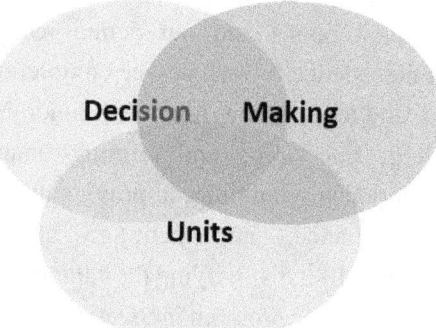

We believe our recognition for bold new paradigms, paragons and parameters for higher education administrators and faculty, along with action research, can improve the internal operations, academic governance, and administrative practices on the modern campus -- particularly given the wealth, breadth, and plethora of available technological resources and social media algorithms. We believe that, as proved at institutions of higher learning where we have worked, many administrative decisions can be made more instantaneously, promptly, speedily, directly, effectively, efficiently, and forthwith in the context of *"tout de suite"*. Indeed, quite often, dealing with administrative problems in higher education is like playing the game of "whackamole"; as soon as you solve one problem that pops up, another one pops up, then another. As discussed in chapter III, action research can also be used for self-reflection about one's own administrative leadership style and delivery. Although our methodology is conceptualized for execution with thirteen steps over a three-day period, it should be noted that conventional action research is a continuous process that requires cyclical practice in higher education administration. We recognize that the action research methodologies for classroom application in the second half chapters of VI, VII, VII, and IX does take more time beyond the three-day prototype in the first half of the desktop guide. We have prototyped some "hypothetical" case scenarios in the first half for our desktop users to consider as examples that we have identified to be typical, routine, usual or characteristic in contemporary higher education administration. As symbolized in Figure 1, we believe based on our individual and collective experiences that many, if not most, administrative decisions on campus can be completed within three days from a well-structured, well disciplined, and well-focused process instead of the traditional bureaucratic-conventional committee structures that frequently waste important human capital time, yield minimal productivity, lack persistent performance, and disconnect from mission centrality. We also believe the self-reflection elements of action research can help higher education administrators become better administrators in the frequently deranged, occasional tempestuous and often anarchic world of academe. We have elected to focus this desk guide on those institutions that hold, as part of their central mission, a commitment to providing access and quality higher learning to students at institutions of higher learning who are lower income, higher risk, and marginalized as a result of conditions beyond their control. Many of these students are enrolled at minority serving institutions for African Americans, Native Americans, and Latinx Americans. Our methodology should be integrated into daily administrative practices and institutionalized on campus as part of an infrastructural system for tacit and explicit knowledge management. We believe action or "applied-translational" research provides the opportunity for higher education administrators, both new and seasoned, to upgrade and advance their skills in leadership development. Given the participatory and democratic nature of our methodology, we suggest that our process provides the academic avenues for knowledge exchange of learning experiences for sustaining a collegial community of practice and leverage human capital on the college or university campus. Today's American colleges and universities must secure, balance, and sustain their institutional existence somewhere between either shrinking and expanding with realistic capability and capacity or sinking and imploding deep into a market abyss with a struggling economy and an intensifying academic enterprise. The past, fertile and prosperous era of "is all, for all" has finally ended, leaving the academic landscape and economic terrain with chaotic and confusing lines of authority for targeting service delivery. In today's market, Historically Black Colleges and Universities (HBCUs) must recreate uniqueness and distinguish themselves from others by systemically transcending; (a) heritage anchored in futurism and (b) campus wide decision-making driven by action research into their modern mission delivery and administrative practice.

Action research can help administrative leaders to identify solutions that can most likely mitigate against recurrence of institutional problems, based on its methodology used in the immediate analysis of data to guide framing solutions and deploying resources. First, action research can be practical and provide insights from data that can lead to practical changes and interventions in higher education administration. Second, action research supports shared governance by providing a process that is participatory, democratic, and inclusive. Third, action research can be empowering by bringing stakeholders together and equipping them with a process and tools for intervention and involvement. Fourth, action research can be interpreted through the lenses of all disciplines that make up the academy as a result of focusing on generic qualitative or quantitative data sets. Fifth, action research can support the process of critical analysis either prior or after administrators on campus develop policies, procedures, protocols, or practices that contribute to academic effectiveness and financial efficiency. The areas of academic effectiveness and financial efficiency are most common in administrative judgment for data analysis and most central to university missions in higher education settings. With our current socio-economic climate in higher education, the "many for the many" academic marketplace has been colliding by the many for the most (public universities and community colleges); the few for some (Ivy League schools); the some for the selected (other private schools); the growing for the many (for profit schools); and the many for the few, HBCUs and other minority serving institutions of higher learning (MSIs). Certainly, there are more niche-branding configurations to consider, but state systems of higher education, in particular, need to re-calibrate their delivery systems at a time when they are competing with other compelling state subsidized or public supported services, programs, resources and deliveries.

In the fiercely competitive market, HBCUs must find modern brand, niche, and market share. HBCUs need new, novel, fresh and invigorating thinking about how they manage their enterprises and existence. As major contributing knowledge engines to higher education delivery systems in the United States from the mid to late 1800s to present day, Historically Black Colleges and Universities have played a major and fundamental role in not only the African American community but in the historical development in the United States. The United States and, indeed, the world have both profited from the intellectual capital, knowledge commodities, and cerebral currency that have and continue to evince from the minds, heart and souls of HBCUs and other predominately Blacks institutions of higher learning in America.

HBCUs have broken down barriers for previous generations and will continue to break through boundaries for future generations to come with their six mission-embedded dimensions: (a) access from post slavery; (b) exits from poverty; (c) engines for social and human justice; (d) voices for the voiceless; (e) empowerment in the arts, sciences and the professions and; (f) community empowerment, civic engagement, and cultural enlightenment. In the embryonic stages of their incubation, HBCUs served as the primary propelling pipeline for offering advanced higher education to newly freed slaves during (and prior to) the birth of many institutions. Providing this type of historical access during a post-slavery era also anchored the institutions' spiritual mission, which provided the genesis for the campuses to serve as the freedom venues in the civil rights movement and the impetus for the institutionalization of social justice. To this end, HBCUs must maintain their commitment, dedication, discipline and focus on those who want, deserve, and need higher education the most -- the under-served, the under-represented, the under-utilized, the impoverished, and the marginalized.

HBCUs have and continue to maintain a mission for all the "unders," complimented by the post-slavery and civil rights movements. With this mission dimension, HBCUs provide purposeful higher learning to students in technology, the arts, the letters, the humanities, the sciences, and the professions. With a foundation in DDDM and the fundamentals of HEART, it is now time for HBCUs to re-create with dimensions of "future history" as new HBCU learning community of practice. While the historical mission anchored a foundation from the past, it is now time to *change course*, as uncharted territory, in an era of increased competition, accelerated change, diversified constituency, emerging technologies, dividing ethnic and economic disparity, expanding racial and religious intensity, and growing intense globalization. Given that every campus has some leadership influence by the president or other senior executive administrators, we have conceptualized four different **hypothetical** leadership frames for readers to consider, as either sub textual or contextual options, when completing the collaborative process of action research decision-making.

Choosing one or more of these frames may be useful for capturing the scope, context and essence for simulation, prototyping, sampling, or modeling during decision-making in the office or the classroom.

Figure 1. Three Days, Thirteen Steps, Twenty-Three

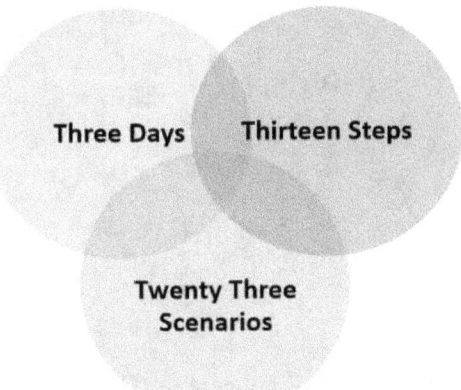

Stevenson (2003) described the administrative office as the "locus of control" and the instructional classroom as the "unit of analysis" for making critical decisions, leveraging intellectual capital, and building learning communities of practice in modern higher education. He used these terms as six-time serving provost, twice in California; twice in Mississippi; once in New York; and as a Visiting Provost-in-Residence for the National Association for Equal Opportunity in Higher Education (NAFEO) in Washington, D.C.

PREFACE AND INTRODUCTION OF DIAGNOSTIC AND DATA DRIVEN DECISION MAKING AND HIGHER EDUCATION ACTION RESEARCH

The data driven decision-making (DDDM) process for prescriptive, diagnostic and assessment purposes by higher education administrators is perhaps more critical and needed today in academe than any other time in history. Often, what is missing from this process is responsive and responsible action, which supports the merits of diligent work with focus, discipline, dedication, and commitment.

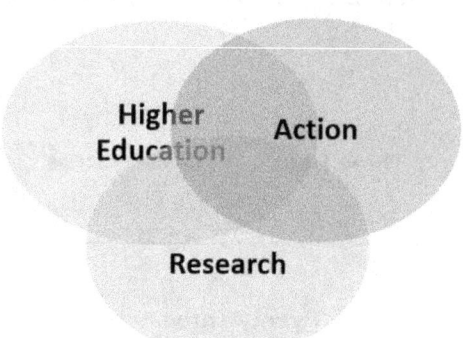

We are introducing this concept in **HEART & SOUL**. The H, E, A, R and T in our title stands for "higher education action research techniques " (hereinafter referred to as HEART) and the word "S.O.U.L " stands for "strategies of university leadership" and represents the sense of yielding results, urgency, relevance, responsiveness, and expeditiousness that is too often needed by administrators in higher education to gather data, collectively analyze the data and collectively decide on new direction. "SOUL" in our book title also captures the both the essence and essentials of the collaborative and collegial group work by completed by "decision-making units" or "DMUs". Indeed, we believe all collaborative group work for decision-making in higher education is leadership and represents "net outcome work". Authentic "net group work" in higher learning cannot manifest without deliberative collaboration. This is important to note as some HBCUs are criticized for a lack of deliberative engagement, campus inclusiveness, and shared governance. While the term "inclusiveness" is typically associated with institutional diversity, it can also capture the essence of too often overlooked, untapped, and underutilized intellectual diversity as institutional capital. Like the common reference to "student learning outcomes" in higher education, we believe the net outcome from collective and deliberative group work should drive the manifestation of other institutional outcomes. These types of outcomes can be targeted from analyses of our scenarios and steps, as well as from those identified real life and relevant scenarios identified on the reader's campus.

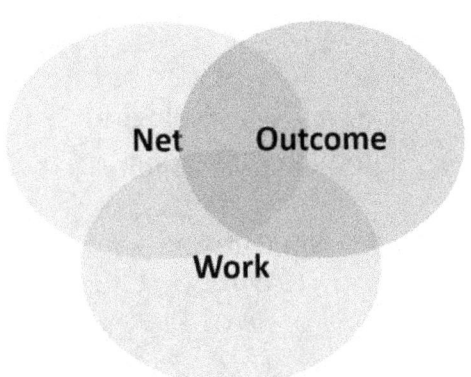

For instance, a typical student learning outcome (SLO) might be *"after the successful completion of studies in the major, students in a discipline will have the ability to create a trans disciplinarily contexed situation, condition, or circumstance that requires critical analysis of cause and effect; fact and opinion; accuracy and completeness; and logic, rationale and reasoning.* The result of "net outcome work" might be that *"after the collective, judicious, and deliberative work by the appointed decision-making unit (DMU) concerning enrollment management challenges, the institutional departments of X and divisions of X will have the processes, protocols and procedures to mitigate against declining student retention rates, related student academic success, and persistence toward degree completion".* To formulate these net outcome work frameworks, we highly recommend that the users of our book read up on two separate yet complimentary areas: "backward induction theory" and "ecological validity". These two areas are particularly relevant to the mission, meaning, curriculum, and culture of HBCUs.

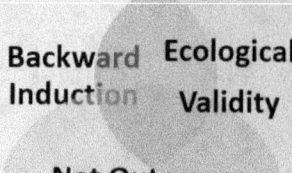

Too frequently in higher education, we unknowingly use adverbs and verbs to describe actions in unintentional and immeasurable terms. Expresso English at https://www.espressoenglish.net/100-common-english-adverbs/ identifies the 100 most commonly used adverbs and many of these adverbs are referenced in academic lexicon, language and vernacular. The top 100 are:

1. *up*
2. *so*
3. out
4. just
5. *now*
6. *how*
7. *then*
8. *more*
9. also
10. here
11. well
12. *only*
13. *very*
14. *even*
15. back
16. there
17. down
18. *still*
19. in
20. as
21. to
22. when
23. *never*
24. *really*
25. *most*
26. on
27. why
28. *about*
29. *over*
30. *again*
31. where
32. right
33. off
34. *always*
35. today
36. all
37. far
38. long
39. away
40. yet
41. often
42. ever
43. *however,*
44. *almost*
45. later
46. much
47. once
48. least
49. ago
50. together
51. around
52. already
53. *enough*
54. both
65. maybe
56. *actually*
57. *probably*
58. home
59. of course,
60. perhaps
61. little
62. else
63. *sometimes*

1. Backdrop for American historically Black Universities and Colleges and Higher Education

64. *finally,*
65. *less*
66. *better*
67. *early*
68. *especially*
69. *either*
70. *quite*
71. *simply*
72. *nearly*
73. soon
74. certainly
75. quickly
76. no
77. *recently*
78. *before*
79. *usually*
80. *thus*
81. *exactly*
82. *hard*
83. *particularly*
84. *pretty*
85. forward
86. ok
87. *clearly*
88. *indeed*
89. *rather*
90. that
91. tonight
92. close
93. suddenly
94. **best**
95. **instead**
96. **ahead**
97. fast
98. alone
99. *eventually*
100. *directly*

The adverbs in **boldface** and *italic* are used in higher education about campus topics that range from enrollment and employment variances to campus conditions concerning climate, curriculum, and culture. While these words certainly have relevance and applicability to the general language and culture of higher education, they should be conceptualized in measurable, tangible, and relational terms. With this in mind, we have developed our model based on executing of DDDM in a timeframe of three days, from problem identification to problem resolution. Suggestions for allotted time on task, by day and by hour, are provided as a part of a thirteen-step process. For administrative application and workplace practice, we have provided three different *types* and a *total* of twenty-three scenarios for HEART and DDDM for the traditional administrative areas of the academy that include: academic affairs, student affairs, financial affairs, advancement affairs, community affairs, physical plant and presidential affairs. We believe most DDDMs on the campus can be made in three days or less with careful pre-planning, real issue identification, participative problem-solving, informed issue analysis, and resolve based on remaining steadfast focus on mission centrality. We believe HEART from DDDM processes can increase personnel performance, program productivity and overall institutional progress relative to both effectiveness and efficiency. We believe this savvy desktop will reinforce the "CORE" of academic culture, defining core as a "**C**ulture **of R**esults and **E**vidence."

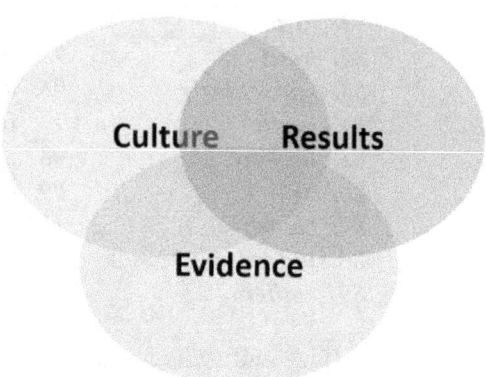

To survive the present and future academic economy, HBCUs must consider two institutional fundamentals: (a) expeditious decision-making and (b) accelerated learning models to survive the fierce academic marketplace throughout the U.S. on campus, online, anytime, anywhere, everywhere. This book series addresses the fundamental of sound, balanced and solvent decision-making. HEART & SOUL is the second volume in the series and deals with accelerated learning models and action research. All the DDDM processes that we are suggesting to the users must be approached with critical thinking, emotional sensitivity, sensible pragmatism, academic soundness, institutional balance, thorough vetting, and carefully calibrated to maximize optimal academic benefits and economic returns on investment. We recognize that there is emphatic, emotional, and expanding discourse about these sensitive topics. In fact, during the collaborative exchanges concerning academics and finance, the driving points should be made grounded in evidence, efficiency, effectiveness, mission, accreditation, market share, greater good and the bigger picture. Since much of the modern academy is guided by finance and academics, and both areas are rooted in data driven decision-making, we feel compelled to provide some comments in these two areas. The synergistic relationships between data, information and knowledge will also facilitate collaboration based on collective intellectual capital and complementary, yet interdependent, arrangements of the financial and budget administration offices within the academic administration side of the institution.

In today's online and on campus market, HBCUs should consider new program structures, possible program consolidations, program transfers, strengthening and enhancement where there is realistic and foreseeable potential for increased productivity, vitality, and performance. Among recommended changes could be the transition from traditional structures to realign institutional resources for promoting market responsiveness and societal relevance. Other administrative realignments could be considered to promote enhanced accountability, improved performance, and maintained quality assurance. From, with, and through HEART, the modern HBCU should primarily examine the following: (1) fundamental centrality (academic) to the mission; (2) foundational essentiality (fiscal) to the mission; (3) streamlining within the infrastructure (operational); (5) emerging academic programs; (6) academic monitoring and special review; (7) financial monitoring; (8) programmatic phase-out; (9) programmatic phase-in; (10) programmatic suspension; (11) gradual resource support; and (12) short, immediate or long term resource support and deployment.

Given that most college and university budgets are predominantly support academics, it is critical to bridge sound financial management with mission-driven academic program deliverables – the central core of the institution. Strategically aligned DDDM and HEART with leadership behavior is fundamentally required for reaffirmation of accreditation, particularly when targeted areas for financial improvement and sustainability are clearly integrated within the workplace. The consequences of not doing so – failed accreditation, probation, or warning --- must be accountable, individually, and collectively on the modern campus. Not doing so must be non-negotiable, uncompromising, and unyielding. Especially with HBCUs serving as knowledge engines for the

African American community, too much is at stake for either temporary or permanent loss of accreditation. Politics, partiality, and personalization should be absent in these exchanges and principal stakeholders and their constituents should make every possible effort to remove emotionalism. What makes balanced "common sense" should be central to economic pragmatism, compelling paradoxes, and other educational paradigms. On evidence, there should be documented rationale, empirical business reasoning, and scientific data finding from vetted financial or academic analysis to prove academic quality and to yield cost savings. Sound and balanced discourse without this makes it difficult for intellectual debate with the academy for sustainability and economy of scale (or "academy" of scale).

On our efficiency, college boards, trustees and other policy makers or overseers should demonstrate and document how focus on decision asking about academics and finance will energize renewal and rationalize intra-institutional collaboration to support shared governance and systemic convergence. HBCUs must do so to achieve a primary mission of resolving educational inequality and economic inequality as the result of learning experiences from our academy. On HBCU mission, there should be exhaustive and extensive documentation on how our academy will meet societal needs, workforce demands, and market share-ready careers with emerging global requirements. Under no circumstances should accreditation be complicated, compromised or jeopardized from consolidation or consortia arrangements. In fact, our decision-making process aims to guide the preparation, the implementation, and the sustainability of accreditation. Accreditation must primarily drive financial stability, academic effectiveness and a prudent as well as prosperous economy of scale. This will require incorporating a logic model with well prescribed performance targets and productivity benchmarks.

HBCUs need real change, renewal, redirection, and innovation in the modern higher education sector, especially within the HBCU sector and among minority-serving institutions of higher learning. HBCU leaders, especially presidents, must master the fundamentals of conciliatory leadership that is manifested from DDDM, HEART, shared governance, building alliances and converging with community-spirited coalitions on and off campus. HEART must be centerpiece to the presidential vision, core to his or her decision-making processes, and central to the modern institutional mission. HBCUs cannot afford to get caught up in the above maze of market miscalculation because of poor DDDM, the absence of HEART, the failure to capture brand, and the inability to target niche. HBCUs must do what they can do well: they must maintain but modify their mission with cutting edge modernization with global diversity, local inclusion, and other societal futurisms. DDDM through HEART can be leveraged to achieve these goals.

The new HBCU mission must have DDDM as its core centrality for administrative assessment, evaluation, and judgment. HEART is essential, relevant, and sustainable for future survival. HEART must be the driving force to create campus- based methodologies for seeking answers to help solve problems, resolve issues, assess situations, and resolve conflict. There is no reason HEART cannot be systemically and sequentially integrated with a more pronounced presence in the institution's administrative infrastructure. We must engage our administrators in practices for a new learning community of practice from all dimensions of expeditious analysis, inquiry, innovation, investigation, fact-finding, probing, and examination. We need new proactive interventions and preventative measures for market stability. Administrators need to be empowered and equipped with action oriented qualitative and quantitative research methodologies. HBCUs institutions should center of their mission to advance the academy for international prominence and global positioning.

HEART is both the art and the science of capturing human behavior and captivating the core essence that is symbolized through words – qualitative; and or from numbers – quantitative. The ultimate challenge as catalytical HEART leaders, especially in the HBCU and MSI community, is to translate DDDM *and* transition HEART relevance into real life action for permanent and sustainable positive change on campus. All the HBCU institutions should create a campus that fosters new "futuristic" thinking – *anchoring longevity before achieving legacy*. This means our campuses must embody a culture with administrators to be more innovative, invigorating, entrepreneurial, creative, and investigative in the classroom and in the campus community. HBCU campuses must nurture the past while preparing students to become future catalysts for positive change.

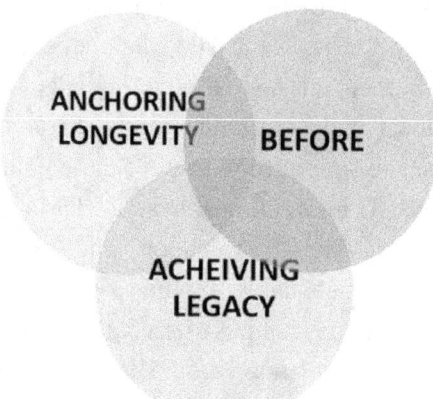

By designating, distributing, and dividing HEART responsibilities vertically and horizontally – from the small unit level to the larger department level --- HBCUs can forge ahead with a new bold agenda for the African American community and the United States. With the intellectual capital and cerebral currency at HBCUs, administrators can leverage collective strengths for future progress. With past and present generations of administrators consistently and constantly focusing on the future based on DDDM and HEART, the HBCU is manifested from intergenerational loop learning and the sector becomes permanently engaged, cyclical, and everlasting. HBCUs as a sector, can do more together than apart in this fierce academic marketplace where more minority students of color, including those who are higher risk and lower income, now have choices to attend non-HBCU institutions with cultural diversity as a foundation for their mission, strategic planning, enrollment benchmarking, financial stability, revenue streaming, and adherence to accreditation standards.

Compounding the HBCU marketplace is the declining state support for higher education and the growing dialogue about institutional consolidation, merger, and acquisition of state resources as most states struggle with investing taxpayer contributions to other systems and other sources with public policy needs and popular demand. The same is occurring at the federal level. Those valorous leaders who opened the doors for newly freed slaves and knocked down the door during civil rights era were, indeed, intrepid futurist contemporaries of their times. For all theoretical and practical purposes for defining futurity, they were empowered with foresight development and employed forecast competencies to see the future for African Americans.

HBCUs will never be relics, irrelevant, or abandon their heritage if they continuously and consistently position themselves for the future of the next HBCU contemporaries. Beginning today, this is our social, educational, political, civic, economic, and historical responsibility in the HBCU community–but HBCUs must maintain, calibrate, and modify mission, first. This is how we will substantiate success and sustain our lasting legacy. Everlasting leadership and forever legacy are our foundation for the future. Leadership has been simply described as a matter of matching the right idea to the right problem at the right time in the correct way (Bolman and Deal, 1984). In this regard, DDDM and HEART in these complex and contemporary times can empower college and university administrators with desk guide toolsets and useful managerial methodologies to make immediate and sound and judgments based on balanced data, informative resources, formative assessment, sequential processes and immediate institutional input and expeditious engagement.

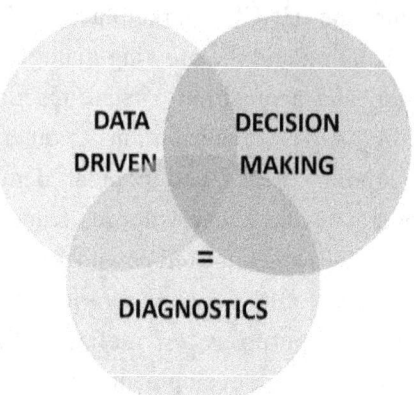

Given the perplexing, perpetuating and persistent challenges that are often specific to HBCUs, we are strongly encouraging that these institutions, in particular, examine our action research conceptual strategies for increasing student persistence toward degree completion and graduation; improving alumni and constituent relations; fundraising and external relationship building; fine-tuning and refining financial stewardship; enhancing media relationship building; improving athletic administration and academic compliance; implementing support services and infrastructure for student life; diversifying the campus culture and climate; and developing new academic program innovations on campus, online and in their targeted community market share.

2.
PREVIEW, OVERVIEW AND HISTORY OF THE "AR" IN HEART

There has been an expanding field of study, a growing body of work and emerging national conversations over the past few decades concerning organizational learning, knowledge management, and the utility of "applied", "actionable" or "translational" research. Appendices A, B, and C of our desktop guide describe action verbs that can be used in action research. Schmuck (2006) provides an extensive profile of prominent authors in action research. He writes that a high school and university teacher, John Dewey became America's best-known and most prolific educational philosopher. Author of four books and a popular lecturer on workplace democracy, Mary Parker Follett sought to use scientific methods to transform worker-manager conflict into creative solutions to enhance productivity. Kurt Lewin is the grandfather of action research.

From 1944 to 1950, Alice Miel cooperated with Ken Benne (who worked with Lewin), Chandas Reid, and Alice Stewart in the Horace-Mann-Lincoln Institute of School Experimentation at Columbia University in New York. Partly because of Miel's innovative efforts, Stephen Corey, former executive director of the Horace-Mann-Lincoln Institute of School Experimentation, organized three national conferences on action research to improve school practices. Ron Lippitt, Lewin's student who did the most to nurture the development of action research, began working with Lewin in 1936. Paulo Freire, an educational reformer, developed a radically innovative strategy of adult learning and social change during the 1960s in Brazil and Chile. Another unique reformer was Reginald Revans of Great Britain, who developed an organizational improvement strategy called action learning. Chris Argyris and Donald

Schon are action research scientists, a variation of action researchers. Chris Argyris created action science with Harvard University students during the 1970s and early 1980s. Donald Schon (1983 and 1987), Argyris's colleague at Harvard, contributed to our understanding of how professional reflection can facilitate improved practice. Taking cues from Schon, Stephen Kemmis' primary concern is in helping teachers critically reflect on their practice. Jean McNiff has extended Corey's, Lippitt's, and Kemmis's work in educational action research. In 1991, William Foote Whyte edited *Participatory Action Research*, which presents case studies of action research in industry and agriculture. Richard Sagor's *How to Conduct Collaborative Action Research*, published in 1992 by the Association for Supervision and Curriculum Development (ASCD), is a small but impressive text. Jeoff Mills' guide (2003) for the teacher researcher is on the list of ten essential books to read to extend and deepen your information about educational action research.

The introduction of action research has proliferated nationally and internationally (Ruben and Jones, 2007) and the benefits of action research have been widely documented (Zambo and Zambo, 2006). As recognized by renowned higher educator Burton Clark (2008), research "involves a process of framing questions, using reliable methods to find answers, and then weighing the relevance of the answers and the significance of the questions" (p 419). Action research follows this sequence. As our new global society continues to struggle with finding answers to complex questions concerning economic decline, racial and religious conflict, health disparities, corporate ethics, global warming, national and global security, technological reliance, educational failure and many other compelling challenges impacting the human condition, the demand to conduct actionable research to resolve real problems becomes more amplified and the revelations of the research findings become more pronounced to society. Time is of the essence and change must come sooner than later.

Action research allows people to complete the fundamentals of sound research methodology and bring results to oscillate from conventional *maintenance* to affect future *movement* with formative, constructive progressive and, ultimately, better outcomes. Again, this book is designed to be a desktop resource for expedient administrative decision-making and expeditious resolution as the result of carefully planned intervention and calculated implementation over the course of three days maximum. During these modern economic times of increased demands for educational accountability, market responsiveness, and bottom-line evidence to reinforce existence, action research could be considered as one of the ends toward the means.

The collaborative feature of action research supports current dialogue in the academy and beyond relative to resource sharing, capacity building and leveraging intellectual capital for positive change. The authors of this book ardently believe in modern organizational learning, benchmarking for better practices, leadership development, action research, and knowledge-empowered decision-making for diagnostic purposes. Action research can provide the mechanism for administrative and instructional decision-making in modern higher education. Although much of the research and related literature on action research has focused on application in the K-12 sector, this desk guide provides frameworks, strategies, parameters, and constructs for applying action research in the administrative decision-making and in other "general' institutional-branch matters concerning academics, finance, student services, development, facilities, community development, information management, and presidential leadership.

This book is also dedicated to the students, staff, and faculty at Jackson State University in Jackson, Mississippi, Tougaloo College in Tougaloo, Mississippi, Mississippi Valley State University in Itta Bena, Mississippi, other HBCUs, and other minority serving institutions of higher learning. To date, Mississippi is considered the poorest state in America, and the Mississippi Delta is the poorest area of the state. Many of the students at Jackson State and Mississippi Valley mirror the populations of urban and rural institutions of higher learning where first generation, low-income, high-risk, Pell-grantee, and marginalized families, are central to the institutional purposes and missions. Indeed, given the "democratic" nature of action research and context of scope for

HEART & SOUL, the methodology builds on the principles of access and equality in higher education. Action research in the classroom can promote students' persistence toward degree completion and institutional efforts toward retaining student clientele—especially those from impoverished, underrepresented, underutilized, and marginalized populations. As pointed out recently by Wyner, Bridgeland, and Diulio entitled, *Achievement Trap: How America is Failing Millions of High-Achieving Students from Lower-Income Families* (2008):

> Today in America, there are millions of students who are overcoming challenging socioeconomic circumstances to excel academically. They defy the stereotype that poverty precludes high academic performance and that lower-income and low academic achievement are inextricably linked. They demonstrate that economically disadvantaged children can learn at the highest levels and provide hope to other lower-income students seeking to follow the same path. Sadly, from the time they enter grade school through their postsecondary education, these students lose more educational ground and excel less frequently than their higher-income peers...There are far fewer lower-income students achieving at the highest levels than there should be, they disproportionately fall out of the high-achieving group during elementary and high school, they rarely rise into the ranks of high achievers during those periods, and, perhaps most disturbingly, far too few ever graduate from college or go on to graduate school. Unless something is done, many more of America's brightest lower-income students will meet this same educational fate, robbing them of opportunity and our nation of a valuable resource" (Executive Summary).

As Cooper writes in **Improving Completion Rates Among Disadvantaged Students,** "...we must assist them with completing the program or course of study they have undertaken, otherwise there is a risk that they will perceive the whole process a failure and will thereby be even more negative toward higher education"(xiii). An annotated bibliography on social and systemic issues related to action research and low-income, high risk college students is provided as a list of suggested readings for future reference. In one of the author's articles entitled *"The Modern Provost"* in **Education,** Stevenson (2000) describes knowledge management as a form of action research with the creation, collection and collaboration of knowledge from best practices; the culmination of those practices or lessons learned as a knowledge base; the application of knowledge to environmental situations; and economic conditions or academic challenges. Stevenson was frequently referenced as stating to fellow administrators, "if you find yourself spending a lot of time in post decision analysis, you probably didn't spend enough time in pre decision analysis". This involves innovating with fresh ideas, seeing things in new ways, resolving problems, and responding to stakeholder needs by changing the way things are done – with more directed focus, strategic thinking, careful planning and DDDM. The constantly and consistently remarked, "to support genuine shared governance, we are going to move expeditiously from input and involvement to implementation…the three crucial, connecting, and critical "I" s…" Action research can be defined and delivered under both "DDDM" and "III" rubrics. All institutions have information, many have knowledge, but only a few leverages that knowledge into action. Placing tacit and/or explicit knowledge in the hands of key-decision makers in a meaningful format by allowing faculty and staff to make actionable decisions that leads to higher performance and enhanced productivity. "Actionable" knowledge grows when it is embedded in the institutional community and academic culture. This desktop includes recommended data bases for quick referencing and to assist with the collaborative decision-making process.

DATA   INFORMATION

KNOWLEDGE

=

ACTION

The interdependent *synergy* between data, information, knowledge and action is critical in these endeavors, as academic leaders first analyze qualitative and quantitative data; second, translate those data into helpful instruction; and third, use that information as knowledge to make diagnostic decision-making. In other words, a characteristic of knowledge management is "action research" according to the working paradigm by Stevenson. After data, information and that knowledge are expanded as resources for decision-making, academic leaders are encouraged to apply to solve problems or academic issues. Two models can be applied as developed by one of the other co-authors, Richard Schmuck, in *Practical Action Research for Change* (2006), a classroom centered process that includes trying new practices, incorporating concerns, collecting data, checking what the data mean, reflecting on alternatives, and trying a new-practice. The steps of proactive research are interdependent, circular, and continuous.

Responsive action research begins in collecting data, analyzing the data, distributing the data, trying a new proactive method, checking for reactions, and collecting the data. Responsive research entails diagnosis, action, and evaluation. Both processes are cyclical and can help academicians change from current, more traditional ways of operating, to a new practice that may be used to fit more modern and contemporary situations. Schmuck refines these processes in the second edition of *Practical Action Research* (2009). Tesch (1990) highlighted action research and case studies among many academic approaches to qualitative research design. Action research enables researchers to improve their practice (Hansen, Kalish, Hall, Gynn, Holly, and Madigan, 2004) and can be defined as a systematic inquiry focused on addressing a specific research question (Brighton and Moon, 2007); a participatory, ideological, and emancipatorial process to radically changed structures (Marshall and Rossman, 2006); a collaborative process to examine classroom planning and change for instructional development (Warren, Doorn, and Green, 2008); a practical approach for conducting research (Fisher, 2008); a process for challenging individuals to reflect on how they think and explore alternative strategies (Schoen, 2007); ways for stakeholders in the learning environment to gather information about how they teach (Clare and Subrzi, 2007); a way to empower teachers in urban school settings (Esposito and Smith, 2006); a reflective process with the two different emphases of action orientation and research orientation (Jarvis, 1999; a systematic collection of information to change existing practices (Bogan and Biklin, 2007) a strategy for assisting professors in the development of the conscientiousness (Mata-Segreda, 2006); and is an active area of publication (Graham, 2005). Hiller and Jameson summarized action research quite well. They state that:

> *"When people are researching into something that they are doing, with a view to making a difference as a result of their research, then they are engaged in something called action research. Action research does not only consist of people's reflections on what they have done. It is research while action is taking place. In other words, it is a deliberate attempt to examine the way in which something is being undertaken, with a view to making changes to that process as the research goes along...A further feature of action research is that it is participative...A systematic enquiry into that practice may ensue, perhaps with colleagues' collaboration. The results may lead to a change that is monitored and evaluated. Throughout this process, the action may be continually refined as a result of critical reflection" (pp. 54-65).*

However, most of the work on action research referenced here is specific to the K-12 sector. As suggested by Wisker (2008), "Academics are in an ideal position to carry out action research: on the one hand, they can create and advance knowledge in higher education on the basis of their concrete, practical experience; on the other hand, they can actively improve practice on the basis of their 'grounded theory'"(p.234). Interestingly, Burton (2008) suggests that, "If teachers operated as scholar-teachers, with action research giving them a work life more like that of university professors, they could then also serve as role models for students preparing for lifelong learning" (p 420). Schon (2000) commenting on the need for new scholarship renewed epistemology in higher education earlier advocated that:

> *Nearly all professional practitioners experience a version of the dilemma of rigor or relevance, and they respond to it in one of several ways... The new scholarship implies action research. The new categories of scholarly activity must take the form of action research... If teaching is to be seen as a form of scholarship, then the practice of teaching must be seen as giving rise to new forms of knowledge... The problem of changing the universities so as to incorporate the new scholarship must include, then, how to introduce action research as a legitimate and appropriately rigorous way of knowing and generating knowledge" (p. 33).*

The timeless work done by Sagor (1992) articulates action research as the process to improve teaching and learning. His recommendations remain not only applicable to modern pedagogy, but certainly relevant to administration in higher education settings as well. Lomax's ***Managing Better Schools and Colleges: An Action Research Way*** (1991) is also resourceful. Higher education applicability is best illustrated in another publication introduced at the same time as Sagor's work entitled ***Action Research in Higher Education: Examples and Reflections (1992)*** by Ortrun Zuber-Skerritt of the University of Queensland in Australia. Zuber-Skerritt's work presented examples that demonstrate how action research can be applied through collaborative inquiry for both professional development and curriculum development. Two areas of action research that stand out for higher education relevance are especially pervasive for higher education administration. First, action research can facilitate continuous improvement in one's professional development as a lifelong learner and in one's workplace for continuous renewal in leadership. This is a two-dimensional process of self-reflection, requiring self- assessment, goal setting, administrative brainstorming, action planning and action evaluation. Second, shared decision-making and group collaboration are fundamental to genuine shared governance. But one cannot govern with others until and unless one governs oneself. This is why self-reflection by administrators must be engaged during the initial, implementation and culminating stages of the action research journey. As mentioned later, "even as a solo teacher or a single administrator, you must engage others in the action research process".

There is debate within the academy on the definitions of research and the merits of action research. Some of this discussion is referenced in ***Campus Progress: Supporting of Teaching and Learning*** (2004) edited by Cambridge and published by the American Association for Higher Education. The reports write that:

> *"...there is some debate about how rigorous methods must be. Some faculty members assert that, to have credibility, this scholarship must conform to the research standards of their academic discipline, whether scientific or humanistic. Others argue that the scholarship of teaching and learning can encompass 'action research'" (p. 193).*

We argue that many of America's low income, high-risk students have needs on today's college and university campus that require immediate, yet sound, research reinforcement with immediate action that can be effectively taken within a three-day window of opportunity. We also believe many of the nation's faculty can use action research to build on the important emerging body of knowledge to enhance knowledge; reflect on their professionalism, teaching modes and modalities; modernize their teaching to meet the needs of new students on the horizon; make substantive positive changes in their classrooms to improve student learning outcomes; and, make significant contributions to their discipline and their university. Such contributions should be reviewed during considerations for professorial development, promotion, tenure, and growth.

We hope that this book broadens the framework for action research by illustrating examples on how the methodology can be used to reflect on one's professional development, collect and analyze data for diagnostic (prescriptive or problem-solving) purposes, and move from traditional teaching practices to more effective practices in the professorial experience. Particularly as it is widely known that some traditional administrators manage without shared decision-making, and collaborative inquiry is often used sparingly between students, staff and faculty, action research can equip administrators with a useful and effective tool box. Action research resources can also empower them to meet the financial demands and academic needs and institutional challenges that vary across campus and during deliberations concerning an academy that that may be faced with new global changes, economic circumstances, educational conditions, and leadership consequences. Wisker (2008) provides some helpful tips on action research that we would like to reiterate for the user of this desk guide. They are: action research should have outcomes that are measurable; action research is a collaborative endeavor that examines ideas and results; action research requires rigor; action research can incorporate quantitative as well as qualitative methods; and action research leads to change. Collaboration for HEART is strongly encouraged during a time of needed change and required cooperation within the academy as the enterprise continues to confront both fiscal and academic challenges. Given the economic times we live in throughout academe and the need for colleges and universities to secure sound enrollment management for sustainable student success, we also recommend campuses to review "Commentary: The Pivotal Role of Faculty in Propelling Student Persistence and Progress Toward Degree Completion" by Stevenson, Buchanan, and Sharpe in the *Journal of College Student Retention* (2007). The essay touches on the usefulness, application, and utility of action research in higher education settings.

Qualitative Research

Quantitative Research

Action Research

3.
NEW PARADIGMS AND PARAGONS FOR HIGHER EDUCATION LEADERS

In the March 12, 2012 issue of the ***Chronicle of Higher Education***, we read with great interest about the high turnover rates of HBCU Presidents throughout the United States. More troubling and unsettling pieces have been appeared in other prominent publications and other social media. Many, if not most, of the plaguing problems from these media revelations appear to lack the beneficial application of action research methodology and the lack of either proactive leadership, diagnostic leadership, responsive, prescriptive leadership, or a combination of all four. We attempt to address some of these presidential issues in this chapter. We feel compelled to recognize the need for bold new paradigms, paragons, and dimensions for higher education leadership for not only HBCU presidents, but others throughout academe. We believe this is a fundamental and a foundational backdrop for forging ahead with the DDDM principles introduced in HEART. Based on our many years of experience in the academic business, and having worked for many presidents during our tenures, we would like to provide some recommendations to presidents and other top administrators at Historically Black Colleges and Universities, before proceeding to the more specific sections of the book concerning higher education action research. A note to the connoisseur: This section is based on very general generalizations and by no means is representative of any single person, institution, or institutions. Moreover, much of what is advocated here is applicable to non-HBCU institutions as well.

This section is about new paradigms, paragons and dimensions of leadership and oscillating from the now, to the next, to the new on behalf of our unique and unifying enterprises. The reader will note in the below

Figure 2 that much of our emphasis is on future-forecasting and forward-thinking about HBCUs and other minority-serving colleges and universities. We in HEART are strong advocates of proactive leadership and the second dimensions in the Figure 2. The personal, academic, professional, and transformational development of the third dimension is up to the reader of HEART as a leader for catalytical and creative change. First, although our original mission for newly freed slaves and subsequent civil rights should remain as part of our historical incubation, it is now time to bridge that mission with a more modern mission that focuses on the future and less on the past. Social justice should remain central to our mission but within a larger context of global diversity. Civil rights are now expanded to human rights and other more modern-relevant areas such as environmental justice, social justice, public health (coronavirus) and global poverty. Second, higher education administrators must continue to think strategically more long-term and not continue with the complacency of short-term solutions to our compelling entrepreneurial mandates. Here, action research can be most helpful, and this is particularly important regarding accreditation where some administrators tend to prepare for accreditation only one year in advance as oppose to embracing accreditation as a process for assessing continuous quality improvement.

Third, in too many instances, higher education administrators tend to resist and, in fact, resent change despite the fact that many of us came to academe to make change in a world that continues to be unjust, unfair, imbalanced, unequal, and inequitable. Administrators must now position themselves as entrepreneurs to not only create change but coordinate strategies to make positive change happen on behalf of our larger human-webbed community. Fourth, the leadership style of administrators on campus should focus less time on maintaining the way things have been or are to moving things to the next level in what has become a fiercely competitive marketplace. Effective higher education administrators and faculty can motivate people, manipulate processes, and manage programs. Fifth, the mind set of *some* faculty and faculty leadership has been closed minded in the classroom resulting in faculty continuing to teach the way they were taught. Bold, new faculty development opportunities must be core to our HBCUs, and faculty must become more open minded to teaching what students need to learn as opposed to what faculty want to teach. Like other colleges and universities, HBCUs need more online classes taught from the real life, relevant principles of contemporary and modern andragogy (adult learning) instead of the outdated, remotely related perils of conventional and traditional pedagogy (youth learning). If resources are available, extending campus offerings beyond the main indigenous campus is part of modern delivery of higher education – closer to where people live, work, and interact neighborhood commerce (Stevenson, 2002). The use of DDDM through geographic information systems (GIS) can be resourceful in this regard. This will certainly ameliorate global diversity, local inclusion, and multi-cultural enrollment management endeavors and facilitate much needed "other" race intellectual discourse in the new global academy. Sixth, the administrative infrastructures on campus need to be less hierarchical with outdated managerial styles that are autocratic and authoritarian. In the modernization process, colleges and universities need to be less vertical and more horizontal to support genuine shared governance and circular conciliatory communication to both internal publics and external stakeholders. Our academy works best with shared accountable acculturation. When challenges or issues occur, administrators must oscillate from the usual examination of cause and effect to the execution of responding and reacting with catalytical leadership and resolve.

Seventh, although many of our students are used to a multi-tasking lifestyle with juggling school, work, family, and technology, it has been our experiences at several institutions that these same students do not necessarily do well with multi-tasking on the campus. What works for most students may not work for work well for many students. Students should be skilled in not trying to create many tasks all at once; rather, they need to be competent in and empowered with achieving a task before going to the next. Sequential tasking as opposed to simultaneous tasking can help facilitate the monitoring of student points of progress on a monthly, semester or quarterly basis. This type of tracing and

Figure 2. Oscillating from the NOW to the NEXT to the NEW

First Dimension	Second Dimension
Historical and Present Mission	Future and Modern Mission
Monocultural Foundation and Heritage	Multicultural Fundamentals and Futurity
Short-Term Solutions	Long-Term Strategy
Change Resistance/Resentment	Catalytical Change/Creation
Managerial Maintenance: Idle-Inert	Leadership Movement: Entrepreneurial
Closed-Minded, Formal Instruction	Open-Minded, Flexible Teaching
On Campus, In Class	Cyber Campus, Online
Hierarchical, Vertical, Up, Down	Horizontal, Circular, Across, Around
Simultaneous Multi-Tasking	Sequential Multi-Tasking
"Not My Job" Aims and Attitude	"Is Our Job" Aptitude and Adroitness
Quantitative Measurement	Qualitative Assessment
Identification of Cause and Effect	Execution of Reaction and Response
Personalized-Political Personnel Hiring	Performance-Nurtured Human Capital
Solo Management- "Me"	Synergistic Leadership- "Us"
Independent Stance	Interdependent Symmetry
Local, Regional Needs	National, Global Demands
Higher Order Achievement	Wider Order Accomplishment
Diagnostic Data-Driven, Decision Making	Prescriptive Data-Driven, Decision Making
Only Revert Backward, Reflectively	Always Revolutionize Forward, Retrospectively
Balance Managerial Efficiency on One Hand	Balance Leader Effectiveness on Other Hand

Modified from the early timeless work of Kotter in *A Force for Change* (1990) and Harris in *Management in Transition* (1985)

tracking mechanism is especially paramount for benchmarking student persistence and navigating institutional retention. Administrators must employ and implement the most effective and efficient methods for solvent documentation and solid record- keeping. Administrators must continue and examine the usual quantitative metrics for institutional decision.

Again, this is where action research can be powerful, influential, and empowering. Administrators may need to use more qualitative measures for decision-making to understand more about both student performance and staff productivity with the utilization of focus groups, interviews, observations, etc. We have found that often we can learn more about our consumer relations, customer service and constituent needs through qualitative methodologies. Regarding human capital or resource management, the common practice of hiring personnel based on personal relationships must be substituted for hiring personnel based on evidenced performance and proven productivity -- balancing the equilibrium between efficiency and effectiveness in work. Constant evaluation of evidence and consistent assessment of bottom line results are imperative. This, too, must be the case for financial stewardship, fiscal accountability, and overall prudence of resource management. Eighth, some of the staff who supports our institutions can be single-minded and are often quoted as saying "that's not my job". These same support staff must move from that mind-set attitude to a mind-set aptitude of accepting that it is everyone's job to create a learning environment that is conducive to entrepreneurial performance. This is the modern community of practice and it requires "systems" mindedness throughout the staff in the respective areas at each level of the institution. Ninth, unit heads must also move from what is frequently perceived as a "solo" managerial style rather than a synergistic style that engages in and embraces interdependent teaming. Management efficiency must be balanced against leadership effectiveness, resulting in managerial leadership. Tenth, the old notion of internal independence as well as external independence must be addressed in order for our institutions to become more collaborative on and off campus. Eleventh, our campuses are no longer isolated to just the local neighborhood and regional needs. We must react and respond to the new national agenda and new global milieu. In our new global academy, institutions of higher learning must now respond to global demands and create pathways to careers that are workforce ready and industry relevant. Thus, we must certainly continue to be locally responsive but globally responsible to new dimensions of academic life. Moreover, some HBCU institutions need to work on being less competitive with each other and more collaborative with sharing resources by combining efforts of mutual mission benefit. HBCUS simply need to do more together as a sector of higher education, perhaps by having public and private institutions working on regional needs, then cross-state needs, then national needs to meet larger global imperatives. Collaborating with non-HBCUs has become fundamentally necessary in today's academic marketplace. Particularly in the areas of science, technology, engineering, and mathematics, smaller and larger HBCUs are strategically positioned to collaborate with other institutions of higher learning to meet national and global demands.

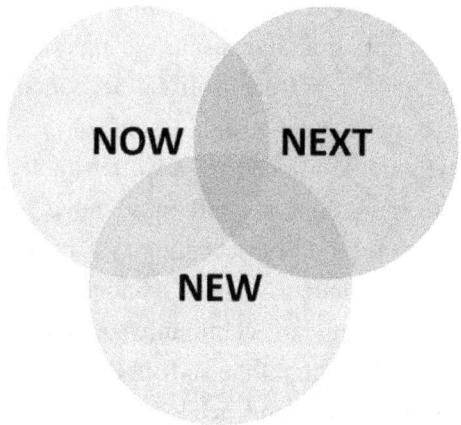

Twelfth, we are not measured ultimately by what our students do while they are enrolled on campuses. We are ultimately measured by what students do after they leave our campuses. Before moving to the specifics of HEART, we would like to encourage two things in this regard. We must train our students in DDDM for diagnostic *and* prescriptive utility before they graduate in an effort to empower them with the research literacy they will need in the workplace or graduate school. Getting students involved in action research can help (See ***Action Research Higher Educators*** by Schmuck and Stevenson, 2010). The ability to compile data, analyze data, and make judgments based on data is critical to the lifelong adult learning of our students – personally, academically, professionally. In addition, with our usual academic aims for higher order achievement in the curriculum, we must also teach our students wider order accomplishment that ignites creativity and stimulates the much-needed innovative thinking that this country so desperately needs now more than probably any other time in world history. This, of course, will require staff, faculty, and administrators to move, in collaboration with our students, from the above first dimensions in the left-hand column, of the above Figure 2, to the second dimensions in the right-hand column. We must build on our historical foundations to position with future fundamentals for progress. We must maintain our mission not only by just looking backward in reflection. We must also modernize our mission from always looking forward with continuous retrospection in the revolving, evolutionary, and revolutionary African dimensions of *Sankofa.* The élan vital of Sankofa is the bedrock for identifying and executing the reader's bold, new ***third dimensions***.

Sankofa

A term that literally means "to go back and get it". The symbol depicts a mythical bird flying forward with its head turned backward. The egg is in its mouth represents the gems or knowledge of the past upon which wisdom is based; it also signifies the generation to come which would benefit from that wisdom. (Wikpdeia, 2013)

Given that every campus has some leadership influence by the president or other senior executive administrator, we have conceptualized four different "hypothetical" leadership frames for readers to consider in **Appendix D** as an option when completing the process of action research decision-making. Choosing one or more of these frames may be useful for capturing the essence. Leadership styles and institutional circumstance

NOW: FIRST DIMENSION

NEXT: SECOND DIMENSION

NEW: THIRD DIMENSION

vary from institution to institution and president to president. Often it effective to frame your decision–making recommendations based on these styles and circumstances, quite frequently, anchored from values and visions early in the search process for presidential leadership selection. These frames in Appendix D should help readers and users of our desktop guide to exercise and engage in lively discussions about the challenges for moving the dimensions from the now, to the next, to the new as highlighted in Figure 2.

4.
DESCRIPTION OF SCOPE AND SEQUENTIAL FRAMEWORKS FOR HEART

As we mentioned earlier, we believe that many, if not most, decisions in higher education administration can be done through responsive decision-making units more effectively and more efficiently within three days to expedite resolve or administrative resolution for prescriptive, prognostic, or diagnostic purposes.

We have put together a sequence of thirteen steps to be executed or implemented over a three-day period to address common areas that come up in everyday higher education administration. We suggest that solving a problem, addressing a concern, or responding to an issue does not require the same efforts of writing a multi-year dissertation or some of the work by "traditional" researchers; however, some of the thinking

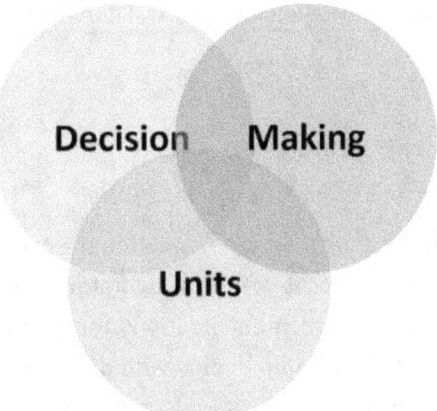

behind our action research model for HEART is rooted in the same type of processing for scholarly academic work. That is, we believe PhD, EdD, MD and other doctoral degree holders should be able to grasp our model as from their initial and hopefully sustained training as academicians.

Although we have crafted this desktop for minority serving institutions that primarily serve minorities, we are confident our methodology can be successfully applied and utilized at any institution of higher learning. We have chosen several areas for our case scenarios. They include academics, finance, advancement/development, student services, facilities, information management, community development, and other areas concerning leadership. Our thirteen-step process is very general in nature for desktop usage. Users of this desk guide should conceptualize their own case scenarios to practice our thirteen-step process, prior to applying our recommendations. Appendices A, B, and C of our desktop guide describe verbs that can be used in action research. We recognize that every college or university campus is different and made up from varying visions, values, and voices. We also recognize that every administrative decision is different with varying variables that make up circumstances, conditions, and consequences. Often, many decisions can't made in three days; but the basic conceptual framework for these types of decisions can be completed in three days like: establishing direction, identifying inhibitors, resource considerations, research methods, policy constraints and areas that require critical analysis from collegial engagements. Nonetheless, what follows is our thirteen-step methodological process of HEART for section one of the desktop guide:

Day One

Early Morning Hours

A. Background Details and Description

First Step. Accept the case-situational scenario (CSS) by the assigned "top executive" administrator with the charge and challenge to make recommendations for resolve, intervention, or solution. This initial step begins with a senior level vice president appointing the case or situation to a direct report. This step should involve the providing the direct report with a background of details and descriptions of the entire case scenario with a brief chronology of the facts, the issues, and the predicament that is faced by the department or unit. Some rationale or reasoning can be provided by the top administrative person to a certain extent; however, some of this pre-determined analysis should be left up to an appointed group as part of the action research process and to support authentic deliberation, circular communication and genuine intellectual discourse.

NOTES:_____
_____
_____
_____
_____
_____
_____

Day One (cont'd)
Mid-Morning Hours

B. Administrative Designation and Deployment

Second Step. Appoint a "unit based" administrative lead person to facilitate the process and navigate the execution for resolve within the prescribed three-day time period. The three-day period should include suggested time and attention to certain areas of the case scenario. This step should include certain benchmark indicators as well as targeted outputs as part of the process. The administrative lead person should appoint certain leadership positions for group process in this initial stage. There should be an appointed group facilitator; there should be an appointed group recorder; and there should be an appointed person to primarily take the lead in collecting data. The facilitator should be recognized on campus as a consensus builder and the recorder should be chosen based on expertise in information management and technological savvy. The data point person should have expertise in literature reviews and data repositories.

NOTES:_____
_____
_____
_____
_____
_____

Day One (cont'd)
Late Morning Hours
C. Group Appointment and Assignment

Third Step. Appoint a diverse group of staff, faculty, and students to serve as a decision-making unit (DMU) for the three-day period. This group must recognize the challenge and charge and be willing to serve impartially and without the influence of both politicization and personalization. The group should be given a template for effective group dynamics based on the early work by Schmuck and Runkel (1994), later by Schmuck and Schmuck (2001), and most recently by Schmuck, Bell, and Bell (2012). In general, the group should build on trust, share influences, welcome ideas, exchange positive regard and exercise mutual respect. The notion here is that no one person in the workgroup can do everything, and everyone can do something to achieve the group charge. For more information, we recommend:

❖ *Schumck, R.A., Bell, S.E., and Bell, W.E. 2012. Handbook of Organizational Development in Schools and Colleges: Building Regenerative Capacity. 5th edition. Santa Cruz: Exchange Pointe International*

NOTES:

Day One (cont'd)
Early Afternoon Hours
D. Establish Setting for Circular Communication

Fourth Step, This group's operations should follow the first step's recommendations but also include areas that are suggested for productivity by the group. This decision-making unit, operating as a community of practice, must recognize intellectual diversity, work through boundaries and borders, rise above politics, apply data-driven analyses, apply creativity and innovation, embrace positive regard for one another, and engage in a process that employs firmness, focus, fluidity and flexibility. The result of this step should be the first outline for a PowerPoint presentation that will be used throughout the remainder of the thirteen-step process. The presentation should be viewed in a circular-conference room format, giving the group the opportunity to view documents at the same time, on the screen or wall, together in concert, to support collegial collaboration. The PowerPoint outline and other templates should also be placed on web link within the institution's "internal" (not external) intranet, with only access to the DMU members or until authorized by the administrative lead person or senior vice president.

NOTES:_____
_____
_____
_____
_____
_____

Day One (cont'd)
Mid Afternoon Hours
E. Create Analytics for Critical Thinking

Fifth Step. Require the decision-making unit to conduct a preliminary screening of the case scenario to assure some analytical fundamentals from the foundations of critical thinking. This includes differentiating between fact and fiction; recognizing and evaluating author bias and rhetoric; determining accuracy and completeness of information; recognizing logical fallacies and faulty reasoning; comparing and contrasting points of view; making judgments and drawing logical conclusions, integrating, and synthesizing information. Following this step, the first force field analysis should be done relative to driving forces on one hand and restraining forces on the other hand.

NOTES:_____
_____
_____
_____
_____
_____

Day One (cont'd)
Late Afternoon Hours
F. Survey and Scan Literature and Information Data Bases

Sixth Step, Review literature, data bases, information repositories and practices at two other Carnegie-classified," peer" institutions that are related to the case scenario and will contribute to the body of work and deliberations from the DMU. The literature review should be current (2015-2020) and include any information, references, and resources that contribute to the general variables that are associated with the case scenario from the department in which the problem was developed. The literature review must also include any information concerning best practices or lessons learned concerning the problem area. The two peer institutional reviews should come from an HBCU and a non-HBCU institution; however, both should be Carnegie-classified. The data point person should be able to pinpoint relative literature and identify only those practices and lessons that are directly related to the CSS. Alternative databases and optional websites for educational research are provided in the Bibliography.

NOTES:_____
_____
_____
_____
_____
_____

Day One (cont'd)
Early Evening Hours
G. Conceptualize and Craft Logic Model

Seventh Step. Frame a working logic model that captures the necessary basic elements and major components that are fundamental to the problem. In general, the logic model should include inputs, outputs, and outcomes. The logic model should be placed on the intranet web link with the templates and the PowerPoint for re-shaping, modification, and adjustment as the group process develops from step one to step thirteen. The logic model should be tailored to and customized for the specificities of the problem in the case scenario. The DMU may elect to suspend this step of framing the logic model to expedite the deliberative process and move on to the next step of HEART. The framing of the logic model could also be postponed until later in the thirteen-step process as part of the culminating activity for finalization. In other words, the creation of the logic model could be part of the resolve of resolution in the recommendations

NOTES:_____
_____
_____
_____
_____
_____

Day Two

Early Morning Hours through Day Three Early Evening Hours

H. Reflect, Determine, Resolve, Measure, Reinforce, Institutionalize

Eighth Step. Conduct a "mid-way" group reflection session and continue to follow the thirteen–step HEART process for implementing "general" data collection and analysis. The data collection could come from institutional research, the literature review, national data bases, and other sources decided by the DMU.

Ninth Step. Collect "specific" data about the problem; analyze data about the problem; identify means for data authentication, validity, verification, reliability, and trustworthiness (if needed) concerning the problem; determine the meaning of the data relative to the problem. There are guidelines and procedures that one should follow when addressing problems and issues regardless of their nature. One of the things that must be done is to gather data related to the problem in order to come up with an appropriate resolution. Prior to data collection several issues must be addressed including the ones listed below:

A. Identifying the population from which the data is to be collected
B. Gaining permission from individuals and/or organizations to carry out the data collection process
C. Determining the type of data needed to address the problem or issue under consideration
D. Creating or identifying an instrument to use in collecting the data
E. Carrying out the data collection procedures

In general, the data collection process is similar regardless of the type of data (quantitative or qualitative) being collected. When dealing with quantitative data, however, one should consider the level of analysis and sampling procedures. Different types of permissions may also be required, depending on whether you are sampling individuals, institutions, or agencies. Gaining informed consent is particularly important to protect the privacy and confidentiality of participants. Operational definitions must be assigned to all variables to be studied. Types of data and measures must be determined prior to the data collection process. Whether the instrument is to measure individual performance, individual attitude, individual behavior, or factual information must be established. Data collection instruments must be identified or designed. The ones utilized must be reliable and valid. Reliable instruments ensure consistency of measurement while valid instruments provide evidence that what purports to be measured is, in fact, measured. Several widely used methods of establishing reliability include the following:

- Test-retest reliability
- Alternate forms reliability
- Inter-rater reliability
- Internal consistency

Traditional types of validity coefficients include:

- Content validity
- Construct validity
- Criterion-related validity

A standardized process for the collection of data must be identified or created and utilized. For more information, we recommend:

❖ Creswell, J. W. (2012). *Educational Research: Planning, Conducting, and Evaluating Quantitative and Qualitative Research (4th ed.).* Boston: Pearson Education, Inc.

Tenth Step, Propose a remedy, resolve, or resolution about the problem; pilot or pre-test the remedy, resolve, or resolution to the problem from a selected qualitative protocol or quantitative instrument (if needed); analyze the data again, from the remedy, resolve, or resolution against some type of effort to again validate, verify, or support reliability and trustworthiness (if needed).

Eleventh Step. Develop recommendations for new practices or pro-active measures to prevent the problem occurring again; identify measurements and metrics for analyzing the new practice, policy, procedure, or process that has been developed as a result of previous steps. These recommendations should specifically identify benchmark indicators that are gauged by actual numbers or percentages, using "action" verbs such as increase, improve, eradicate, enhance, implement, monitor, assess, evaluate, eliminate, replicate, mitigate, etc. Other verbs suggested by Livingston (1980) are presented in Appendices A, B, and C. Each recommendation should include a budget code with the benchmarked number or percentage so that financial returns on investment can be traced by the unit head/budget officer and tracked by the institutional accounting office.

Twelfth Step. Place the proposed new practice, policy, or procedure on the internal web link and allow stakeholders on campus the opportunity to provide feedback on the proposed recommendations by the DMU. This type of social media intervention reinforces shared governance on campus through electronic means and for expeditious decision-making based on DDM. After expanded internal feedback and input has been provided on campus to reinforce the work of the DMU, the DMU should begin the finalization process by the examination of all the implications from the new recommendations in the context of budget and physical constraints law and legal mandates, past and present institutional policies, and concerns relative to ethics, integrity, credibility and other areas from a second force field analysis of driving forces on one hand and restraining forces on the other hand.

Thirteenth Step, Address for a second time any issues concerning proactive or preventative measures after a thorough and final consideration of stakeholder input and integration of the new practice, policy, process, procedure or plan into the institutional strategic plan and unit-based budget where the problem was developed.

NOTES:_____

Moving from the Steps to the Scenarios

What follows in this section is a series of CSSs for each major branch of a college or a university. These branches include academic affairs, finance, student affairs, information management, institutional advancement, and others. We have prototyped three different scenarios for each major branch. These scenarios are typical and based on our individual and collective experiences in higher education administration. The readers of our desktop guide should consider these case scenarios as *strictly hypothetical* to modern administration in higher education. Obviously, the users of this desktop guide can consider these examples as they examine problems on their respective campuses. We have crafted these scenarios under the assumption that the problems and issues raised in each one can be either resolved or solved within three days. We suggest that when groups are formed to deal with these types of challenges, the institution should consider releasing group members from their regular duties to serve with the decision-making unit for the three-day period. As highlighted above, as well as below, assigned decision-making units under the leadership of a lead person should develop clear cut strategies to deal with the problem. The DMU should examine other experiences at other peer institutions as well as gain insight and revelations from literature reviews. The assessment of problem priorities and the sequence that the group utilizes to solve the problem should be based on the conditions and circumstances the DMU is faced with from the problem.

We do recognize that some problems may require more time to resolve beyond our three-day period model. Under these circumstances, if the problem is more complex than the DMU realizes another route might be taken by the institution. Moreover, if the problem has higher significance than the group is prepared to deal with, the institution may also decide on a more comprehensive and extensive approach. We remind readers that in all cases of solving problems on campus, there must be the constant and consistent re-visitation to the institution's mission, purpose, values, and strategic direction. Mission centrality should be at the core of all DMU deliberations, discourse, debate, and consensus building. In this regard, making certain the DMU represents intellectual diversity and campus representation is important. The result or results of DMU work should be an outcome or outcome that is either demonstrable or deliverable. To reiterate, given that every campus has some leadership influence by the president or other senior executive administrator, we have conceptualized four different "hypothetical" leadership frames for readers to consider in Appendix D, as an option, when completing the process of action research decision-making. Choosing one or more of these frames may be useful for capturing the essence. Leadership styles and institutional circumstance vary from institution to institution and president to president. Often it is effective to frame your decision –making recommendations based on these styles and circumstances that are quite frequently anchored from values and visions expressed early in the search process for presidential leadership selection. These frames in **Appendix D** should help readers and users of our desktop guide to exercise and engage in lively discussions about the below hypothetical case scenarios and the challenges for moving the dimensions from the now, to the next, to the new as highlighted in Figure 2. To reiterate, campuses should craft their own scenarios for real life and pay attention to the "sixth and ninth steps" (*with different checkmarks*) relative to data bases, data authentication, data methods, and data assessment.

Case Scenario Number 1: For Academic Affairs
MATCHING MISSION RELEVANCE WITH MARKET DEMANDS AND CAREER NEEDS

A group of employers who represent business, education, government, and other regional commerce recently met with the Chamber of Commerce for an urban city in the Deep South where there is a minority serving research university. The group met several times, and all agreed that many of the students who were graduating from the local university did not have the competencies, skill sets, attitudes, dispositions, and knowledge bases to meet the workforce demands and workplace needs of their respective organizations. Among the areas of concern were teambuilding, cultural diversity, technology savvy, data-driven decision-making, and entrepreneurial innovation. The president of the chamber of commerce met with the president of the local university and suggested that in the spirit of cross-sector collaboration, the university should look into this apparent problem which clearly indicates a breakdown in cross-sector communication, curriculum relevance and career mobility expectations between industrial workforce competencies and academic teaching competencies. What type of data needs to be collected? From whom and from where? What should be the methodology? How will the data be used? What actions should be taken after the data has been collected, shared, and analyzed? Who is at stake? What are the mission, policy, and planning implications? What are the lessons learned? Going forward, what is next? How should future actions be assessed, measured, benchmarked, and monitored for the future?

- ✓ **First Step** accept the case-situational scenario (CSS) by the assigned "top executive" administrator with the charge and challenge to make recommendations for resolve, intervention, or solution.
- ✓ **Second Step** appoint a "unit based" administrative lead person to facilitate the process and navigate the execution for resolve within the prescribed three-day time period.
- ✓ **Third Step** appoint a diverse group of staff, faculty, and students to serve as a decision-making unit (DMU) for the three-day period.

✓ **Fourth Step**, this group's operations should follow the first step's recommendations but also include areas that are suggested for productivity by the group.

✓ **Fifth Step** require the decision-making unit to conduct a preliminary screening of the case scenario to assure that there are some analytical fundamentals from the foundations of critical thinking.

✓ **Sixth Step**, review literature, data bases, information repositories and practices at two other Carnegie-classified," peer" institutions that are related to the case scenario and will contribute to the body of work and deliberations from the DMU. Suggested databases: *Academic Search Premier; Education Research Complete; JSTOR; PsycArticles*

✓ **Seventh Step** frame a working logic model that captures the necessary basic elements and major components that are fundamental to the problem.

✓ **Eighth Step** conduct a "mid-way" group reflection session and continue to follow the thirteen–step HEART process for implementing "general" data collection and analysis.

✓ **Ninth Step** collect "specific" data about the problem; analyze data about the problem; identify means for data authentication, validity, verification, reliability, and trustworthiness (if needed) concerning the problem; determine the meaning of the data relative to the problem. There are guidelines and procedures that one should follow when addressing problems and issues regardless of their nature. One of the things that must be done is to gather data related to the problem in order to come up with an appropriate resolution. Prior to data collection several issues must be addressed including the ones listed below:

A. Identifying the population from which the data is to be collected
B. Gaining permission from individuals and/or organizations to carry out the data collection process
C. Determining the type of data needed to address the problem or issue under consideration
D. Creating or identifying an instrument to use in collecting the data
E. Carrying out the data collection procedures

In general, the data collection process is similar regardless of the type of data (quantitative or qualitative) being collected. When dealing with quantitative data, however, one should consider the level of analysis and sampling procedures. Different types of permissions may also be required, depending on whether you are sampling individuals, institutions, or agencies. Gaining informed consent is particularly important to protect the privacy and confidentiality of participants. Operational definitions must be assigned to all variables to be studied. Types of data and measures must be determined prior to the data collection process. Whether the instrument is to measure individual performance, individual attitude, individual behavior, or factual information must be established. Data collection instruments must be identified or designed. The ones utilized must be reliable and valid. Reliable instruments ensure consistency of measurement while valid instruments provide evidence that what purports to be measured is, in fact, measured. Several widely used methods of establishing reliability include the following:

- Test-retest reliability
- Alternate forms reliability
- Inter-rater reliability
- Internal consistency

Traditional types of validity coefficients include:

- Content validity
- Construct validity
- Criterion-related validity

A standardized process for the collection of data must be identified or created and utilized.

✓ **Tenth Step** propose a remedy, resolve, or resolution about the problem; pilot or pre-test the remedy, resolve, or resolution to the problem from a selected qualitative protocol or quantitative instrument (if needed); analyze the data to validate, verify, or support reliability and trustworthiness (if needed).

✓ **Eleventh Step** develop recommendations for new practices or pro-active measures to prevent the problem occurring again; identify measurements and metrics for analyzing the new practice, policy, procedure, or process that has been developed as a result of previous steps.

✓ **Twelfth Step** place the proposed new practice, policy, or procedure on the internal web link and allow stakeholders on campus the opportunity to provide feedback on the proposed recommendations by the DMU.

✓ **Thirteenth Step**, address for a second time any issues concerning proactive or preventative measures after a thorough and final consideration of stakeholder input and integration of the new practice, policy, process, procedure, protocol or plan into the institutional strategic plan and unit-based budget where the problem was developed.

Case Scenario Number 2: For Academic Affairs
ACADEMIC PROGRAM REVIEW, PERFORMANCE AND PRODUCTIVITY

The provost of the state's only publicly supported liberal arts college has conducted an academic program review to determine performance and productivity levels of all academic programs of study. She has asked the deans and academic chairs to provide her with recommendations on which programs should be strengthened, which programs should be placed on probation, and which programs should be eliminated. Many of the low-producing programs are central to the liberal arts mission but failed to secure appropriate enrollment levels in today's market. Among the areas that are low producing are poetry, history, psychology, sociology, and art. The provost remains supportive of these disciplines but has been charged by the president and board of trustees to develop an action plan that allows the liberal arts mission to be maintained but within the context of much needed modernization within the disciplines. The faculty at the college is committed to their discipline and the students that they serve; however, many students believe that the faculty is not teaching in ways and methods that are market responsive to the modern workplace. What type of data needs to be collected? From whom and from where? What should be the methodology? How will the data be used? What actions should be taken after the data has been collected, shared, and analyzed? What is the mission, policy, and planning implications? Who is at stake? What are the lessons learned? Going forward, what is next? How should future actions be assessed, measured, benchmarked, and monitored for the future?

- ✓ **First Step** accept the case-situational scenario (CSS) by the assigned "top executive" administrator with the charge and challenge to make recommendations for resolve, intervention, or solution.
- ✓ **Second Step** appoint a "unit based" administrative lead person to facilitate the process and navigate the execution for resolve within the prescribed three-day time period.

- ✓ **Third Step** appoint a diverse group of staff, faculty, and students to serve as a decision-making unit (DMU) for the three-day period.
- ✓ **Fourth Step**, this group's operations should follow the first step's recommendations but also include areas that are suggested for productivity by the group.
- ✓ **Fifth Step** require the decision-making unit to conduct a preliminary screening of the case scenario to assure some analytical fundamentals from the foundations of critical thinking.
- ✓ **Sixth Step**, review literature, data bases, information repositories and practices at two other Carnegie-classified," peer" institutions that are related to the case scenario and will contribute to the body of work and deliberations from the DMU. Suggested databases: *Academic Search Premier; Education Research Complete; JSTOR; PsycArticles*
- ✓ **Seventh Step** frame a working logic model that captures the necessary basic elements and major components that are fundamental to the problem.
- ✓ **Eighth Step** conduct a "mid-way" group reflection session and continue to follow the thirteen–step HEART process for implementing "general" data collection and analysis.
- ✓ **Ninth Step** collect "specific" data about the problem; analyze data about the problem; identify means for data authentication, validity, verification, reliability, and trustworthiness (if needed) concerning the problem; determine the meaning of the data relative to the problem. There are guidelines and procedures that one should follow when addressing problems and issues regardless of their nature. One of the things that must be done is to gather data related to the problem in order to come up with an appropriate resolution. Prior to data collection several issues must be addressed including the ones listed below:

    A. Identifying the population from which the data is to be collected
    B. Gaining permission from individuals and/or organizations to carry out the data collection process
    C. Determining the type of data needed to address the problem or issue under consideration
    D. Creating or identifying an instrument to use in collecting the data
    E. Carrying out the data collection procedures

In general, the data collection process is similar regardless of the type of data (quantitative or qualitative) being collected. When dealing with quantitative data, however, one should consider the level of analysis and sampling procedures. Different types of permissions may also be

required, depending on whether you are sampling individuals, institutions, or agencies. Gaining informed consent is particularly important to protect the privacy and confidentiality of participants. Operational definitions must be assigned to all variables to be studied. Types of data and measures must be determined prior to the data collection process. Whether the instrument is to measure individual performance, individual attitude, individual behavior, or factual information must be established. Data collection instruments must be identified or designed. The ones utilized must be reliable and valid. Reliable instruments ensure consistency of measurement while valid instruments provide evidence that what purports to be measured is, in fact, measured. Several widely used methods of establishing reliability include the following:

- Test-retest reliability
- Alternate forms reliability
- Inter-rater reliability
- Internal consistency

Traditional types of validity coefficients include:

- Content validity
- Construct validity
- Criterion-related validity

A standardized process for the collection of data must be identified or created and utilized.

- ✓ **Tenth Step** propose a remedy, resolve, or resolution about the problem; pilot or pre-test the remedy, resolve, or resolution to the problem from a selected qualitative protocol or quantitative instrument (if needed); analyze the data to validate, verify, or support reliability and trustworthiness (if needed).
- ✓ **Eleventh Step** develop recommendations for new practices or proactive measures to prevent the problem occurring again; identify measurements and metrics for analyzing the new practice, policy, procedure, or process that has been developed as a result of previous steps.
- ✓ **Twelfth Step** place the proposed new practice, policy, or procedure on the internal web link and allow stakeholders on campus the opportunity to provide feedback on the proposed recommendations by the DMU.

✓ **Thirteenth Step**, address for a second time any issues concerning proactive or preventative measures after a thorough and final consideration of stakeholder input and integration of the new practice, policy, process, procedure, protocol or plan into the institutional strategic plan and unit-based budget where the problem was developed.

Case Scenario Number 3: For Academic Affairs
ONLINE CLASSES, DISTANCE LEARNING AND STUDENT DEMAND

The student government association for a regional university located in a rural part of the state has gathered petitions from the student body in preparation for a meeting with the university president. The petition complains about the lack of on-line courses at the institution that should be offered at the institution so that more students can complete classes from their homes that are located in rural towns throughout the region. Although the students do enjoy coming to the campus for socialization and interaction with other students in the classroom and throughout the campus, they would still like to have the access and opportunity to complete courses at home so that they can be closer to their families, save on transportation fuel, and utilize the computer laboratory at the local library for on-line classes with the institution. The president is supportive of the on-line advocacy by the students, but the campus faculty believes the president has not provided the technological infrastructure to implement successful on-line offerings. Students have threatened to leave the campus and enroll at another institution if the campus does not respond to the petition. What type of data needs to be collected? From whom and from where? What should be the methodology? How will the data be used? What actions should be taken after the data has been collected, shared, and analyzed? Who is at stake? What are the mission, policy, and planning implications? What are the lessons learned? Going forward, what is next? How should future actions be assessed, measured, benchmarked, and monitored for the future?

✓ **First Step** accept the case-situational scenario (CSS) by the assigned "top executive" administrator with the charge and challenge to make recommendations for resolve, intervention, or solution.

☑ **Second Step** appoint a "unit based" administrative lead person to facilitate the process and navigate the execution for resolve within the prescribed three-day time period.

☑ **Third Step** appoint a diverse group of staff, faculty, and students to serve as a decision-making unit (DMU) for the three-day period.

☑ **Fourth Step**, this group's operations should follow the first step's recommendations but also include areas that are suggested for productivity by the group.

☑ **Fifth Step** require the decision-making unit to conduct a preliminary screening of the case scenario to assure some analytical fundamentals from the foundations of critical thinking.

☑ **Sixth Step**, review literature, data bases, information repositories and practices at two other Carnegie-classified," peer" institutions that are related to the case scenario and will contribute to the body of work and deliberations from the DMU. Suggested databases: *Academic Search Premier; Education Research Complete; JSTOR; PsycArticles*

☑ **Seventh Step** frame a working logic model that captures the necessary basic elements and major components that are fundamental to the problem.

☑ **Eighth Step** conduct a "mid-way" group reflection session and continue to follow the thirteen–step HEART process for implementing "general" data collection and analysis.

☑ **Ninth Step** collect "specific" data about the problem; analyze data about the problem; identify means for data authentication, validity, verification, reliability, and trustworthiness (if needed) concerning the problem; determine the meaning of the data relative to the problem. There are guidelines and procedures that one should follow when addressing problems and issues regardless of their nature. One of the things that must be done is to gather data related to the problem in order to come up with an appropriate resolution. Prior to data collection several issues must be addressed including the ones listed below:

A. Identifying the population from which the data is to be collected
B. Gaining permission from individuals and/or organizations to carry out the data collection process
C. Determining the type of data needed to address the problem or issue under consideration
D. Creating or identifying an instrument to use in collecting the data
E. Carrying out the data collection procedures

In general, the data collection process is similar regardless of the type of data (quantitative or qualitative) being collected. When dealing with quantitative data, however, one should consider the level of analysis and sampling procedures. Different types of permissions may also be required, depending on whether you are sampling individuals, institutions, or agencies. Gaining informed consent is particularly important to protect the privacy and confidentiality of participants. Operational definitions must be assigned to all variables to be studied. Types of data and measures must be determined prior to the data collection process. Whether the instrument is to measure individual performance, individual attitude, individual behavior, or factual information must be established. Data collection instruments must be identified or designed. The ones utilized must be reliable and valid. Reliable instruments ensure consistency of measurement while valid instruments provide evidence that what purports to be measured is, in fact, measured. Several widely used methods of establishing reliability include the following:

- Test-retest reliability
- Alternate forms reliability
- Inter-rater reliability
- Internal consistency

Traditional types of validity coefficients include:

- Content validity
- Construct validity
- Criterion-related validity

A standardized process for the collection of data must be identified or created and utilized.

✓ **Tenth Step** propose a remedy, resolve, or resolution about the problem; pilot or pre-test the remedy, resolve, or resolution to the problem from a selected qualitative protocol or quantitative instrument (if needed); analyze the data to validate, verify, or support reliability and trustworthiness (if needed).

✓ **Eleventh Step** develop recommendations for new practices or pro-active measures to prevent the problem occurring again; identify measurements and metrics for analyzing the new practice, policy, procedure, or process that has been developed as a result of previous steps.

- ✓ **Twelfth Step** place the proposed new practice, policy, or procedure on the internal web link and allow stakeholders on campus the opportunity to provide feedback on the proposed recommendations by the DMU.
- ✓ **Thirteenth Step**, address for a second time any issues concerning proactive or preventative measures after a thorough and final consideration of stakeholder input and integration of the new practice, policy, process, procedure, protocol or plan into the institutional strategic plan and unit-based budget where the problem was developed.

Case Scenario Number 4: For Student Affairs
DOCUMENTATION, ENROLLMENT MANAGEMENT AND TECHNOLOGY

A small minority-serving university in the southeastern United States is converting to a recordkeeping system that is widely used by colleges and universities. The computer technology team must work closely with institutional leaders to ensure that the new system meets their specific record-keeping needs. The design of the student records module occurred without consultation with the chief student affairs officer. The departments reporting to the student affairs leader were the traditional enrollment management offices (e.g. recruitment, admission, registrar, financial aid), student support services (e.g. housing, health services, dean of students), and student development (e.g. student government, career services). After inquiring about the status of the new system, the student affairs leader learned that an aggrieved member of the staff, who aspired to be the chief student affairs officer, had clandestinely designed the student affairs module in collaboration with the vice president of information technology. The vice president later finagled a transfer of that individual to his division along with the entire enrollment management unit. What type of data needs to be collected? From whom and from where? What should be the methodology? How will the data be used? What actions should be taken after the data has been collected, shared, and analyzed? Who is at stake? What are the mission, policy, and planning implications? What are the lessons learned? Going forward, what is next? How should future actions be assessed, measured, benchmarked, and monitored for the future?

- ✓ **First Step** accept the case-situational scenario (CSS) by the assigned "top executive" administrator with the charge and challenge to make recommendations for resolve, intervention, or solution.

✓ **Second Step** appoint a "unit based" administrative lead person to facilitate the process and navigate the execution for resolve within the prescribed three-day time period.

✓ **Third Step** appoint a diverse group of staff, faculty, and students to serve as a decision-making unit (DMU) for the three-day period.

✓ **Fourth Step**, this group's operations should follow the first step's recommendations but also include areas that are suggested for productivity by the group.

✓ **Fifth Step** require the decision-making unit to conduct a preliminary screening of the case scenario to assure some analytical fundamentals from the foundations of critical thinking.

✓ **Sixth Step**, review literature, data bases, information repositories and practices at two other Carnegie-classified," peer" institutions that are related to the case scenario and will contribute to the body of work and deliberations from the DMU. Suggested databases: *ACM Digital Library*; *Edible Digital Library; Education Research Complete; ERIC*

✓ **Seventh Step** frame a working logic model that captures the necessary basic elements and major components that are fundamental to the problem.

✓ **Eighth Step** conduct a "mid-way" group reflection session and continue to follow the thirteen–step HEART process for implementing "general" data collection and analysis.

✓ **Ninth Step** collect "specific" data about the problem; analyze data about the problem; identify means for data authentication, validity, verification, reliability, and trustworthiness (if needed) concerning the problem; determine the meaning of the data relative to the problem. There are guidelines and procedures that one should follow when addressing problems and issues regardless of their nature. One of the things that must be done is to gather data related to the problem in order to come up with an appropriate resolution. Prior to data collection several issues must be addressed including the ones listed below:

A. Identifying the population from which the data is to be collected
B. Gaining permission from individuals and/or organizations to carry out the data collection process
C. Determining the type of data needed to address the problem or issue under consideration
D. Creating or identifying an instrument to use in collecting the data
E. Carrying out the data collection procedures

In general, the data collection process is similar regardless of the type of data (quantitative or qualitative) being collected. When dealing

with quantitative data, however, one should consider the level of analysis and sampling procedures. Different types of permissions may also be required, depending on whether you are sampling individuals, institutions, or agencies. Gaining informed consent is particularly important to protect the privacy and confidentiality of participants. Operational definitions must be assigned to all variables to be studied. Types of data and measures must be determined prior to the data collection process. Whether the instrument is to measure individual performance, individual attitude, individual behavior, or factual information must be established. Data collection instruments must be identified or designed. The ones utilized must be reliable and valid. Reliable instruments ensure consistency of measurement while valid instruments provide evidence that what purports to be measured is, in fact, measured. Several widely used methods of establishing reliability include the following:

- Test-retest reliability
- Alternate forms reliability
- Inter-rater reliability
- Internal consistency

Traditional types of validity coefficients include:

- Content validity
- Construct validity
- Criterion-related validity

A standardized process for the collection of data must be identified or created and utilized.

> ✓ **Tenth Step** propose a remedy, resolve, or resolution about the problem; pilot or pre-test the remedy, resolve, or resolution to the problem from a selected qualitative protocol or quantitative instrument (if needed); analyze the data to validate, verify, or support reliability and trustworthiness (if needed).
> ✓ **Eleventh Step** develop recommendations for new practices or pro-active measures to prevent the problem occurring again; identify measurements and metrics for analyzing the new practice, policy, procedure, or process that has been developed as a result of previous steps.
> ✓ **Twelfth Step** place the proposed new practice, policy, or procedure on the internal web link and allow stakeholders on campus the

opportunity to provide feedback on the proposed recommendations by the DMU.

✓ **Thirteenth Step**, address for a second time any issues concerning proactive or preventative measures after a thorough and final consideration of stakeholder input and integration of the new practice, policy, process, procedure, protocol or plan into the institutional strategic plan and unit-based budget where the problem was developed.

Case Scenario Number 5: For Student Affairs
STUDENT HOUSING, STUDENT LIFE, AND RELATIONS

A part-time employer, dormitory roommate, family, and instructors are panicked that a female student is missing from an urban university. It is unusual for the student not to seen or heard from by all of them daily. As time passes, investigators learn that the female has been experiencing relationship problems with her male friend who is a student at the same university. The female had told close friends of recent incidences of physical abuse and her desire to end the relationship. The last sighting of the student was outside of a campus building as she was getting into a car with her male friend. For days, university officials, her parents, and the community searched for the student. After continued questioning, her male friend led police to her deteriorating body after more than a week. Her body lay in a field near a college on the outskirts of the city. He confessed that he caused the death by hitting the female whose head hit-the-door during the altercation. What precautions can be taken to prevent a similar incident in the future? What type of data needs to be collected? From whom and from where? What should be the methodology? How will the data be used? What actions should be taken after the data has been collected, shared, and analyzed? What is the mission, policy, and planning implications? Who is at stake? What are the lessons learned? Going forward, what is next? How should future actions be assessed, measured, benchmarked, and monitored for the future?

- ✓ **First Step** accept the case-situational scenario (CSS) by the assigned "top executive" administrator with the charge and challenge to make recommendations for resolve, intervention, or solution.
- ✓ **Second Step** appoint a "unit based" administrative lead person to facilitate the process and navigate the execution for resolve within the prescribed three-day time period.
- ✓ **Third Step** appoint a diverse group of staff, faculty, and students to serve as a decision-making unit (DMU) for the three-day period.
- ✓ **Fourth Step**, this group's operations should follow the first step's recommendations but also include areas that are suggested for productivity by the group.

✓ **Fifth Step** require the decision-making unit to conduct a preliminary screening of the case scenario to assure some analytical fundamentals from the foundations of critical thinking.

✓ **Sixth Step**, review literature, data bases, information repositories and practices at two other Carnegie-classified," peer" institutions that are related to the case scenario and will contribute to the body of work and deliberations from the DMU. Suggested databases: *Academic Search Premier; Education Research Complete; PsycArticles*

✓ **Seventh Step** frame a working logic model that captures the necessary basic elements and major components that are fundamental to the problem.

✓ **Eighth Step** conduct a "mid-way" group reflection session and continue to follow the thirteen–step HEART process for implementing "general" data collection and analysis.

✓ **Ninth Step** collect "specific" data about the problem; analyze data about the problem; identify means for data authentication, validity, verification, reliability, and trustworthiness (if needed) concerning the problem; determine the meaning of the data relative to the problem. There are guidelines and procedures that one should follow when addressing problems and issues regardless of their nature. One of the things that must be done is to gather data related to the problem in order to come up with an appropriate resolution. Prior to data collection several issues must be addressed including the ones listed below:

A. Identifying the population from which the data is to be collected
B. Gaining permission from individuals and/or organizations to carry out the data collection process
C. Determining the type of data needed to address the problem or issue under consideration
D. Creating or identifying an instrument to use in collecting the data
E. Carrying out the data collection procedures

In general, the data collection process is similar regardless of the type of data (quantitative or qualitative) being collected. When dealing with quantitative data, however, one should consider the level of analysis and sampling procedures. Different types of permissions may also be required, depending on whether you are sampling individuals, institutions, or agencies. Gaining informed consent is particularly important to protect the privacy and confidentiality of participants. Operational definitions must be assigned to all variables to be studied. Types of data and measures

must be determined prior to the data collection process. Whether the instrument is to measure individual performance, individual attitude, individual behavior, or factual information must be established. Data collection instruments must be identified or designed. The ones utilized must be reliable and valid. Reliable instruments ensure consistency of measurement while valid instruments provide evidence that what purports to be measured is, in fact, measured. Several widely used methods of establishing reliability include the following:

- Test-retest reliability
- Alternate forms reliability
- Inter-rater reliability
- Internal consistency

Traditional types of validity coefficients include:

- Content validity
- Construct validity
- Criterion-related validity

A standardized process for the collection of data must be identified or created and utilized.

✓ **Tenth Step** propose a remedy, resolve, or resolution about the problem; pilot or pre-test the remedy, resolve, or resolution to the problem from a selected qualitative protocol or quantitative instrument (if needed); analyze the data to validate, verify, or support reliability and trustworthiness (if needed).

✓ **Eleventh Step** develop recommendations for new practices or proactive measures to prevent the problem occurring again; identify measurements and metrics for analyzing the new practice, policy, procedure, or process that has been developed as a result of previous steps.

✓ **Twelfth Step** place the proposed new practice, policy, or procedure on the internal web link and allow stakeholders on campus the opportunity to provide feedback on the proposed recommendations by the DMU.

✓ **Thirteenth Step**, address for a second time any issues concerning proactive or preventative measures after a thorough and final consideration of stakeholder input and integration of the new practice, policy, process, procedure, protocol or plan into the institutional strategic plan and unit-based budget where the problem was developed.

Case Scenario Number 6: For Student Affairs
RESOURCES, PROFESSIONAL DEVELOPMENT AND CREATIVITY

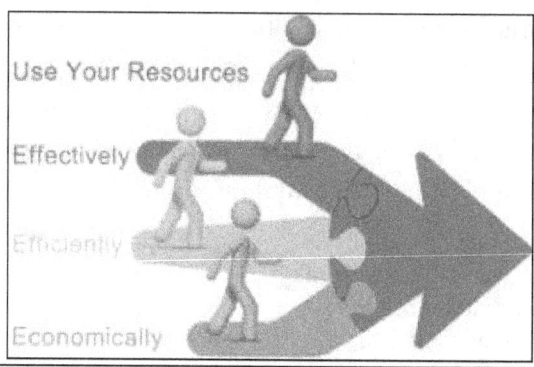

Funds for professional development are limited at a small southern university, but student affairs staffs rarely have time to participate in such activities away from the campus. There are limited numbers of staff and many of them are essential to student affairs operations. The traditional methods of serving students, including *in loco parentis*, have long faded. Federal and state regulations have many legal prescriptions for preserving student rights. As typical, students' knowledge of their rights is more contemporary than that of student affairs' staffs. Therefore, if Mohammad cannot go to the mountain, the mountain must come to Mohammad. Student affairs leaders must create opportunities for professional development of staffs, using creativity and innovation. How does the student affairs leader identify the developmental needs of staff? What are some alternative professional development strategies? What type of data needs to be collected? From whom and from where? What should be the methodology? How will the data be used? What actions should be taken after the data has been collected, shared, and analyzed? Who is at stake? What is the mission, policy, and planning implications? What are the lessons learned? Going forward, what is next? How should future actions be assessed, measured, benchmarked, and monitored for the future?

✓ **First Step** accept the case-situational scenario (CSS) by the assigned "top executive" administrator with the charge and challenge to make recommendations for resolve, intervention, or solution.

✓ **Second Step** appoint a "unit based" administrative lead person to facilitate the process and navigate the execution for resolve within the prescribed three-day time period.

✓ **Third Step** appoint a diverse group of staff, faculty, and students to serve as a decision-making unit (DMU) for the three-day period.

✓ **Fourth Step**, this group's operations should follow the first step's recommendations but also include areas that are suggested for productivity by the group.

- ✓ **Fifth Step** require the decision-making unit to conduct a preliminary screening of the case scenario to assure some analytical fundamentals from the foundations of critical thinking.
- ✓ **Sixth Step**, review literature, data bases, information repositories and practices at two other Carnegie-classified," peer" institutions that are related to the case scenario and will contribute to the body of work and deliberations from the DMU. Suggested databases: *ABI/Inform Complete; Business Source Complete; ERIC; LexisNexis Academic*
- ✓ **Seventh Step** frame a working logic model that captures the necessary basic elements and major components that are fundamental to the problem.
- ✓ **Eighth Step** conduct a "mid-way" group reflection session and continue to follow the thirteen–step HEART process for implementing "general" data collection and analysis.
- ✓ **Ninth Step** collect "specific" data about the problem; analyze data about the problem; identify means for data authentication, validity, verification, reliability, and trustworthiness (if needed) concerning the problem; determine the meaning of the data relative to the problem. There are guidelines and procedures that one should follow when addressing problems and issues regardless of their nature. One of the things that must be done is to gather data related to the problem in order to come up with an appropriate resolution. Prior to data collection several issues must be addressed including the ones listed below:

    A. Identifying the population from which the data is to be collected
    B. Gaining permission from individuals and/or organizations to carry out the data collection process
    C. Determining the type of data needed to address the problem or issue under consideration
    D. Creating or identifying an instrument to use in collecting the data
    E. Carrying out the data collection procedures

In general, the data collection process is similar regardless of the type of data (quantitative or qualitative) being collected. When dealing with quantitative data, however, one should consider the level of analysis and sampling procedures. Different types of permissions may also be required, depending on whether you are sampling individuals, institutions, or agencies. Gaining informed consent is particularly important to protect the privacy and confidentiality of participants. Operational definitions must be assigned to all variables to be studied. Types of data and measures

must be determined prior to the data collection process. Whether the instrument is to measure individual performance, individual attitude, individual behavior, or factual information must be established. Data collection instruments must be identified or designed. The ones utilized must be reliable and valid. Reliable instruments ensure consistency of measurement while valid instruments provide evidence that what purports to be measured is, in fact, measured. Several widely used methods of establishing reliability include the following:

- Test-retest reliability
- Alternate forms reliability
- Inter-rater reliability
- Internal consistency

Traditional types of validity coefficients include:

- Content validity
- Construct validity
- Criterion-related validity

A standardized process for the collection of data must be identified or created and utilized.

- ✓ **Tenth Step** propose a remedy, resolve, or resolution about the problem; pilot or pre-test the remedy, resolve, or resolution to the problem from a selected qualitative protocol or quantitative instrument (if needed); analyze the data to validate, verify, or support reliability and trustworthiness (if needed).
- ✓ **Eleventh Step** develop recommendations for new practices or pro-active measures to prevent the problem occurring again; identify measurements and metrics for analyzing the new practice, policy, procedure, or process that has been developed as a result of previous steps.
- ✓ **Twelfth Step** place the proposed new practice, policy, or procedure on the internal web link and allow stakeholders on campus the opportunity to provide feedback on the proposed recommendations by the DMU.
- ✓ **Thirteenth Step**, address for a second time any issues concerning proactive or preventative measures after a thorough and final consideration of stakeholder input and integration of the new practice, policy, process, procedure, protocol or plan into the institutional strategic plan and unit-based budget where the problem was developed.

4. Description of scope and sequential frameworks for heart   77

Case Scenario Number 7: For Financial Affairs
REVENUE SOURCES, STREAMS AND SOLVENCY

The funding sources for most public colleges and universities, tuition, appropriations, grants, and auxiliaries, as well as the institutional Foundations receiving charitable contributions on their behalf, are increasingly scrutinized in today's economy. A recent Board of Trustees' Forecast Report for a midsized research state university in the Northeast showed a 10-year negative trend in state funding to higher education. Simultaneously, according to a 1998 USDE report on tuition cost, the trajectory of higher education cost has and continues to outpace inflation by 400%. Another factor to consider is a state mandate of 10% minority student enrollment at selected institutions, as part of a landmark settlement in a racial discrimination case. How does an institution address the issues of shrinking revenues while also funding an endowment to subsidize institutional sustainability and fiscal solvency? What type of data needs to be collected? From whom and from where? What should be the methodology? How will the data be used? What actions should be taken after the data has been collected, shared, and analyzed? What is the mission, policy, and planning implications? Who is at stake? What are the lessons learned? Going forward, what is next? How should future actions be assessed, measured, benchmarked, and monitored for the future?

- ✓ **First Step** accept the case-situational scenario (CSS) by the assigned "top executive" administrator with the charge and challenge to make recommendations for resolve, intervention, or solution.

- ✓ **Second Step** appoint a "unit based" administrative lead person to facilitate the process and navigate the execution for resolve within the prescribed three-day time period.
- ✓ **Third Step** appoint a diverse group of staff, faculty, and students to serve as a decision-making unit (DMU) for the three-day period.
- ✓ **Fourth Step**, this group's operations should follow the first step's recommendations but also include areas that are suggested for productivity by the group.
- ✓ **Fifth Step** require the decision-making unit to conduct a preliminary screening of the case scenario to assure some analytical fundamentals from the foundations of critical thinking.
- ✓ **Sixth Step**, review literature, data bases, information repositories and practices at two other Carnegie-classified," peer" institutions that are related to the case scenario and will contribute to the body of work and deliberations from the DMU. Suggested databases: *Almanac of Higher Education; Education Research Complete; ERIC; LexisNexis Academic*
- ✓ **Seventh Step** frame a working logic model that captures the necessary basic elements and major components that are fundamental to the problem.
- ✓ **Eighth Step** conduct a "mid-way" group reflection session and continue to follow the thirteen–step HEART process for implementing "general" data collection and analysis.
- ✓ **Ninth Step** collect "specific" data about the problem; analyze data about the problem; identify means for data authentication, validity, verification, reliability, and trustworthiness (if needed) concerning the problem; determine the meaning of the data relative to the problem. There are guidelines and procedures that one should follow when addressing problems and issues regardless of their nature. One of the things that must be done is to gather data related to the problem in order to come up with an appropriate resolution. Prior to data collection several issues must be addressed including the ones listed below:

    A. Identifying the population from which the data is to be collected
    B. Gaining permission from individuals and/or organizations to carry out the data collection process
    C. Determining the type of data needed to address the problem or issue under consideration
    D. Creating or identifying an instrument to use in collecting the data
    E. Carrying out the data collection procedures

In general, the data collection process is similar regardless of the type of data (quantitative or qualitative) being collected. When dealing

with quantitative data, however, one should consider the level of analysis and sampling procedures. Different types of permissions may also be required, depending on whether you are sampling individuals, institutions, or agencies. Gaining informed consent is particularly important to protect the privacy and confidentiality of participants. Operational definitions must be assigned to all variables to be studied. Types of data and measures must be determined prior to the data collection process. Whether the instrument is to measure individual performance, individual attitude, individual behavior, or factual information must be established. Data collection instruments must be identified or designed. The ones utilized must be reliable and valid. Reliable instruments ensure consistency of measurement while valid instruments provide evidence that what purports to be measured is, in fact, measured. Several widely used methods of establishing reliability include the following:

- Test-retest reliability
- Alternate forms reliability
- Inter-rater reliability
- Internal consistency

Traditional types of validity coefficients include:

- Content validity
- Construct validity
- Criterion-related validity

A standardized process for the collection of data must be identified or created and utilized.

- ✓ **Tenth Step** propose a remedy, resolve, or resolution about the problem; pilot or pre-test the remedy, resolve, or resolution to the problem from a selected qualitative protocol or quantitative instrument (if needed); analyze the data to validate, verify, or support reliability and trustworthiness (if needed).
- ✓ **Eleventh Step** develop recommendations for new practices or pro-active measures to prevent the problem occurring again; identify measurements and metrics for analyzing the new practice, policy, procedure, or process that has been developed as a result of previous steps.
- ✓ **Twelfth Step**, place the proposed new practice, policy, or procedure on the internal web link and allow stakeholders on campus the opportunity to provide feedback on the proposed recommendations by the DMU.

✓ **Thirteenth Step**, address for a second time any issues concerning proactive or preventative measures after a thorough and final consideration of stakeholder input and integration of the new practice, policy, process, procedure, protocol or plan into the institutional strategic plan and unit-based budget where the problem was developed.

Case Scenario Number 8: For Financial Affairs
RESOURCE ALLOCATION, DEMANDS AND MANAGEMENT

With various resource constraints, the need to properly allocate and manage institutional resources has become a critical initiative for most public higher education institutions. Having expanded programs, services, and infrastructure during the economic boon (pre-2008 economic collapse), most public universities are now faced with an imbalance of an expand institutional foot print and shrinking state funding to support the physical, programmatic, and human capital expansion, which were also driven by the pre- 2008 growth. How does the institution identify its demand for services, i.e., the true fully loaded cost of providing such services? How should those resources be allocated to realize the maximum impact for both the students' and the university's long-term sustainability? What type of data needs to be collected? From whom and from where? What should be the methodology? Who is at stake? How will the data be used? What actions should be taken after the data has been collected, shared, and analyzed? What are the mission, policy, and planning implications? What are the lessons learned? Going forward, what is next? How should future actions be assessed, measured, benchmarked, and monitored for the future?

- ✓ **First Step** accept the case-situational scenario (CSS) by the assigned "top executive" administrator with the charge and challenge to make recommendations for resolve, intervention, or solution.
- ✓ **Second Step** appoint a "unit based" administrative lead person to facilitate the process and navigate the execution for resolve within the prescribed three-day time period.
- ✓ **Third Step** appoint a diverse group of staff, faculty, and students to serve as a decision-making unit (DMU) for the three-day period.
- ✓ **Fourth Step**, this group's operations should follow the first step's recommendations but also include areas that are suggested for productivity by the group.

✓ **Fifth Step** require the decision-making unit to conduct a preliminary screening of the case scenario to assure some analytical fundamentals from the foundations of critical thinking.

✓ **Sixth Step**, review literature, data bases, information repositories and practices at two other Carnegie-classified," peer" institutions that are related to the case scenario and will contribute to the body of work and deliberations from the DMU. Suggested databases: *ABI/Inform Complete; Business Source Complete; Education Research Complete; LexisNexis Academic; National Center for Education Statistics*

✓ **Seventh Step** frame a working logic model that captures the necessary basic elements and major components that are fundamental to the problem.

✓ **Eighth Step** conduct a "mid-way" group reflection session and continue to follow the thirteen–step HEART process for implementing "general" data collection and analysis.

✓ **Ninth Step** collect "specific" data about the problem; analyze data about the problem; identify means for data authentication, validity, verification, reliability, and trustworthiness (if needed) concerning the problem; determine the meaning of the data relative to the problem. There are guidelines and procedures that one should follow when addressing problems and issues, regardless of their nature. One of the things that must be done is to gather data related to the problem in order to come up with an appropriate resolution. Prior to data collection several issues must be addressed including the ones listed below:

A. Identifying the population from which the data is to be collected
B. Gaining permission from individuals and/or organizations to carry out the data collection process
C. Determining the type of data needed to address the problem or issue under consideration
D. Creating or identifying an instrument to use in collecting the data
E. Carrying out the data collection procedures

In general, the data collection process is similar regardless of the type of data (quantitative or qualitative) being collected. When dealing with quantitative data, however, one should consider the level of analysis and sampling procedures. Different types of permissions may also be required, depending on whether you are sampling individuals, institutions, or agencies. Gaining informed consent is particularly important to protect the privacy and confidentiality of participants. Operational definitions must be assigned to all variables to be studied. Types of data and measures must be determined prior to the data collection process. Whether the instrument is to measure individual performance, individual attitude, individual behavior, or factual information must be established. Data collection instruments must be identified or designed. The ones utilized must be reliable and valid. Reliable instruments ensure consistency of measurement while valid instruments provide evidence that what purports to be measured is, in fact, measured. Several widely used methods of establishing reliability include the following:

- Test-retest reliability
- Alternate forms reliability
- Inter-rater reliability
- Internal consistency

Traditional types of validity coefficients include:

- Content validity
- Construct validity
- Criterion-related validity

A standardized process for the collection of data must be identified or created and utilized.

✓ **Tenth Step** propose a remedy, resolve, or resolution about the problem; pilot or pre-test the remedy, resolve, or resolution to the problem from a selected qualitative protocol or quantitative instrument (if needed); analyze the data to validate, verify, or support reliability and trustworthiness (if needed).

✓ **Eleventh Step** develop recommendations for new practices or pro-active measures to prevent the problem occurring again; identify measurements and metrics for analyzing the new practice, policy, procedure, or process that has been developed as a result of previous steps.

✓ **Twelfth Step** place the proposed new practice, policy, or procedure on the internal web link and allow stakeholders on campus the opportunity to provide feedback on the proposed recommendations by the DMU.

✓ **Thirteenth Step**, address for a second time any issues concerning proactive or preventative measures after a thorough and final consideration of stakeholder input and integration of the new practice, policy, process, procedure, protocol or plan into the institutional strategic plan and unit-based budget where the problem was developed.

Case Scenario Number 9: For Financial Affairs
FACULTY AGING, TECHNOLOGY, AND FUNDING

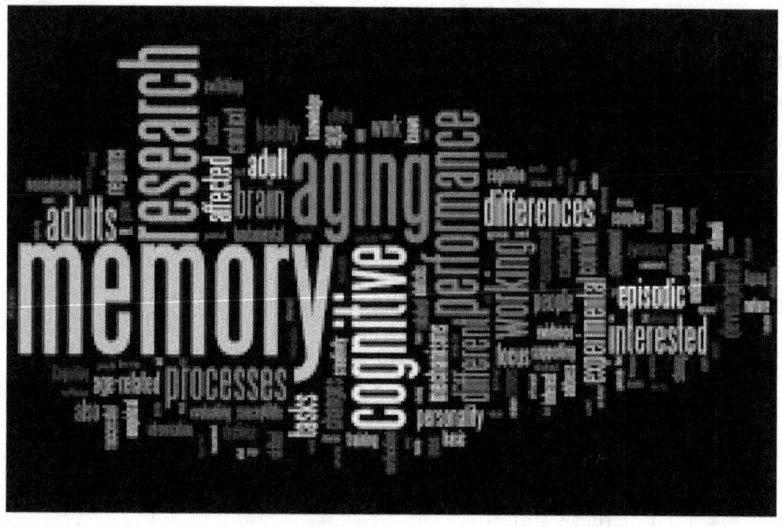

Sixty percent of XYZ university's personnel is 65 years old or older and nearing retirement. Most persons in this age group do not use technology as readily as the student population or their younger faculty colleagues. The slow integration of technology in the classroom directly correlates with faculty aged 65 and older, while the expansion of online programs and services directly correlates with faculty between the ages of 25-45. When funding resources are constrained, how does the institution expedite the integration of technology across all platforms, foster a pedagogy that leverages the latest advancements in education technology, recruit tech savvy faculty (at a reasonable cost) to drive new forms of course delivery and assessment, while maintaining the quality of programs and services needed to compete in local, national, and global competitive markets for students? What type of data needs to be collected? From whom and from where? What should be the methodology? Who is at stake? How will the data be used? What actions should be taken after the data has been collected, shared, and analyzed? What is the mission, policy, and planning implications? What are the lessons learned? Going forward, what is next? How should future actions be assessed, measured, benchmarked, and monitored for the future?

- ✓ **First Step** accept the case-situational scenario (CSS) by the assigned "top executive" administrator with the charge and challenge to make recommendations for resolve, intervention, or solution.
- ✓ **Second Step** appoint a "unit based" administrative lead person to facilitate the process and navigate the execution for resolve within the prescribed three-day time period.

- ✓ **Third Step** appoint a diverse group of staff, faculty, and students to serve as a decision-making unit (DMU) for the three-day period.
- ✓ **Fourth Step**, this group's operations should follow the first step's recommendations but also include areas that are suggested for productivity by the group.
- ✓ **Fifth Step** require the decision-making unit to conduct a preliminary screening of the case scenario to assure some analytical fundamentals from the foundations of critical thinking.
- ✓ **Sixth Step**, review literature, data bases, information repositories and practices at two other Carnegie-classified," peer" institutions that are related to the case scenario and will contribute to the body of work and deliberations from the DMU. Suggested databases: *ACM Digital Library; Academic Search Premier; EdITLib Digital Library; ERIC*
- ✓ **Seventh Step** frame a working logic model that captures the necessary basic elements and major components that are fundamental to the problem.
- ✓ **Eighth Step** conduct a "mid-way" group reflection session and continue to follow the thirteen–step HEART process for implementing "general" data collection and analysis.
- ✓ **Ninth Step** collect "specific" data about the problem; analyze data about the problem; identify means for data authentication, validity, verification, reliability, and trustworthiness (if needed) concerning the problem; determine the meaning of the data relative to the problem. There are guidelines and procedures that one should follow when addressing problems and issues regardless of their nature. One of the things that must be done is to gather data related to the problem in order to come up with an appropriate resolution. Prior to data collection several issues must be addressed including the ones listed below:

    A. Identifying the population from which the data is to be collected
    B. Gaining permission from individuals and/or organizations to carry out the data collection process
    C. Determining the type of data needed to address the problem or issue under consideration
    D. Creating or identifying an instrument to use in collecting the data
    E. Carrying out the data collection procedures

In general, the data collection process is similar regardless of the type of data (quantitative or qualitative) being collected. When dealing with quantitative data, however, one should consider the level of analysis and sampling procedures. Different types of permissions may also be

required, depending on whether you are sampling individuals, institutions, or agencies. Gaining informed consent is particularly important to protect the privacy and confidentiality of participants. Operational definitions must be assigned to all variables to be studied. Types of data and measures must be determined prior to the data collection process. Whether the instrument is to measure individual performance, individual attitude, individual behavior, or factual information must be established. Data collection instruments must be identified or designed. The ones utilized must be reliable and valid. Reliable instruments ensure consistency of measurement while valid instruments provide evidence that what purports to be measured is, in fact, measured. Several widely used methods of establishing reliability include the following:

- Test-retest reliability
- Alternate forms reliability
- Inter-rater reliability
- Internal consistency

Traditional types of validity coefficients include:
- Content validity
- Construct validity
- Criterion-related validity

A standardized process for the collection of data must be identified or created and utilized.

✓ **Tenth Step** propose a remedy, resolve, or resolution about the problem; pilot or pre-test the remedy, resolve, or resolution to the problem from a selected qualitative protocol or quantitative instrument (if needed); analyze the data to validate, verify, or support reliability and trustworthiness (if needed).

✓ **Eleventh Step** develop recommendations for new practices or pro-active measures to prevent the problem occurring again; identify measurements and metrics for analyzing the new practice, policy, procedure, or process that has been developed as a result of previous steps.

✓ **Twelfth Step** place the proposed new practice, policy, or procedure on the internal web link and allow stakeholders on campus the opportunity to provide feedback on the proposed recommendations by the DMU.

✓ **Thirteenth Step**, address for a second time any issues concerning proactive or preventative measures after a thorough and final consideration of stakeholder input and integration of the new practice, policy, process, procedure, protocol or plan into the institutional strategic plan and unit-based budget where the problem was developed.

Case Scenario Number 10: For Information Technology Management

TECHNOLOGICAL INFLUENCE, PROGRAMS AND SERVICES

Modern technology has been increasingly influencing the architecture, physical plants, and infrastructure in higher learning. XYZ University spent most of the past 12 years growing its infrastructure (i.e. buildings and degree programs). As buildings and programs increased, so did the cost of support services. With the cost of technology, personnel, and equipment outpacing inflation, CPI, and HEPI, what can the institution do to determine the optimal size of support services and the academy's demand for such services? What type of data needs to be collected? From whom and from where? What should be the methodology? How will the data be used? What actions should be taken after the data has been collected, shared, and analyzed? Who is at stake? What is the mission, policy, and planning implications? What are the lessons learned? Going forward, what is next? How should future actions be assessed, measured, benchmarked, and monitored for the future?

- ✓ **First Step** accept the case-situational scenario (CSS) by the assigned "top executive" administrator with the charge and challenge to make recommendations for resolve, intervention, or solution.
- ✓ **Second Step** appoint a "unit based" administrative lead person to facilitate the process and navigate the execution for resolve within the prescribed three-day time period.
- ✓ **Third Step** appoint a diverse group of staff, faculty, and students to serve as a decision-making unit (DMU) for the three-day period.
- ✓ **Fourth Step**, this group's operations should follow the first step's recommendations but also include areas that are suggested for productivity by the group.

- ✓ **Fifth Step** require the decision-making unit to conduct a preliminary screening of the case scenario to assure some analytical fundamentals from the foundations of critical thinking.
- ✓ **Sixth Step**, review literature, data bases, information repositories and practices at two other Carnegie-classified," peer" institutions that are related to the case scenario and will contribute to the body of work and deliberations from the DMU. Suggested databases: *ABI/Inform Complete; ACM Digital Library; EdITLib Digital Library; Education Research Complete; Professional Development Collection*
- ✓ **Seventh Step** frame a working logic model that captures the necessary basic elements and major components that are fundamental to the problem.
- ✓ **Eighth Step** conduct a "mid-way" group reflection session and continue to follow the thirteen–step HEAR process for implementing "general" data collection and analysis.
- ✓ **Ninth Step** collect "specific" data about the problem; analyze data about the problem; identify means for data authentication, validity, verification, reliability, and trustworthiness (if needed) concerning the problem; determine the meaning of the data relative to the problem. There are guidelines and procedures that one should follow when addressing problems and issues regardless of their nature. One of the things that must be done is to gather data related to the problem in order to come up with an appropriate resolution. Prior to data collection several issues must be addressed including the ones listed below:

    A. Identifying the population from which the data is to be collected
    B. Gaining permission from individuals and/or organizations to carry out the data collection process
    C. Determining the type of data needed to address the problem or issue under consideration
    D. Creating or identifying an instrument to use in collecting the data
    E. Carrying out the data collection procedures

In general, the data collection process is similar regardless of the type of data (quantitative or qualitative) being collected. When dealing with quantitative data, however, one should consider the level of analysis and sampling procedures. Different types of permissions may also be required, depending on whether you are sampling individuals, institutions, or agencies. Gaining informed consent is particularly important to protect the privacy and confidentiality of participants. Operational definitions must be assigned to all variables to be studied. Types of data and measures must be determined prior to the data collection process. Whether the instrument is to measure individual performance, individual attitude, individual behavior, or factual information must be established. Data collection instruments must be identified or designed. The ones utilized must be reliable and valid. Reliable instruments ensure consistency of measurement while valid instruments provide evidence that what purports to be measured is, in fact, measured. Several widely used methods of establishing reliability include the following:

- Test-retest reliability
- Alternate forms reliability
- Inter-rater reliability
- Internal consistency

Traditional types of validity coefficients include:

- Content validity
- Construct validity
- Criterion-related validity

A standardized process for the collection of data must be identified or created and utilized.

> ✓ **Tenth Step** propose a remedy, resolve, or resolution about the problem; pilot or pre-test the remedy, resolve, or resolution to the problem from a selected qualitative protocol or quantitative instrument (if needed); analyze the data to validate, verify, or support reliability and trustworthiness (if needed).
>
> ✓ **Eleventh Step** develop recommendations for new practices or pro-active measures to prevent the problem occurring again; identify measurements and metrics for analyzing the new practice, policy, procedure, or process that has been developed as a result of previous steps.
>
> ✓ **Twelfth Step** place the proposed new practice, policy, or procedure on the internal web link and allow stakeholders on campus the opportunity to provide feedback on the proposed recommendations by the DMU.
>
> ✓ **Thirteenth Step**, address for a second time any issues concerning proactive or preventative measures after a thorough and final consideration of stakeholder input and integration of the new practice, policy, process, procedure, protocol or plan into the institutional strategic plan and unit-based budget where the problem was developed.

Case Scenario Number 11: For Information Technology Management

SOFTWARE LICENCES, TRANSFER AND STUDENT CONSUMER

ABC University has struggled with software license agreements for the past 10 years and has decided to transfer the software license agreements to their student body. The University has asked the software companies to bundle the software licenses with textbooks, so that when the students purchase their textbooks, they will be buying software licenses with it. Should the university transfer the cost of software ownership to the student body and reduce its operating budget? What type of data needs to be collected? From whom and from where? What should be the methodology? How will the data be used? What actions should be taken after the data has been collected, shared, and analyzed? What is the mission, policy, and planning implications? Who is at stake? What are the lessons learned? Going forward, what is next? How should future actions be assessed, measured, benchmarked, and monitored for the future?

- ✓ **First Step** accept the case-situational scenario (CSS) by the assigned "top executive" administrator with the charge and challenge to make recommendations for resolve, intervention, or solution.
- ✓ **Second Step** appoint a "unit based" administrative lead person to facilitate the process and navigate the execution for resolve within the prescribed three-day time period.
- ✓ **Third Step** appoint a diverse group of staff, faculty, and students to serve as a decision-making unit (DMU) for the three-day period.
- ✓ **Fourth Step**, this group's operations should follow the first step's recommendations but also include areas that are suggested for productivity by the group.

✓ **Fifth Step** require the decision-making unit to conduct a preliminary screening of the case scenario to assure some analytical fundamentals from the foundations of critical thinking.

✓ **Sixth Step**, review literature, data bases, information repositories and practices at two other Carnegie-classified," peer" institutions that are related to the case scenario and will contribute to the body of work and deliberations from the DMU. Suggested databases: *Education Full Text; Education Research Complete; LexisNexis Academic*

✓ **Seventh Step** frame a working logic model that captures the necessary basic elements and major components that are fundamental to the problem.

✓ **Eighth Step** conduct a "mid-way" group reflection session and continue to follow the thirteen–step HEART process for implementing "general" data collection and analysis.

✓ **Ninth Step** collect "specific" data about the problem; analyze data about the problem; identify means for data authentication, validity, verification, reliability, and trustworthiness (if needed) concerning the problem; determine the meaning of the data relative to the problem. There are guidelines and procedures that one should follow when addressing problems and issues regardless of their nature. One of the things that must be done is to gather data related to the problem in order to come up with an appropriate resolution. Prior to data collection several issues must be addressed including the ones listed below:

A. Identifying the population from which the data is to be collected
B. Gaining permission from individuals and/or organizations to carry out the data collection process
C. Determining the type of data needed to address the problem or issue under consideration
D. Creating or identifying an instrument to use in collecting the data
E. Carrying out the data collection procedures

In general, the data collection process is similar regardless of the type of data (quantitative or qualitative) being collected. When dealing with quantitative data, however, one should consider the level of analysis and sampling procedures. Different types of permissions may also be required, depending on whether you are sampling individuals, institutions, or agencies. Gaining informed consent is particularly important to protect the privacy and confidentiality of participants. Operational definitions must be assigned to all variables to be studied. Types of data and measures must be determined prior to the data collection process. Whether the instrument is to measure individual performance, individual attitude, individual behavior, or factual information must be established. Data collection instruments must be identified or designed. The ones utilized must be reliable and valid. Reliable instruments ensure consistency of measurement while valid instruments provide evidence that what purports to be measured is, in fact, measured. Several widely used methods of establishing reliability include the following:

- Test-retest reliability
- Alternate forms reliability
- Inter-rater reliability
- Internal consistency

Traditional types of validity coefficients include:

- Content validity
- Construct validity
- Criterion-related validity

A standardized process for the collection of data must be identified or created and utilized.

✓ **Tenth Step** propose a remedy, resolve, or resolution about the problem; pilot or pre-test the remedy, resolve, or resolution to the problem from a selected qualitative protocol or quantitative instrument (if needed); analyze the data to validate, verify, or support reliability and trustworthiness (if needed).

✓ **Eleventh Step** develop recommendations for new practices or proactive measures to prevent the problem occurring again; identify measurements and metrics for analyzing the new practice, policy, procedure, or process that has been developed as a result of previous steps.

✓ **Twelfth Step** place the proposed new practice, policy, or procedure on the internal web link and allow stakeholders on campus the opportunity to provide feedback on the proposed recommendations by the DMU.

✓ **Thirteenth Step**, address for a second time any issues concerning proactive or preventative measures after a thorough and final consideration of stakeholder input and integration of the new practice, policy, process, procedure, protocol or plan into the institutional strategic plan and unit-based budget where the problem was developed.

Case Scenario Number 12: For Information Technology Management
OUTSOURCING TECHNOLOGY, SKILL SETS, AND INVESTMENT

> Many universities are challenged by the cost of recruiting skilled personnel to manage their technology infrastructure. Some of the methods devised to address this problem include: Outsourcing technology departments, laptop/iPod/iPad provisions for students accompanied by a student technology fee attached to tuition cost; and reducing operational costs associated with records storage, duplication and publication equipment, and paper usage. What factors should dictate the feasibility of technology outsourcing? Should the cost of outsourcing be transferred to the student? What criteria should be used to assess the benefits of outsourcing? What type of data needs to be collected? From whom and from where? What should be the methodology? How will the data be used? What actions should be taken after the data has been collected, shared, and analyzed? What is the mission, policy, and planning implications? Who is at stake? What are the lessons learned? Going forward, what is next? How should future actions be assessed, measured, benchmarked, and monitored for the future?

- ✓ **First Step** accept the case-situational scenario (CSS) by the assigned "top executive" administrator with the charge and challenge to make recommendations for resolve, intervention, or solution.
- ✓ **Second Step** appoint a "unit based" administrative lead person to facilitate the process and navigate the execution for resolve within the prescribed three-day time period.
- ✓ **Third Step** appoint a diverse group of staff, faculty, and students to serve as a decision-making unit (DMU) for the three-day period.
- ✓ **Fourth Step**, this group's operations should follow the first step's recommendations but also include areas that are suggested for productivity by the group.
- ✓ **Fifth Step** require the decision-making unit to conduct a preliminary screening of the case scenario to assure some analytical fundamentals from the foundations of critical thinking.

✓ **Sixth Step**, review literature, data bases, information repositories and practices at two other Carnegie-classified," peer" institutions that are related to the case scenario and will contribute to the body of work and deliberations from the DMU. Suggested databases: *ABI/Inform Complete; Business Source Complete; EdITLib Digital Library; Education Full Text*

✓ **Seventh Step** frame a working logic model that captures the necessary basic elements and major components that are fundamental to the problem.

✓ **Eighth Step** conduct a "mid-way" group reflection session and continue to follow the thirteen–step HEART process for implementing "general" data collection and analysis.

✓ **Ninth Step** collect "specific" data about the problem; analyze data about the problem; identify means for data authentication, validity, verification, reliability, and trustworthiness (if needed) concerning the problem; determine the meaning of the data relative to the problem. There are guidelines and procedures that one should follow when addressing problems and issues regardless of their nature. One of the things that must be done is to gather data related to the problem in order to come up with an appropriate resolution. Prior to data collection several issues must be addressed including the ones listed below:

A. Identifying the population from which the data is to be collected
B. Gaining permission from individuals and/or organizations to carry out the data collection process
C. Determining the type of data needed to address the problem or issue under consideration
D. Creating or identifying an instrument to use in collecting the data
E. Carrying out the data collection procedures

In general, the data collection process is similar regardless of the type of data (quantitative or qualitative) being collected. When dealing with quantitative data, however, one should consider the level of analysis and sampling procedures. Different types of permissions may also be required, depending on whether you are sampling individuals, institutions, or agencies. Gaining informed consent is particularly important to protect the privacy and confidentiality of participants. Operational definitions must be assigned to all variables to be studied. Types of data and measures must be determined prior to the data collection process. Whether the instrument is to measure individual performance, individual attitude, individual behavior, or factual information must be established. Data collection instruments must be identified or designed. The ones utilized must be reliable and valid. Reliable instruments ensure consistency of measurement while valid instruments provide evidence that what purports to be measured is, in fact, measured. Several widely used methods of establishing reliability include the following:

- Test-retest reliability
- Alternate forms reliability
- Inter-rater reliability
- Internal consistency

Traditional types of validity coefficients include:

- Content validity
- Construct validity
- Criterion-related validity

A standardized process for the collection of data must be identified or created and utilized.

✓ **Tenth Step** propose a remedy, resolve, or resolution about the problem; pilot or pre-test the remedy, resolve, or resolution to the problem from a selected qualitative protocol or quantitative instrument (if needed); analyze the data to validate, verify, or support reliability and trustworthiness (if needed).

✓ **Eleventh Step** develop recommendations for new practices or proactive measures to prevent the problem occurring again; identify measurements and metrics for analyzing the new practice, policy, procedure, or process that has been developed as a result of previous steps.

✓ **Twelfth Step** place the proposed new practice, policy, or procedure on the internal web link and allow stakeholders on campus the opportunity to provide feedback on the proposed recommendations by the DMU.

✓ **Thirteenth Step**, address for a second time any issues concerning proactive or preventative measures after a thorough and final consideration of stakeholder input and integration of the new practice, policy, process, procedure, protocol or plan into the institutional strategic plan and unit-based budget where the problem was developed.

Case Scenario Number 13: For Community Affairs
COMMUNITY EXPANSION, MARKETSHARE, AND ENROLLMENT

The city council for a metropolitan city requested to meet with the board of regents over the local university to discuss the feasibility of the university extending its offerings and branching out to some of the surrounding suburban areas of the downtown area of the city where the university is located. Although many of the suburban area residents work downtown near the university, these same residents have expressed an interest in taking classes from the university on the weekends and in the evenings closer to their neighborhoods. The residents' homes are complete with the computer technology to also take courses on-line from the university; however, many of the residents are older and would prefer to interact with other students in a classroom setting. The faculty at the institution already feels stretched with their current workload and the academic chairs are concerned that the offerings at the downtown campus would be compromised if faculty members are stretched too far, particularly under their current compensation provisions. The regents have asked the president to pursue the outreach efforts to enhance enrollment and subsequent revenue streams. What type of data needs to be collected? From whom and from where? What should be the methodology? How will the data be used? What actions should be taken after the data has been collected, shared, and analyzed? What are the mission, policy, and planning implications? Who is at stake? What are the lessons learned? Going forward, what is next? How should future actions be assessed, measured, benchmarked, and monitored for the future?

✓ **First Step** accept the case-situational scenario (CSS) by the assigned "top executive" administrator with the charge and challenge to make recommendations for resolve, intervention, or solution.

✓ **Second Step** appoint a "unit based" administrative lead person to facilitate the process and navigate the execution for resolve within the prescribed three-day time period.

✓ **Third Step** appoint a diverse group of staff, faculty, and students to serve as a decision-making unit (DMU) for the three-day period.

✓ **Fourth Step**, this group's operations should follow the first step's recommendations but also include areas that are suggested for productivity by the group.

✓ **Fifth Step** require the decision-making unit to conduct a preliminary screening of the case scenario to assure some analytical fundamentals from the foundations of critical thinking.

✓ **Sixth Step**, review literature, data bases, information repositories and practices at two other Carnegie-classified," peer" institutions that are related to the case scenario and will contribute to the body of work and deliberations from the DMU. Suggested databases: *Academic Search Premier; Business Source Complete; Education Full Text; Science Direct*

✓ **Seventh Step** frame a working logic model that captures the necessary basic elements and major components that are fundamental to the problem.

✓ **Eighth Step** conduct a "mid-way" group reflection session and continue to follow the thirteen–step HEART process for implementing "general" data collection and analysis.

✓ **Ninth Step** collect "specific" data about the problem; analyze data about the problem; identify means for data authentication, validity, verification, reliability, and trustworthiness (if needed) concerning the problem; determine the meaning of the data relative to the problem. There are guidelines and procedures that one should follow when addressing problems and issues regardless of their nature. One of the things that must be done is to gather data related to the problem in order to come up with an appropriate resolution. Prior to data collection several issues must be addressed including the ones listed below:

A. Identifying the population from which the data is to be collected
B. Gaining permission from individuals and/or organizations to carry out the data collection process
C. Determining the type of data needed to address the problem or issue under consideration
D. Creating or identifying an instrument to use in collecting the data
E. Carrying out the data collection procedures

In general, the data collection process is similar regardless of the type of data (quantitative or qualitative) being collected. When dealing

with quantitative data, however, one should consider the level of analysis and sampling procedures. Different types of permissions may also be required, depending on whether you are sampling individuals, institutions, or agencies. Gaining informed consent is particularly important to protect the privacy and confidentiality of participants. Operational definitions must be assigned to all variables to be studied. Types of data and measures must be determined prior to the data collection process. Whether the instrument is to measure individual performance, individual attitude, individual behavior, or factual information must be established. Data collection instruments must be identified or designed. The ones utilized must be reliable and valid. Reliable instruments ensure consistency of measurement while valid instruments provide evidence that what purports to be measured is, in fact, measured. Several widely used methods of establishing reliability include the following:

- Test-retest reliability
- Alternate forms reliability
- Inter-rater reliability
- Internal consistency

Traditional types of validity coefficients include:

- Content validity
- Construct validity
- Criterion-related validity

A standardized process for the collection of data must be identified or created and utilized.

> ✓ **Tenth Step** propose a remedy, resolve, or resolution about the problem; pilot or pre-test the remedy, resolve, or resolution to the problem from a selected qualitative protocol or quantitative instrument (if needed); analyze the data to validate, verify, or support reliability and trustworthiness (if needed).
> ✓ **Eleventh Step** develop recommendations for new practices or pro-active measures to prevent the problem occurring again; identify measurements and metrics for analyzing the new practice, policy, procedure, or process that has been developed as a result of previous steps.
> ✓ **Twelfth Step** place the proposed new practice, policy, or procedure on the internal web link and allow stakeholders on campus the opportunity to provide feedback on the proposed recommendations by the DMU.

☑ **Thirteenth Step**, address for a second time any issues concerning proactive or preventative measures after a thorough and final consideration of stakeholder input and integration of the new practice, policy, process, procedure, protocol or plan into the institutional strategic plan and unit-based budget where the problem was developed.

Case Scenario Number 14: For Community Affairs
HEALTHCARE, POVERTY, AND FACULTY INCENTIVE

> The medical center and hospital associated with a major research university has been criticized by the local media for not reaching out to impoverished communities outside the city to meet some of the challenges of community health issues. Most of these communities outside the city are composed of the elderly and others who do not have the transportation means to visit the hospital often enough to deal with their illnesses, ailments, and sicknesses. The medical center recently received multi-million-dollar funding from a large philanthropic organization to assist these communities with getting access to medical services and healthcare; however, the philanthropic organization has requested a one-week deadline for the chancellor of the medical center to develop an action plan for implementation. The action plan must address the issues that have been expressed by the communities and provide the measurable strategies the medical center will develop to successfully implement the plan. Some of the newer faculty at the medical center have not only offered to provide care in the communities, they have also offered to live in the communities if incentives are provided for them to do so. What type of data needs to be collected? From whom and from where? What should be the methodology? How will the data be used? What actions should be taken after the data has been collected, shared, and analyzed? What are the mission, policy, and planning implications? Who is at stake? What are the lessons learned? Going forward, what is next? How should future actions be assessed, measured, benchmarked, and monitored for the future?

- ✓ **First Step** accept the case-situational scenario (CSS) by the assigned "top executive" administrator with the charge and challenge to make recommendations for resolve, intervention, or solution.
- ✓ **Second Step** appoint a "unit based" administrative lead person to facilitate the process and navigate the execution for resolve within the prescribed three-day time period.
- ✓ **Third Step** appoint a diverse group of staff, faculty, and students to serve as a decision-making unit (DMU) for the three-day period.
- ✓ **Fourth Step**, this group's operations should follow the first step's recommendations but also include areas that are suggested for productivity by the group.

✓ **Fifth Step** require the decision-making unit to conduct a preliminary screening of the case scenario to assure some analytical fundamentals from the foundations of critical thinking.

✓ **Sixth Step**, review literature, data bases, information repositories and practices at two other Carnegie-classified," peer" institutions that are related to the case scenario and will contribute to the body of work and deliberations from the DMU. Suggested databases: *ABI/Inform Complete; Academic Search Complete; Education Research Complete; LexisNexis; Science Direct*

✓ **Seventh Step** frame a working logic model that captures the necessary basic elements and major components that are fundamental to the problem.

✓ **Eighth Step** conduct a "mid-way" group reflection session and continue to follow the thirteen–step HEART process for implementing "general" data collection and analysis.

✓ **Ninth Step** collect "specific" data about the problem; analyze data about the problem; identify means for data authentication, validity, verification, reliability, and trustworthiness (if needed) concerning the problem; determine the meaning of the data relative to the problem. There are guidelines and procedures that one should follow when addressing problems and issues regardless of their nature. One of the things that must be done is to gather data related to the problem in order to come up with an appropriate resolution. Prior to data collection several issues must be addressed including the ones listed below:

A. Identifying the population from which the data is to be collected
B. Gaining permission from individuals and/or organizations to carry out the data collection process
C. Determining the type of data needed to address the problem or issue under consideration
D. Creating or identifying an instrument to use in collecting the data
E. Carrying out the data collection procedures

In general, the data collection process is similar regardless of the type of data (quantitative or qualitative) being collected. When dealing with quantitative data, however, one should consider the level of analysis and sampling procedures. Different types of permissions may also be required, depending on whether you are sampling individuals, institutions, or agencies. Gaining informed consent is particularly important to protect the privacy and confidentiality of participants. Operational definitions must be assigned to all variables to be studied. Types of data and measures

must be determined prior to the data collection process. Whether the instrument is to measure individual performance, individual attitude, individual behavior, or factual information must be established. Data collection instruments must be identified or designed. The ones utilized must be reliable and valid. Reliable instruments ensure consistency of measurement while valid instruments provide evidence that what purports to be measured is, in fact, measured. Several widely used methods of establishing reliability include the following:

- Test-retest reliability
- Alternate forms reliability
- Inter-rater reliability
- Internal consistency

Traditional types of validity coefficients include:

- Content validity
- Construct validity
- Criterion-related validity

A standardized process for the collection of data must be identified or created and utilized.

> ✓ **Tenth Step** propose a remedy, resolve, or resolution about the problem; pilot or pre-test the remedy, resolve, or resolution to the problem from a selected qualitative protocol or quantitative instrument (if needed); analyze the data to validate, verify, or support reliability and trustworthiness (if needed).
>
> ✓ **Eleventh Step** develop recommendations for new practices or pro-active measures to prevent the problem occurring again; identify measurements and metrics for analyzing the new practice, policy, procedure, or process that has been developed as a result of previous steps.
>
> ✓ **Twelfth Step** place the proposed new practice, policy, or procedure on the internal web link and allow stakeholders on campus the opportunity to provide feedback on the proposed recommendations by the DMU.
>
> ✓ **Thirteenth Step**, address for a second time any issues concerning proactive or preventative measures after a thorough and final consideration of stakeholder input and integration of the new practice, policy, process, procedure, protocol or plan into the institutional strategic plan and unit-based budget where the problem was developed.

Case Scenario Number 15: For Community Affairs
COMMUNITY OUTREACH, EDUCATION, AND RESEARCH

A large group of parents and community leaders that represent the area that is adjacent to the local college have conducted a series of meetings with local churches and other organizations to complain about the lack of involvement by the school of education at the college relative to working with students and teachers to help get academic achievement scores up to state and federal standards. The school of education at the college places more emphasis on teaching and research than community service. The provost of the college and the dean of the school have advocated the advancement of promotion and tenure from standards in research and teaching. The local community parents and leaders believe that a publicly subsidized college should first be primarily and fundamentally supportive of the local community before prioritizing faculty performance based on standards beyond the local community. The faculty has expressed both empathy and sympathy for the local parents and family; however, they are also concerned about employment security and advancing as professors through scholarship and research. The mayor of the city has also advocated strategic partnership between the university and the community to support economic development. What type of data needs to be collected? From whom and from where? What should be the methodology? How will the data be used? What actions should be taken after the data has been collected, shared, and analyzed? What are the mission, policy, and planning implications? Who is at stake? What are the lessons learned? Going forward, what is next? How should future actions be assessed, measured, benchmarked, and monitored for the future?

✓ **First Step** accept the case-situational scenario (CSS) by the assigned "top executive" administrator with the charge and challenge to make recommendations for resolve, intervention, or solution.

- ✓ **Second Step** appoint a "unit based" administrative lead person to facilitate the process and navigate the execution for resolve within the prescribed three-day time period.
- ✓ **Third Step** appoint a diverse group of staff, faculty, and students to serve as a decision-making unit (DMU) for the three-day period.
- ✓ **Fourth Step**, this group's operations should follow the first step's recommendations but also include areas that are suggested for productivity by the group.
- ✓ **Fifth Step** require the decision-making unit to conduct a preliminary screening of the case scenario to assure some analytical fundamentals from the foundations of critical thinking.
- ✓ **Sixth Step**, review literature, data bases, information repositories and practices at two other Carnegie-classified," peer" institutions that are related to the case scenario and will contribute to the body of work and deliberations from the DMU. Suggested databases: *Academic Search Premier; Education Full Text; ERIC; JSTOR; LexisNexis*
- ✓ **Seventh Step** frame a working logic model that captures the necessary basic elements and major components that are fundamental to the problem.
- ✓ **Eighth Step** conduct a "mid-way" group reflection session and continue to follow the thirteen–step HEART process for implementing "general" data collection and analysis.
- ✓ **Ninth Step** collect "specific" data about the problem; analyze data about the problem; identify means for data authentication, validity, verification, reliability, and trustworthiness (if needed) concerning the problem; determine the meaning of the data relative to the problem. There are guidelines and procedures that one should follow when addressing problems and issues regardless of their nature. One of the things that must be done is to gather data related to the problem in order to come up with an appropriate resolution. Prior to data collection several issues must be addressed including the ones listed below:
  A. Identifying the population from which the data is to be collected
  B. Gaining permission from individuals and/or organizations to carry out the data collection process
  C. Determining the type of data needed to address the problem or issue under consideration
  D. Creating or identifying an instrument to use in collecting the data
  E. Carrying out the data collection procedures

In general, the data collection process is similar regardless of the type of data (quantitative or qualitative) being collected. When dealing

with quantitative data, however, one should consider the level of analysis and sampling procedures. Different types of permissions may also be required, depending on whether you are sampling individuals, institutions, or agencies. Gaining informed consent is particularly important to protect the privacy and confidentiality of participants. Operational definitions must be assigned to all variables to be studied. Types of data and measures must be determined prior to the data collection process. Whether the instrument is to measure individual performance, individual attitude, individual behavior, or factual information must be established. Data collection instruments must be identified or designed. The ones utilized must be reliable and valid. Reliable instruments ensure consistency of measurement while valid instruments provide evidence that what purports to be measured is, in fact, measured. Several widely used methods of establishing reliability include the following:

- Test-retest reliability
- Alternate forms reliability
- Inter-rater reliability
- Internal consistency

Traditional types of validity coefficients include:
- Content validity
- Construct validity
- Criterion-related validity

A standardized process for the collection of data must be identified or created and utilized.

> ✓ **Tenth Step** propose a remedy, resolve, or resolution about the problem; pilot or pre-test the remedy, resolve, or resolution to the problem from a selected qualitative protocol or quantitative instrument (if needed); analyze the data to validate, verify, or support reliability and trustworthiness (if needed).
> ✓ **Eleventh Step** develop recommendations for new practices or pro-active measures to prevent the problem occurring again; identify measurements and metrics for analyzing the new practice, policy, procedure, or process that has been developed as a result of previous steps.
> ✓ **Twelfth Step** place the proposed new practice, policy, or procedure on the internal web link and allow stakeholders on campus the opportunity to provide feedback on the proposed recommendations by the DMU.

✓ **Thirteenth Step**, address for a second time any issues concerning proactive or preventative measures after a thorough and final consideration of stakeholder input and integration of the new practice, policy, process, procedure, protocol or plan into the institutional strategic plan and unit-based budget where the problem was developed.

Case Scenario Number 16: For Physical Plant Affairs
LIBRARY SPACE, RENOVATION, AND REPURPOSING

A large urban university is experiencing growing pains. Relatively land-locked, the university is unable to build additional facilities to house some newer academic programs that were added in recent years. Occupying a central location on the campus, the library, with six stories and over 200,000 square feet of interior space, is regarded by many as prime real estate. Moreover, the perception exists that as the library acquires more electronic resources, it is transitioning from a physical space to a virtual presence. In so doing it is anticipated that large areas of the building will become available for non-library use. The administrative cabinet has met with the library dean and other library managers to discuss plans to repurpose the upper two floors of the library into faculty offices and classroom space for an external unit. Currently one of the two floors provides shelving for half of the monograph collection and 20% of public study space. Though they believe relinquishing the space will have a negative impact, the library staff must determine how best to re-organize the library to meet the future needs and expectations of the library community, while supporting current library services. What type of data needs to be collected? From whom and from where? What should be the methodology? How will the data be used? What actions should be taken after the data has been collected, shared, and analyzed? What are the mission, policy, and planning implications? Who is at stake? What are the lessons learned? Going forward, what is next? How should future actions be assessed, measured, benchmarked, and monitored for the future?

- ✓ **First Step** accept the case-situational scenario (CSS) by the assigned "top executive" administrator with the charge and challenge to make recommendations for resolve, intervention, or solution.
- ✓ **Second Step** appoint a "unit based" administrative lead person to facilitate the process and navigate the execution for resolve within the prescribed three-day time period.

- ✓ **Third Step** appoint a diverse group of staff, faculty, and students to serve as a decision-making unit (DMU) for the three-day period.
- ✓ **Fourth Step**, this group's operations should follow the first step's recommendations but also include areas that are suggested for productivity by the group.
- ✓ **Fifth Step** require the decision-making unit to conduct a preliminary screening of the case scenario to assure some analytical fundamentals from the foundations of critical thinking.
- ✓ **Sixth Step**, review literature, data bases, information repositories and practices at two other Carnegie-classified," peer" institutions that are related to the case scenario and will contribute to the body of work and deliberations from the DMU. Suggested databases: *Education Research Complete; ERIC; Library Literature and Information Science; Science Direct*
- ✓ **Seventh Step** frame a working logic model that captures the necessary basic elements and major components that are fundamental to the problem.
- ✓ **Eighth Step** conduct a "mid-way" group reflection session and continue to follow the thirteen–step HEART process for implementing "general" data collection and analysis.
- ✓ **Ninth Step** collect "specific" data about the problem; analyze data about the problem; identify means for data authentication, validity, verification, reliability, and trustworthiness (if needed) concerning the problem; determine the meaning of the data relative to the problem. There are guidelines and procedures that one should follow when addressing problems and issues regardless of their nature. One of the things that must be done is to gather data related to the problem in order to come up with an appropriate resolution. Prior to data collection several issues must be addressed including the ones listed below:

  A. Identifying the population from which the data is to be collected
  B. Gaining permission from individuals and/or organizations to carry out the data collection process
  C. Determining the type of data needed to address the problem or issue under consideration
  D. Creating or identifying an instrument to use in collecting the data
  E. Carrying out the data collection procedures

In general, the data collection process is similar regardless of the type of data (quantitative or qualitative) being collected. When dealing with quantitative data, however, one should consider the level of analysis and sampling procedures. Different types of permissions may also be

required, depending on whether you are sampling individuals, institutions, or agencies. Gaining informed consent is particularly important to protect the privacy and confidentiality of participants. Operational definitions must be assigned to all variables to be studied. Types of data and measures must be determined prior to the data collection process. Whether the instrument is to measure individual performance, individual attitude, individual behavior, or factual information must be established. Data collection instruments must be identified or designed. The ones utilized must be reliable and valid. Reliable instruments ensure consistency of measurement while valid instruments provide evidence that what purports to be measured is, in fact, measured. Several widely used methods of establishing reliability include the following:

- Test-retest reliability
- Alternate forms reliability
- Inter-rater reliability
- Internal consistency

Traditional types of validity coefficients include:
- Content validity
- Construct validity
- Criterion-related validity

A standardized process for the collection of data must be identified or created and utilized.

> ✓ **Tenth Step** propose a remedy, resolve, or resolution about the problem; pilot or pre-test the remedy, resolve, or resolution to the problem from a selected qualitative protocol or quantitative instrument (if needed); analyze the data to validate, verify, or support reliability and trustworthiness (if needed).
> ✓ **Eleventh Step** develop recommendations for new practices or pro-active measures to prevent the problem occurring again; identify measurements and metrics for analyzing the new practice, policy, procedure, or process that has been developed as a result of previous steps.
> ✓ **Twelfth Step** place the proposed new practice, policy, or procedure on the internal web link and allow stakeholders on campus the opportunity to provide feedback on the proposed recommendations by the DMU.

✓ **Thirteenth Step**, address for a second time any issues concerning proactive or preventative measures after a thorough and final consideration of stakeholder input and integration of the new practice, policy, process, procedure, protocol or plan into the institutional strategic plan and unit-based budget where the problem was developed.

Case Scenario Number 17: For Physical Plant Affairs
DEFERRED MAINTENANCE AND FUNDING SHORTFALL

A publicly supported, mid-sized college is faces challenges of an aging campus infrastructure. With more than half of its buildings constructed during the late sixties and early seventies, major renovations and rehabilitation are frequent occurrences, and a once robust reserve of maintenance funds has long been depleted. In rapid succession the HVAC systems of three major buildings needed replacement, and safety inspectors ordered enhancements to fire suppression systems in more than a dozen buildings. As is the case with many state-supported schools, this college accumulated a significant backlog of deferred maintenance projects due in large part to rising costs and massive funding shortfalls in the wake of the 2008 recession. Nationwide, it is estimated that the costs associated with deferred campus maintenance may approach $30 billion. Deferred maintenance impacts not only public safety and health but also the ability of the school to recruit and retain faculty and students. The President and facility managers realize that deferred maintenance must be addressed, but also understand that prevailing anti-tax sentiments and adverse reactions to tuition increases limit their options. What type of data needs to be collected? From whom and from where? What should be the methodology? How will the data be used? What actions should be taken after the data has been collected, shared, and analyzed? Who is at stake? What are the mission, policy, and planning implications? What are the lessons learned? Going forward, what is next? How should future actions be assessed, measured, benchmarked, and monitored for the future?

✓ **First Step** accept the case-situational scenario (CSS) by the assigned "top executive" administrator with the charge and challenge to make recommendations for resolve, intervention, or solution.

✓ **Second Step** appoint a "unit based" administrative lead person to facilitate the process and navigate the execution for resolve within the prescribed three-day time period.

✓ **Third Step** appoint a diverse group of staff, faculty, and students to serve as a decision-making unit (DMU) for the three-day period.

✓ **Fourth Step**, this group's operations should follow the first step's recommendations but also include areas that are suggested for productivity by the group.

- ✓ **Fifth Step** require the decision-making unit to conduct a preliminary screening of the case scenario to assure some analytical fundamentals from the foundations of critical thinking.
- ✓ **Sixth Step**, review literature, data bases, information repositories and practices at two other Carnegie-classified," peer" institutions that are related to the case scenario and will contribute to the body of work and deliberations from the DMU. Suggested databases: *Academic Search Premier; Business Source Complete; ERIC; LexisNexis Academic*
- ✓ **Seventh Step** frame a working logic model that captures the necessary basic elements and major components that are fundamental to the problem.
- ✓ **Eighth Step** conduct a "mid-way" group reflection session and continue to follow the thirteen–step HEART process for implementing "general" data collection and analysis.
- ✓ **Ninth Step** collect "specific" data about the problem; analyze data about the problem; identify means for data authentication, validity, verification, reliability, and trustworthiness (if needed) concerning the problem; determine the meaning of the data relative to the problem. There are guidelines and procedures that one should follow when addressing problems and issues regardless of their nature. One of the things that must be done is to gather data related to the problem in order to come up with an appropriate resolution. Prior to data collection several issues must be addressed including the ones listed below:

    A. Identifying the population from which the data is to be collected
    B. Gaining permission from individuals and/or organizations to carry out the data collection process
    C. Determining the type of data needed to address the problem or issue under consideration
    D. Creating or identifying an instrument to use in collecting the data
    E. Carrying out the data collection procedures

In general, the data collection process is similar regardless of the type of data (quantitative or qualitative) being collected. When dealing with quantitative data, however, one should consider the level of analysis and sampling procedures. Different types of permissions may also be required, depending on whether you are sampling individuals, institutions, or agencies. Gaining informed consent is particularly important to protect the privacy and confidentiality of participants. Operational definitions must be assigned to all variables to be studied. Types of data and measures

must be determined prior to the data collection process. Whether the instrument is to measure individual performance, individual attitude, individual behavior, or factual information must be established. Data collection instruments must be identified or designed. The ones utilized must be reliable and valid. Reliable instruments ensure consistency of measurement while valid instruments provide evidence that what purports to be measured is, in fact, measured. Several widely used methods of establishing reliability include the following:

- Test-retest reliability
- Alternate forms reliability
- Inter-rater reliability
- Internal consistency

Traditional types of validity coefficients include:

- Content validity
- Construct validity
- Criterion-related validity

A standardized process for the collection of data must be identified or created and utilized.

✓ **Tenth Step** propose a remedy, resolve, or resolution about the problem; pilot or pre-test the remedy, resolve, or resolution to the problem from a selected qualitative protocol or quantitative instrument (if needed); analyze the data to validate, verify, or support reliability and trustworthiness (if needed).

✓ **Eleventh Step** develop recommendations for new practices or pro-active measures to prevent the problem occurring again; identify measurements and metrics for analyzing the new practice, policy, procedure, or process that has been developed as a result of previous steps.

✓ **Twelfth Step** place the proposed new practice, policy, or procedure on the internal web link and allow stakeholders on campus the opportunity to provide feedback on the proposed recommendations by the DMU.

✓ **Thirteenth Step**, address for a second time any issues concerning proactive or preventative measures after a thorough and final consideration of stakeholder input and integration of the new practice, policy, process, procedure, protocol or plan into the institutional strategic plan and unit-based budget where the problem was developed.

Case Scenario Number 18: For Physical Plant Affairs
DISASTER RESPONSE, EMERGENCY REACTION, AND SUPPORT

> Community leaders and representatives of several relief agencies have approached the President of a large university located in a rural area of a southern state. This is a region of the country that frequently experiences extreme weather events, including major hurricanes and tornados, and with climate change, the severity and frequency of such storms are expected to increase. The University has the area's most commodious and structurally substantial buildings and has in the past provided temporary housing and relief services to those affected by disasters on an informal, case by case basis. The community leaders and relief agency representatives wish to enter into a formalized agreement that would delineate how and to what extent the university would respond to disasters. University officials believe that providing disaster assistance is one way the university fulfills its service mission, however there is some apprehension that providing housing and other support for extended periods of time, would be disruptive to the operation of the institution, displace students and prove financially burdensome. What type of data needs to be collected? From whom and from where? What should be the methodology? How will the data be used? What actions should be taken after the data has been collected, shared, and analyzed? What are the mission, policy, and planning implications? Who is at stake? What are the lessons learned? Going forward, what is next? How should future actions be assessed, measured, benchmarked, and monitored for the future?

✓ **First Step** accept the case-situational scenario (CSS) by the assigned "top executive" administrator with the charge and challenge to make recommendations for resolve, intervention, or solution.

✓ **Second Step** appoint a "unit based" administrative lead person to facilitate the process and navigate the execution for resolve within the prescribed three-day time period.

✓ **Third Step** appoint a diverse group of staff, faculty, and students to serve as a decision-making unit (DMU) for the three-day period.

✓ **Fourth Step**, this group's operations should follow the first step's recommendations but also include areas that are suggested for productivity by the group.

✓ **Fifth Step** require the decision-making unit to conduct a preliminary screening of the case scenario to assure some analytical fundamentals from the foundations of critical thinking.

✓ **Sixth Step**, review literature, data bases, information repositories and practices at two other Carnegie-classified," peer" institutions that are related to the case scenario and will contribute to the body of work and deliberations from the DMU. Suggested databases: *ABI/Inform; Education Research Complete; ERIC: Science Direct*

✓ **Seventh Step** frame a working logic model that captures the necessary basic elements and major components that are fundamental to the problem.

✓ **Eighth Step** conduct a "mid-way" group reflection session and continue to follow the thirteen–step HEART process for implementing "general" data collection and analysis.

✓ **Ninth Step** collect "specific" data about the problem; analyze data about the problem; identify means for data authentication, validity, verification, reliability, and trustworthiness (if needed) concerning the problem; determine the meaning of the data relative to the problem. There are guidelines and procedures that one should follow when addressing problems and issues regardless of their nature. One of the things that must be done is to gather data related to the problem in order to come up with an appropriate resolution. Prior to data collection several issues must be addressed including the ones listed below:

A. Identifying the population from which the data is to be collected
B. Gaining permission from individuals and/or organizations to carry out the data collection process
C. Determining the type of data needed to address the problem or issue under consideration
D. Creating or identifying an instrument to use in collecting the data
E. Carrying out the data collection procedures

In general, the data collection process is similar regardless of the type of data (quantitative or qualitative) being collected. When dealing with quantitative data, however, one should consider the level of analysis and sampling procedures. Different types of permissions may also be required, depending on whether you are sampling individuals, institutions, or agencies. Gaining informed consent is particularly important to protect the privacy and confidentiality of participants. Operational definitions must be assigned to all variables to be studied. Types of data and measures must be determined prior to the data collection process. Whether the instrument is to measure individual performance, individual attitude, individual behavior, or factual information must be established. Data collection instruments must be identified or designed. The ones utilized must be reliable and valid. Reliable instruments ensure consistency of measurement while valid instruments provide evidence that what purports to be measured is, in fact, measured. Several widely used methods of establishing reliability include the following:

- Test-retest reliability
- Alternate forms reliability
- Inter-rater reliability
- Internal consistency

Traditional types of validity coefficients include:

- Content validity
- Construct validity
- Criterion-related validity

A standardized process for the collection of data must be identified or created and utilized.

✓ **Tenth Step** propose a remedy, resolve, or resolution about the problem; pilot or pre-test the remedy, resolve, or resolution to the problem from a selected qualitative protocol or quantitative instrument (if needed); analyze the data to validate, verify, or support reliability and trustworthiness (if needed).

✓ **Eleventh Step** develop recommendations for new practices or pro-active measures to prevent the problem occurring again; identify measurements and metrics for analyzing the new practice, policy, procedure, or process that has been developed as a result of previous steps.

✓ **Twelfth Step** place the proposed new practice, policy, or procedure on the internal web link and allow stakeholders on campus the opportunity to provide feedback on the proposed recommendations by the DMU.

✓ **Thirteenth Step**, address for a second time any issues concerning proactive or preventative measures after a thorough and final consideration of stakeholder input and integration of the new practice, policy, process, procedure, protocol or plan into the institutional strategic plan and unit-based budget where the problem was developed.

Case Scenario Number 19: For Presidential Leadership Affairs

SHARED GOVERNANCE, LEADESHIP, AND FOLLOWSHIP

A growing segment of the faculty at a public small liberal arts institution in the mid-west has gathered in the campus faculty club to address complaints about the new president's failure to involve faculty in the design of the new interdisciplinary undergraduate research facility next to the library. At the center of the discussion are the scope of shared governance and whether the facility design is considered "administrative prerogative" given its implications to budget or an "academic issue" for the faculty to be involved, given the teaching and curriculum implications. The president has been given a mandate to keep the new facility costs under a certain budget, but the faculty argues the quality of academic delivery will be compromised unless the faculty concerns are addressed. Students are advocating that since their tuition funds contribute to the construction of the building, they believe their input should be above the priority and the faculty. Students' tuition has increased at the institution by 7% for three consecutive years. The board has caught wind of the mounting campus sentiments and they have asked the president to assemble a representative group to analyze the situation and provide recommendations before approaching potential corporate funders to support the new facility. What type of data needs to be collected? From whom and from where? What should be the methodology? How will the data be used? What actions should be taken after the data has been collected, shared, and analyzed? Who is at

> stake? What are the mission, policy, and planning implications? What are the lessons learned? Going forward, what is next? How should future actions be assessed, measured, benchmarked, and monitored for the future?

- ✓ **First Step** accept the case-situational scenario (CSS) by the assigned "top executive" administrator with the charge and challenge to make recommendations for resolve, intervention, or solution.
- ✓ **Second Step** appoint a "unit based" administrative lead person to facilitate the process and navigate the execution for resolve within the prescribed three-day time period.
- ✓ **Third Step** appoint a diverse group of staff, faculty, and students to serve as a decision-making unit (DMU) for the three-day period.
- ✓ **Fourth Step**, this group's operations should follow the first step's recommendations but also include areas that are suggested for productivity by the group.
- ✓ **Fifth Step** require the decision-making unit to conduct a preliminary screening of the case scenario to assure some analytical fundamentals from the foundations of critical thinking.
- ✓ **Sixth Step**, review literature, data bases, information repositories and practices at two other Carnegie-classified," peer" institutions that are related to the case scenario and will contribute to the body of work and deliberations from the DMU. Suggested databases: *Academic Search Premier; Almanac of Higher Education; Education Research Complete; ERIC*
- ✓ **Seventh Step** frame a working logic model that captures the necessary basic elements and major components that are fundamental to the problem.
- ✓ **Eighth Step** conduct a "mid-way" group reflection session and continue to follow the thirteen–step HEART process for implementing "general" data collection and analysis.
- ✓ **Ninth Step** collect "specific" data about the problem; analyze data about the problem; identify means for data authentication, validity, verification, reliability, and trustworthiness (if needed) concerning the problem; determine the meaning of the data relative to the problem. There are guidelines and procedures that one should follow when addressing problems and issues regardless of their nature. One of the things that must be done is to gather data related to the problem in order to come up with an appropriate resolution. Prior to data collection several issues must be addressed including the ones listed below:
    A. Identifying the population from which the data is to be collected
    B. Gaining permission from individuals and/or organizations to carry out the data collection process

4. Description of scope and sequential frameworks for heart

  C. Determining the type of data needed to address the problem or issue under consideration
  D. Creating or identifying an instrument to use in collecting the data
  E. Carrying out the data collection procedures.

In general, the data collection process is similar regardless of the type of data (quantitative or qualitative) being collected. When dealing with quantitative data, however, one should consider the level of analysis and sampling procedures. Different types of permissions may also be required, depending on whether you are sampling individuals, institutions, or agencies. Gaining informed consent is particularly important to protect the privacy and confidentiality of participants. Operational definitions must be assigned to all variables to be studied. Types of data and measures must be determined prior to the data collection process. Whether the instrument is to measure individual performance, individual attitude, individual behavior, or factual information must be established. Data collection instruments must be identified or designed. The ones utilized must be reliable and valid. Reliable instruments ensure consistency of measurement while valid instruments provide evidence that what purports to be measured is, in fact, measured. Several widely used methods of establishing reliability include the following:

- Test-retest reliability
- Alternate forms reliability
- Inter-rater reliability
- Internal consistency

Traditional types of validity coefficients include:

- Content validity
- Construct validity
- Criterion-related validity

A standardized process for the collection of data must be identified or created and utilized.

  ✓ **Tenth Step** propose a remedy, resolve, or resolution about the problem; pilot or pre-test the remedy, resolve, or resolution to the problem from a selected qualitative protocol or quantitative instrument (if needed); analyze the data to validate, verify, or support reliability and trustworthiness (if needed).

- ✓ **Eleventh Step** develop recommendations for new practices or proactive measures to prevent the problem occurring again; identify measurements and metrics for analyzing the new practice, policy, procedure, or process that has been developed as a result of previous steps.
- ✓ **Twelfth Step** place the proposed new practice, policy, or procedure on the internal web link and allow stakeholders on campus the opportunity to provide feedback on the proposed recommendations by the DMU.
- ✓ **Thirteenth Step**, address for a second time any issues concerning proactive or preventative measures after a thorough and final consideration of stakeholder input and integration of the new practice, policy, process, procedure, protocol or plan into the institutional strategic plan and unit-based budget where the problem was developed.

Case Scenario Number 20: For Presidential Leadership Affairs
CROSS SECTOR COLLABORATION, COMMUNITY CONNECTION, AND FACULTY

The Governor's Office recently called the president of a regional agricultural university located in the most rural area of the state to inform him and his board that there was an engineering company in Australia that was very interested in considering the rural part of the state for the location of a new high tech agricultural research center that focuses on new forms for growing cotton. The concerns listed by the Australian company included the quality of the schools, workforce readiness, higher education responsiveness to their needs, and excessive government regulation. The Governor was looking into the regulation issue, but she asked the president to develop an agreement between the university and the business sectors in the rural area to resolve the other issues. When the president approached the provost about faculty capacity and expertise, the provost responded that she did not feel the faculty was resourced and calibrated to work on such a project. The business community had been complaining for years that the university's faculty was not modern enough and responsive to their needs. Several board members who were appointed by the Governor has asked the president to assign a group with key stakeholders from the sectors of business, government, and the university to craft an action plan for going forward on the project. What type of data needs to be collected? From

> whom and from where? What should be the methodology? How will the data be used? What actions should be taken after the data has been collected, shared, and analyzed? What are the mission, policy, and planning implications? Who is at stake? What are the lessons learned? Going forward, what is next? How should future actions be assessed, measured, benchmarked, and monitored for the future?

- ✓ **First Step** accept the case-situational scenario (CSS) by the assigned "top executive" administrator with the charge and challenge to make recommendations for resolve, intervention, or solution.
- ✓ **Second Step** appoint a "unit based" administrative lead person to facilitate the process and navigate the execution for resolve within the prescribed three-day time period.
- ✓ **Third Step** appoint a diverse group of staff, faculty, and students to serve as a decision-making unit (DMU) for the three-day period.
- ✓ **Fourth Step**, this group's operations should follow the first step's recommendations but also include areas that are suggested for productivity by the group.
- ✓ **Fifth Step** require the decision-making unit to conduct a preliminary screening of the case scenario to assure some analytical fundamentals from the foundations of critical thinking.
- ✓ **Sixth Step**, review literature, data bases, information repositories and practices at two other Carnegie-classified," peer" institutions that are related to the case scenario and will contribute to the body of work and deliberations from the DMU. Suggested databases: *Business Source Complete; EdITLib Digital Library; Education Research Complete; ERIC; Professional Development Collection*
- ✓ **Seventh Step** frame a working logic model that captures the necessary basic elements and major components that are fundamental to the problem.
- ✓ **Eighth Step** conduct a "mid-way" group reflection session and continue to follow the thirteen-step HEART process for implementing "general" data collection and analysis.
- ✓ **Ninth Step** collect "specific" data about the problem; analyze data about the problem; identify means for data authentication, validity, verification, reliability, and trustworthiness (if needed) concerning the problem; determine the meaning of the data relative to the problem. There are guidelines and procedures that one should follow when addressing problems and issues regardless of their nature. One of the things that must be done is to gather data related to the problem in order to come up with an appropriate resolution. Prior to data collection several issues must be addressed including the ones listed below:
  A. Identifying the population from which the data is to be collected

B. Gaining permission from individuals and/or organizations to carry out the data collection process
C. Determining the type of data needed to address the problem or issue under consideration
D. Creating or identifying an instrument to use in collecting the data
E. Carrying out the data collection procedures

In general, the data collection process is similar regardless of the type of data (quantitative or qualitative) being collected. When dealing with quantitative data, however, one should consider the level of analysis and sampling procedures. Different types of permissions may also be required, depending on whether you are sampling individuals, institutions, or agencies. Gaining informed consent is particularly important to protect the privacy and confidentiality of participants. Operational definitions must be assigned to all variables to be studied. Types of data and measures must be determined prior to the data collection process. Whether the instrument is to measure individual performance, individual attitude, individual behavior, or factual information must be established. Data collection instruments must be identified or designed. The ones utilized must be reliable and valid. Reliable instruments ensure consistency of measurement while valid instruments provide evidence that what purports to be measured is, in fact, measured. Several widely used methods of establishing reliability include the following:

- Test-retest reliability
- Alternate forms reliability
- Inter-rater reliability
- Internal consistency

Traditional types of validity coefficients include:

- Content validity
- Construct validity
- Criterion-related validity

A standardized process for the collection of data must be identified or created and utilized.

✓ **Tenth Step** propose a remedy, resolve, or resolution about the problem; pilot or pre-test the remedy, resolve, or resolution to the problem from a selected qualitative protocol or quantitative instrument (if needed); analyze the data to validate, verify, or support reliability and trustworthiness (if needed).

✓ **Eleventh Step** develop recommendations for new practices or proactive measures to prevent the problem occurring again; identify measurements and metrics for analyzing the new practice, policy, procedure, or process that has been developed as a result of previous steps.

✓ **Twelfth Step** place the proposed new practice, policy, or procedure on the internal web link and allow stakeholders on campus the opportunity to provide feedback on the proposed recommendations by the DMU.

✓ **Thirteenth Step**, address for a second time any issues concerning proactive or preventative measures after a thorough and final consideration of stakeholder input and integration of the new practice, policy, process, procedure, protocol or plan into the institutional strategic plan and unit-based budget where the problem was developed.

Case Scenario Number 21: For Presidential Leadership Affairs
STUDENT UNREST, RELIGION, MISSION AND HUMAN DIVERSITY

A group of international students who were recruited to a U.S. public university at reduced tuition rates have been tolerating abuse and mistreatment by fellow students of a different faith for several months, but the incidents were escalating, and one student was even threatened with violence on night after being in the library. Some of these harassment incidents were reported to the campus police but most were not considered serious according to the dean of students. A group of interfaith leaders got together at one of the local synagogues to discuss the problem. The university president, who was not of the same faith as most of the student body and faculty, was increasingly criticized for not being proactive and responsive to the problem. A close faculty friend of the president mentioned privately to other faculty that the president did not share her personal faith with the board prior to being hired (for fear of not being hired), even though she is an alumna of the institution. The campus has many diversity centered programs, but they are primarily provided to ethnic minority students from the local region and around the country. The local clergy have asked the president and dean of students to examine the problem and provide an action plan for positive change. What type of data needs to be collected? From whom and from where? What should be the methodology? How will the data be used? Who is at stake? What actions should be taken after the data has been collected, shared, and analyzed? What is the mission, policy, and planning implications? What are the lessons learned? Going forward, what is next? How should future actions be assessed, measured, benchmarked, and monitored for the future?

- ✓ **First Step** accept the case-situational scenario (CSS) by the assigned "top executive" administrator with the charge and challenge to make recommendations for resolve, intervention, or solution.
- ✓ **Second Step** appoint a "unit based" administrative lead person to facilitate the process and navigate the execution for resolve within the prescribed three-day time period.
- ✓ **Third Step** appoint a diverse group of staff, faculty, and students to serve as a decision-making unit (DMU) for the three-day period.
- ✓ **Fourth Step**, this group's operations should follow the first step's recommendations but also include areas that are suggested for productivity by the group.
- ✓ **Fifth Step** require the decision-making unit to conduct a preliminary screening of the case scenario to assure some analytical fundamentals from the foundations of critical thinking.
- ✓ **Sixth Step**, review literature, data bases, information repositories and practices at two other Carnegie-classified," peer" institutions that are related to the case scenario and will contribute to the body of work and deliberations from the DMU. Suggested databases: *Academic Search Premier; Education Research Complete; JSTOR; PsycArticles*
- ✓ **Seventh Step** frame a working logic model that captures the necessary basic elements and major components that are fundamental to the problem.
- ✓ **Eighth Step** conduct a "mid-way" group reflection session and continue to follow the thirteen–step HEART process for implementing "general" data collection and analysis.
- ✓ **Ninth Step** collect "specific" data about the problem; analyze data about the problem; identify means for data authentication, validity, verification, reliability, and trustworthiness (if needed) concerning the problem; determine the meaning of the data relative to the problem. There are guidelines and procedures that one should follow when addressing problems and issues regardless of their nature. One of the things that must be done is to gather data related to the problem in order to come up with an appropriate resolution. Prior to data collection several issues must be addressed including the ones listed below:

   A. Identifying the population from which the data is to be collected
   B. Gaining permission from individuals and/or organizations to carry out the data collection process

C. Determining the type of data needed to address the problem or issue under consideration
D. Creating or identifying an instrument to use in collecting the data
E. Carrying out the data collection procedures

In general, the data collection process is similar regardless of the type of data (quantitative or qualitative) being collected. When dealing with quantitative data, however, one should consider the level of analysis and sampling procedures. Different types of permissions may also be required, depending on whether you are sampling individuals, institutions, or agencies. Gaining informed consent is particularly important to protect the privacy and confidentiality of participants. Operational definitions must be assigned to all variables to be studied. Types of data and measures must be determined prior to the data collection process. Whether the instrument is to measure individual performance, individual attitude, individual behavior, or factual information must be established. Data collection instruments must be identified or designed. The ones utilized must be reliable and valid. Reliable instruments ensure consistency of measurement while valid instruments provide evidence that what purports to be measured is, in fact, measured. Several widely used methods of establishing reliability include the following:

- Test-retest reliability
- Alternate forms reliability
- Inter-rater reliability
- Internal consistency

Traditional types of validity coefficients include:

- Content validity
- Construct validity
- Criterion-related validity

A standardized process for the collection of data must be identified or created and utilized.

✓ **Tenth Step** propose a remedy, resolve, or resolution about the problem; pilot or pre-test the remedy, resolve, or resolution to the problem from a selected qualitative protocol or quantitative instrument (if needed); analyze the data to validate, verify, or support reliability and trustworthiness (if needed).

✓ **Eleventh Step** develop recommendations for new practices or proactive measures to prevent the problem occurring again; identify measurements and metrics for analyzing the new practice, policy, procedure, or process that has been developed as a result of previous steps.

✓ **Twelfth Step** place the proposed new practice, policy, or procedure on the internal web link and allow stakeholders on campus the opportunity to provide feedback on the proposed recommendations by the DMU.

✓ **Thirteenth Step**, address for a second time any issues concerning proactive or preventative measures after a thorough and final consideration of stakeholder input and integration of the new practice, policy, process, procedure, protocol or plan into the institutional strategic plan and unit-based budget where the problem was developed.

4. Description of scope and sequential frameworks for heart   131

Case Scenario Number 22: For Advancement and Development
ALUMNI RELATIONS, RESPONSE, AND RESPONSIBILITY

The national alumni association for a small technological university has been active in giving and supporting the institution for decades. Many of the university alums are prominent leaders in local government, business, and other commerce. Although the university was financially secure, many of the alums' children were choosing to go to other universities within the state and throughout the region because their parents' alma mater did not offer many online classes or three-year degree programs. The three-year degree concept was gaining popularity in the regional academic marketplace. The president has met with all of the college deans and chairs of academic departments to discuss the issue, in conjunction with the alumni director, vice president for development and the provost. Several alums have threatened to stop giving donations to the university unless something is done. The provost has suggested outsourcing the development of online offerings to an outside business, but the faculty has also threatened a vote of no confidence for his leadership if that happens. The local alumni group has asked some of the more prominent members of the association to meet with the president to outline a plan of response and subsequent action by the institution. What type of data needs to be collected? From whom and from where? What should be the methodology? How will the data be used? What actions should be taken after the data has been collected, shared, and analyzed? Who is at stake? What are the mission, policy, and planning implications? What are the lessons learned? Going forward, what is next? How should future actions be assessed, measured, benchmarked, and monitored for the future?

✓ **First Step** accept the case-situational scenario (CSS) by the assigned "top executive" administrator with the charge and challenge to make recommendations for resolve, intervention, or solution.

✓ **Second Step** appoint a "unit based" administrative lead person to facilitate the process and navigate the execution for resolve within the prescribed three-day time period.

✓ **Third Step** appoint a diverse group of staff, faculty, and students to serve as a decision-making unit (DMU) for the three-day period.

✓ **Fourth Step**, this group's operations should follow the first step's recommendations but also include areas that are suggested for productivity by the group.

✓ **Fifth Step** require the decision-making unit to conduct a preliminary screening of the case scenario to assure some analytical fundamentals from the foundations of critical thinking.

✓ **Sixth Step**, review literature, data bases, information repositories and practices at two other Carnegie-classified," peer" institutions that are related to the case scenario and will contribute to the body of work and deliberations from the DMU. Suggested databases: *Academic Search Premier; Education Research Complete; JSTOR; PsycArticles*

✓ **Seventh Step** frame a working logic model that captures the necessary basic elements and major components that are fundamental to the problem.

✓ **Eighth Step** conduct a "mid-way" group reflection session and continue to follow the thirteen–step HEART process for implementing "general" data collection and analysis.

✓ **Ninth Step** collect "specific" data about the problem; analyze data about the problem; identify means for data authentication, validity, verification, reliability, and trustworthiness (if needed) concerning the problem; determine the meaning of the data relative to the problem. There are guidelines and procedures that one should follow when addressing problems and issues regardless of their nature. One of the things that must be done is to gather data related to the problem in order to come up with an appropriate resolution. Prior to data collection several issues must be addressed including the ones listed below:

A. Identifying the population from which the data is to be collected
B. Gaining permission from individuals and/or organizations to carry out the data collection process
C. Determining the type of data needed to address the problem or issue under consideration
D. Creating or identifying an instrument to use in collecting the data
E. Carrying out the data collection procedures

In general, the data collection process is similar regardless of the type of data (quantitative or qualitative) being collected. When dealing with quantitative data, however, one should consider the level of analysis and sampling procedures. Different types of permissions may also be required, depending on whether you are sampling individuals, institutions, or agencies. Gaining informed consent is particularly important to protect the privacy and confidentiality of participants. Operational definitions must be assigned to all variables to be studied. Types of data and measures must be determined prior to the data collection process. Whether the instrument is to measure individual performance, individual attitude, individual behavior, or factual information must be established. Data collection instruments must be identified or designed. The ones utilized must be reliable and valid. Reliable instruments ensure consistency of measurement while valid instruments provide evidence that what purports to be measured is, in fact, measured. Several widely used methods of establishing reliability include the following:

- Test-retest reliability
- Alternate forms reliability
- Inter-rater reliability
- Internal consistency

Traditional types of validity coefficients include:
- Content validity
- Construct validity
- Criterion-related validity

A standardized process for the collection of data must be identified or created and utilized.

> ✓ **Tenth Step** propose a remedy, resolve, or resolution about the problem; pilot or pre-test the remedy, resolve, or resolution to the problem from a selected qualitative protocol or quantitative instrument (if needed); analyze the data to validate, verify, or support reliability and trustworthiness (if needed).
> ✓ **Eleventh Step** develop recommendations for new practices or pro-active measures to prevent the problem occurring again; identify measurements and metrics for analyzing the new practice, policy, procedure, or process that has been developed as a result of previous steps.

- ✓ **Twelfth Step** place the proposed new practice, policy, or procedure on the internal web link and allow stakeholders on campus the opportunity to provide feedback on the proposed recommendations by the DMU.
- ✓ **Thirteenth Step**, address for a second time any issues concerning proactive or preventative measures after a thorough and final consideration of stakeholder input and integration of the new practice, policy, process, procedure, protocol or plan into the institutional strategic plan and unit-based budget where the problem was developed.

Case Scenario Number 23: For Advancement and Development
MAJOR GIFTING, POLITICS, POOR PEOPLE AND EXTERNAL RELATIONS

The faculty of a large multi-campus, community college is known for being very liberal and to the left of politics on the local and national levels. Many of the faculty chose the nationally ranked community college (with lower salaries and without tenure) instead of the traditional university setting because of the college's proximity to the Gulf Coast, the openness of the local community, and the college's reputation for helping the underprivileged local community through faculty-led service-learning activities. But when the College Board announced it was going to consider a multimillion-dollar gift from a nationally known conservative who was accused of making his money as a predatory lender in low-income communities, the faculty lodged hundreds of complaints using various media platforms. The local Congresswoman, and a former college faculty member who has received financial contributions from the conservative businessman has asked the college president to study the problem and report the findings to her. What type of data needs to be collected? From whom and from where? What should be the methodology? How will the data be used? What actions should be taken after the data has been collected, shared, and analyzed? What are the mission, policy, and planning implications? Who is at stake? What are the lessons learned? Going forward, what is next? How should future actions be assessed, measured, benchmarked, and monitored for the future?

- ✓ **First Step** accept the case-situational scenario (CSS) by the assigned "top executive" administrator with the charge and challenge to make recommendations for resolve, intervention, or solution.
- ✓ **Second Step** appoint a "unit based" administrative lead person to facilitate the process and navigate the execution for resolve within the prescribed three-day time period.

- ✓ **Third Step** appoint a diverse group of staff, faculty, and students to serve as a decision-making unit (DMU) for the three-day period.
- ✓ **Fourth Step**, this group's operations should follow the first step's recommendations but also include areas that are suggested for productivity by the group.
- ✓ **Fifth Step** require the decision-making unit to conduct a preliminary screening of the case scenario to assure some analytical fundamentals from the foundations of critical thinking.
- ✓ **Sixth Step**, review literature, data bases, information repositories and practices at two other Carnegie-classified," peer" institutions that are related to the case scenario and will contribute to the body of work and deliberations from the DMU. Suggested databases: *Academic Search Premier; Education Research Complete; JSTOR; PsycArticles*
- ✓ **Seventh Step** frame a working logic model that captures the necessary basic elements and major components that are fundamental to the problem.
- ✓ **Eighth Step** conduct a "mid-way" group reflection session and continue to follow the thirteen–step HEART process for implementing "general" data collection and analysis.
- ✓ **Ninth Step** collect "specific" data about the problem; analyze data about the problem; identify means for data authentication, validity, verification, reliability, and trustworthiness (if needed) concerning the problem; determine the meaning of the data relative to the problem. There are guidelines and procedures that one should follow when addressing problems and issues regardless of their nature. One of the things that must be done is to gather data related to the problem in order to come up with an appropriate resolution. Prior to data collection several issues must be addressed including the ones listed below:

    A. Identifying the population from which the data is to be collected
    B. Gaining permission from individuals and/or organizations to carry out the data collection process
    C. Determining the type of data needed to address the problem or issue under consideration
    D. Creating or identifying an instrument to use in collecting the data
    E. Carrying out the data collection procedures

In general, the data collection process is similar regardless of the type of data (quantitative or qualitative) being collected. When dealing with quantitative data, however, one should consider the level of analysis and sampling procedures. Different types of permissions may also be

required, depending on whether you are sampling individuals, institutions, or agencies. Gaining informed consent is particularly important to protect the privacy and confidentiality of participants. Operational definitions must be assigned to all variables to be studied. Types of data and measures must be determined prior to the data collection process. Whether the instrument is to measure individual performance, individual attitude, individual behavior, or factual information must be established. Data collection instruments must be identified or designed. The ones utilized must be reliable and valid. Reliable instruments ensure consistency of measurement while valid instruments provide evidence that what purports to be measured is, in fact, measured. Several widely used methods of establishing reliability include the following:

- Test-retest reliability
- Alternate forms reliability
- Inter-rater reliability
- Internal consistency

Traditional types of validity coefficients include:

- Content validity
- Construct validity
- Criterion-related validity

A standardized process for the collection of data must be identified or created and utilized.

> ✓ **Tenth Step** propose a remedy, resolve, or resolution about the problem; pilot or pre-test the remedy, resolve, or resolution to the problem from a selected qualitative protocol or quantitative instrument (if needed); analyze the data to validate, verify, or support reliability and trustworthiness (if needed).
> ✓ **Eleventh Step** develop recommendations for new practices or proactive measures to prevent the problem occurring again; identify measurements and metrics for analyzing the new practice, policy, procedure, or process that has been developed as a result of previous steps.
> ✓ **Twelfth Step** place the proposed new practice, policy, or procedure on the internal web link and allow stakeholders on campus the opportunity to provide feedback on the proposed recommendations by the DMU.

✓ **Thirteenth Step**, address for a second time any issues concerning proactive or preventative measures after a thorough and final consideration of stakeholder input and integration of the new practice, policy, process, procedure, protocol or plan into the institutional strategic plan and unit-based budget where the problem was developed.

SECTION TWO

1.
SELF REFLECTIONS AND CONTINUOUS IMPROVEMENT FOR TEACHING - INSTRUCTION-CLASSROOM

For our readers, to get ready to carry out action research in your higher education administrative context, self-reflect on your own professional practice. In section one of the desktop guide, we dealt with institutional-action decision-making in the workplace from an *administrative* perspective. In section two, this chapter and the ones following will deal more with academic decision-making in the classroom-action from a *faculty* perspective. Appendices A, B, and C of this desktop guide describe verbs that can be used in action research. We recognize that the action research methodologies for classroom application do take more time beyond the three-day prototype in section one of our HEART desktop guide. We believe that higher education administrators and classroom academicians are better situated, prepared, and equipped to deal with the type of problems and issues in the above thirteen step process when that can reflect on their own academic style and leadership delivery. Again, we frame administrative reflection in the spirit of *Sankofa*. We must build on our historical foundations to position with future fundamentals for progress. We must maintain our mission not only by just looking backward in reflection. We must also modernize our mission from always looking forward with continuous retrospection in the revolving, evolutionary, and revolutionary African dimensions of *Sankofa*. The élan vital of Sankofa is the bedrock for identifying and executing our reader's bold, new *third dimensions* described in chapter IV. Reflection is self-focused meditation that involves visualizing where you are, where you have been, and where you might go. Like reading a map upon entering a college campus, reflection helps you see where you are now and alternative paths to reach other campus spots you might wish to visit later or have visited before. In striving to become a better administrative practitioner in higher education, you must move from careful assessments of where you are presently to reflect on how to use past and future strategies to realize improvement. By getting in touch with yourself and by remembering a few wonderful moments with your students or colleagues, you can begin to fix on a topic for your own action research.

Future, Past, and Present Mediation

You think about your future practice when you plan an administrative project, develop an initiative with strategies, put together an agenda for a faculty meeting, solving a personnel problem, solving a student issue, responding to a community conflict or mentally rehearse a lecture or input for a meeting. Reflecting about future behaviors and foreseeing outcomes are essential steppingstones to effective action. You can also benefit from fixing your mind on your past plans and how those plans unfolded, how your behaviors came across to your students or colleagues, and what happened as consequences. Reflection on past practices helps you gain competence, mastery, and understanding, which serve as your foundations of psychological strength when facing the next challenge or a similar event. Act first, and then think critically about the effects of those actions before acting again. The most challenging type of meditation is thinking about your present behavior, which calls for you to focus on the HEART instead of the *"there and then"*. Reflecting effectively in the present demands moment-to-moment shifts between doing-and-thinking and thinking-and-doing. Although reflecting on the future, past, and present are important for any higher education administrator to master, they cannot in themselves solve educational problems or lead to change in your higher education context. One can use meditation to fine-tune practice but not to create new and innovative practice. The effectiveness of your meditations can be significantly enhanced by the systematic collection and analysis of data about your practice. That is the path to action research.

Self-Knowledge

Having a sincere interest in understanding yourself is a needed foundation for benefiting from action research. As a reflective higher education administrator in search of self-knowledge, ask yourself in the present: "What am I doing now? How am I acting in this situation? How am I living my leadership values? Are my current leadership actions congruent with my beliefs? Am I practicing what I preach? Do I learn from the issues, concerns, or problems I resolve with action research? Do I consistently integrate DDDM in my leadership style and delivery for others to follow by example, especially students? Does my current behavior offer a standard for my students, fellow administrators, supervisors or subordinates, and colleagues to imitate?" Looking to the past, ask yourself: "How did I develop to be who I am now? Which of my past experiences had the most influence on my current beliefs, values, and behaviors? Who were the most powerful role models of my youth and early adulthood?" Focusing your mind on the present, seek to understand how your current practices affect students, and colleagues. Ask yourself: "How am I coming across to those I serve? What are my students' perceptions of my practices? What are my faculty perceptions of my administrative or academic leadership practices? How do my colleagues view my leadership contributions to the faculty and shared governance? How do my professional peers see me as a colleague?" You might ask yourself: "What changes might help me better achieve my professional goals? How can I increase consistency between my administrative and academic leadership values and my professional behaviors? What changes should I consider in my concepts about what motivates student or staff behavior to get ready for future challenges?"

Solitary Dialogue

One sort of solitary dialogue that could be useful in getting yourself ready for action research is a conversation between your frustrated past self and your hopeful future self. Your "frustrated past self" uses verbs like could not, defended, did not, feared, worried, rejected, resisted, struggled, and wanted. Your hopeful future self uses verbs like can, search, seek, strive, want, will, and yearn for. These positive-forward verbs are not unlike the action verbs described in step 11 of the above thirteen step process. Another type of solitary dialogue is a conversation between your past courageous self and your future doubting self. Or, consider conversations between your tough and tender selves, task-oriented and person-oriented selves, pushing and pulling selves, caring, and challenging selves, worried and laid-back selves, convergent and divergent selves, and creative and conservative selves.

Professional Growing HEART Educators

As you aspire to become a senior higher education administrator or executive, you should be concerned with continuous improvement in achieving results or in reaching valued outcomes. To reach your desired results, try to segment your planning, acting, and evaluating into the following ten stages, which will help you move from reflection to action research for self-development:

1. Assess your higher education situation.
2. Set clear goals.
3. Brainstorm action strategies.
4. Implement action plans.
5. Monitor your own actions.
6. Assess others' reactions.
7. Evaluate what others have achieved.
8. Confront yourself with the results.
9. Reflect on new actions to take.
10. Assess the new higher education situation and set new goals.

Moving Toward Action Research

Use four tools of reflection—force field analysis, situation-target-path (STP) concepts, brainstorming versus critical thinking, and self-confrontation—to move toward your own action research in higher education. In force field analysis, visualize your current higher education situation as being made up of a field of facilitating and restraining forces. The facilitating forces are helping you move toward your goal, which is the desired state on the right side of the field; the restraining forces are keeping you from getting to the right and pushing you toward the undesirable state on the left side of the field. See Figures 2 and 3, in this regard, to not relate the first and second dimensions and conceptualize your third dimension, but to leverage the informed process of force field analysis too.

Figure 3. Force Field Analyses

Current Situation (S)	
Driving Forces	Restraining Forces
_____ >	< _____
Undesirable _____ >	< _____ Most
state _____ >	< _____ desired state
on this side _____ >	< _____ in this side
_____ >	< _____

Once you have listed four to six forces that characterize your situation on each side of the field, you are ready to focus on problems for action research in step 1 of the thirteen-step process. You seek either to increase the driving forces or to decrease the restraining forces. A second tool to help you move toward action research is the STP paradigm. Note in Figure 4.0 that S stands for your current situation, T Stands for your target, and P stands for your path, plan, procedure, project, or proposal.

Your action research will focus either on your S (collect data to understand better your situation), or on your P (collect data to understand your plan's effectiveness).

Figure 4. Situation, Target, Path-Plan-Procedure-Project-Proposal Concepts

S		T
Current	[path-plan-procedure-project-proposal]	—>Desired
Situation—>		Target

Force field analysis, for self-reflection, and the STP concepts can be integrated into a single, powerful tool. Conceive of your current situation as a field of facilitating and restraining forces held in equilibrium. You create Ps to reduce the restraining forces or to increase the facilitating forces, thus moving the equilibrium toward the desired target on the right. A third tool is to distinguish between brainstorming and critical thinking. Brainstorming helps foster creativity and opens one up to fresh ideas.

Critical thinking helps foster decision-making and involves rational, logical thinking. We have framed a rubric for critical thinking in step 5 of the above thirteen step process. A fourth tool to help one move toward action research is the skill of self-confrontation. It takes place when you are clear about what you value, and you gather data to assess how true you are being to those values. When the data show that you are falling short of achieving your values, you become motivated to do action research on your higher education situation.

More Continuous Improvement

Reflection, problem solving, and action research are three phases of continuous improvement in higher education for classroom application.

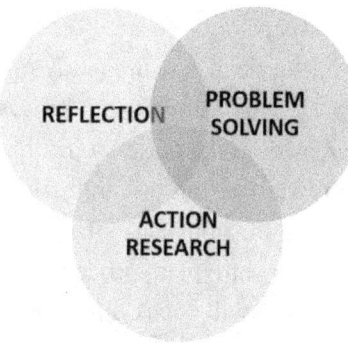

For your reflection to be systematic and effective for self-reflection, use any of the steps in the thirteen processes that would useful. Remember, when using some of the action research elements for self-reflection and continuous professional improvement, a problem is a gap between a current situation (S) and more desirable targets (T) or in other words your most cherished goals or critical values. The problem is being solved as paths (Ps) are created to move from the S to the T. There are seven problem solving steps:

1. Specify the higher education problem
2. Analyze the situation with a force field analysis
3. Brainstorm multiple paths
4. Plan for Action
5. Anticipate obstacles
6. Take Action
7. Evaluate

The process of continuous improvement, the most challenging, complex, and difficult, is action research. As referenced earlier, "traditional" researchers do laboratory and field experiments to create sociological and psychological theories to explain the functioning of higher education. Action researchers do naturalistic field studies within higher education settings to create techniques of planned change, administrative problem solving, and college and university development and improvement. In action research, higher education administrators study their own situation, as well as those in the workplace or classroom, to improve the quality of processes and results within it. By using DDDM and data collection methods for administration, in collaboration with DMU colleagues, you are striving to improve the effectiveness of your workplace, classroom, departmental unit, college or university. Traditional research on colleges and universities can provide ideas and insights, but it usually will not connect directly with your unique situation. Traditional research is usually carried out with the research community in mind; the results are published in scientific journals that are read by other traditional researchers. Action research is done by you to help you and your DMU colleagues, and often not published, although more and more action research is being published nowadays. We believe this is the result of high demand and increasing needs for more problems, concerns, or issues to be resolved with expedition and immediacy amid the escalation of fierce competition in the new global academic marketplace. Traditional research often is carried out by disinterested (objective) scientists, usually with concern for secrecy expressed as the principle of objectivity and a wish to establish generalized truths, often without immediate payoffs or instant returns on investment for research subjects.

In action research, you remove the traditional gap between scientist and research subject because as the action researcher you are both "scientist" and "subject" of the research. Still some traditional research can be useful for administrative decision-making. Action researchers in higher education should use reviews and meta-analyses of traditional higher-education research and read traditional methodological research to find and check on data collection methods for local application. There are four core differences between action research and traditional research:

1. **Improvement versus Explanation**—Action researchers seek a shared understanding of how those who work together in higher education affect one another. They are concerned with intervention for improvement. Traditional researchers seek to explain how social (or administrative) relations in higher education function, and what characterizes an effective college or university. They are concerned with generalized explanation and truth.
2. **Development versus Knowledge**—Action researchers strive to foster development and self-renewal of their own college or university. They are concerned with meaningful, local planned change. Traditional researchers seek to build a body of knowledge about higher education that grows over time. They are concerned with accumulation of knowledge.
3. **Perspectives versus Experimentation**—Action researchers strive to reach beyond their own limited points of view by collecting data of multiple perspectives from significant higher education participants. They are concerned with obtaining trustworthy data from the right people within their own higher education setting. Traditional researchers strive to move outside their subjective realities by collecting data in controlled experiments or field case studies. They are concerned with obtaining valid data from a representative higher education sample.
4. **Local vs Universal**—Action researchers work by themselves or, as in the case in chapter V, join with colleagues in cooperative self-study and problem solving to increase local effectiveness in their own classroom, workplace, department unit, college, or university. Traditional researchers engage other researchers worldwide in impersonal studies to build universal theory. They are concerned with establishing generalized principles.

Proactive   Responsive

**Action
Research**

2.
ACTION RESEARCH METHODS FOR TEACHING-INSTRUCTION-CLASSROOM

Action research is to study your own higher education situation, as well as other situations around you that were introduced in the earlier thirteen steps, in order to change the expediency or quality of resolve, relationships and results within it. We discussed this earlier from the administrative point of view; now we will address from the academic view. When you carry out action research you empower yourself, and those with whom you are working, to collect data about your actions and strategies so that your future actions and strategies will be more effective. Action research also aspires to improve your professional judgments and to help you attain insight into how better to achieve your higher administrative or academic goals. By doing action research, you can convert your current educational practices into better procedures, better instruction, better curriculum and better administration. Action research is like: watching a movie of oneself or one's own workplace, department unit, college or university in action, collecting objective ratings on one's own educational television program, eavesdropping on student's conversations as they leave a lecture you have presented, retrieving other faculty members' ratings of an important curriculum meeting that you have chaired, or reading critics' reviews of a textbook you have written. Carry out action research to understand how significant others, such as your students, colleagues, or administrators, see you and how they are affected by you. Undertake action research in order to grow beyond your reflections and solitary dialogues to involve significant others in open conversations about how you and others affect them. Use action research to discover how you should practice differently to be more effective. Action research entails carefully planned scientific inquiry, a deliberate search for information, perspectives, or knowledge. It involves self-reflective questioning, which is internal and subjective, as well as inquiry-oriented practice, which is external, and data based. Action research is a formal investigation into your own classroom or into your own department, college, or university. Action research entails planned, continuous, and systematic procedures for learning about your higher-education practices, and for trying out alternative practices to improve higher education outcomes. It develops through a spiral of cycles: reflecting, planning, acting, data collecting, re-planning, acting, more data collecting, reflecting, etc. As an alternative to traditional research, action research is practical, participative, empowering, interpretative, tentative, and critical.

Group Processes

Although you are the responsible actor for starting up action research in your own classroom, workplace, department, college, or university, you never do action research alone. Reflection and mental problem solving can be done alone, but action research is never carried out alone. As a college administrator or faculty member, you enlist your DMU colleagues as co-participants in DDDM planning and executing action research. As a department head, dean, or provost, you engage some part of your faculty in action research. As a college or university vice-president or president, you involve faculty, staff, or boards as partners in your action research. Thus, action research always involves group processes. Cooperative group work when studying ourselves is a basic process of action research in higher education. That is the case even when you initiate and coordinate your own action research in your own workplace, classroom, committee, department, college, or university. Even as a solo teacher or as a single administrator, you must engage others in the action research process.

In fact, while a large amount of action research is carried out by individual college teachers working privately with their students, increasingly more and more action research is being organized from the start as a team effort, in groups with such names as DMUs, administrative cabinets, curriculum committees, planning task forces, leadership teams, and problem-solving groups. Since democratic participation and egalitarian collaboration are essential ingredients to carry out action research, those higher educators who execute action research must have more than knowledge about research methods to do it well. They should also be skillful in leading groups and in working with others cooperatively. Higher educators, from the ranks of administration or faculty, who strive to do action research should be competent in communication, joint goal setting, cooperative problem solving, DMU deliberation, and consensual decision-making. Action research calls for cooperative group processes through which you share data and jointly search for solutions to problems or for new ways to reach shared goals.

Effective action research is a living form of democracy, especially when it fosters group reflection, joint inquiry, shared debriefing, and cooperative action planning.

Two Models

For academic purposes, versus the earlier HEAR and NOW frameworks for administrative purposes, the two models of action research by Schmuck (2006) -- proactive and responsive -- differ primarily about when data are collected and analyzed during the action research cycle. In proactive action research, action precedes the data collection process. The higher education administrator or academician acts and then studies the effects of those actions. In responsive action research, data are collected and analyzed about the higher-education situation before action is taken. You diagnose the higher-education classroom situation or perhaps carry out a tailored needs-assessment before you take action. In both models, action and data collection are alternating events, which mean that after startup, both models are similar. Again, this section two of the desktop guide now deals more with action research from the academician-classroom side as opposed to the earlier administrative-workplace side of HEAR and NOW. In this academician context, we are now introducing the theoretical, practical, and applied concepts of proactive action research and responsive action research.

Proactive Action Research.

In being proactive, the higher educator is inspired to try a new practice. Your inspiration might come from your meditations on your past and future, your debriefings with your students or colleagues, or hopes and aspirations that came into your thought patterns during a professional conference or a graduate course in education. Sometimes your creative inspirations about a new practice will come into your mind as you think about how to tighten the linkage between your practices and your values. Steps of the proactive model are:

> 1. List your hopes and concerns for the new practice.
> 2. After a knowledge search, try the new practice to have different effects on your students or colleagues and to bring about better outcomes in your higher education situation.
> 3. Carry out a method's search to create a research strategy; next collect data to track whether you are moving to achieve your hopes and to overcome your concerns.
> 4. Check on what the data mean
> 5. Reflect on alternative ways to take new actions.
> 6. Make needed changes to the new practice or try a different new practice.

Responsive Action Research

In the responsive model, the higher educator collects diagnostic data before she or he tries a new practice. Your decision to collect data first might arise out of your belief that your higher education situation is unclear and that it is your professional responsibility to understand the situation better before acting. You might also recall when a new action you took did not work well because your students or colleagues did not understand what you were trying to achieve. Also, it often is best to start with a data-based diagnosis when the higher education practice you are focusing upon has been in place for a long time. Steps of the responsive model are:

> 1. After a methods search, collect data to diagnose the situation.
> 2. Analyze the data for themes and ideas for new actions.
> 3. Carry out a knowledge search, distribute (feedback) the data, and announce changes that will be tried.
> 4. List hopes and concerns for the new practice.

5. Try the new practice to have a different effect on students or colleagues and to bring about better outcomes.
6. Collect data to evaluate the effects of the new practice.

Models Compared

The two models differ primarily at startup. After a continuous cycle is commenced, both models call for revised action and new research. No action without research; no research without action. Each model gains in strength as it incorporates central aspects of the other. Both models list hopes and concerns before a new practice is tried because the hopes and concerns must be known before the new practice is launched. Moreover, the hopes become the outcomes that are measured to note if the new practice has been effective. By taking the concerns into account, the new practice can be modified to increase the likelihood of its being effective. Both models call for a knowledge search and a methods search. In the proactive model, the knowledge search is placed early, because a new practice's success is based on the practice having been tried successfully in other higher education settings. In the responsive model, the methods search must come early, because an accurate diagnosis of the higher education situation is critical to the success of the project. That both types of searches are in both models reminds us of how important contributions of traditional research can be to the success of action research in higher education. Although traditional research and action research differ in purposes, they overlap in the research methods they employ. Both use methods to obtain data that follow three procedures: 1. asking questions, 2. observing behaviors, and 3. using existing data collected by someone else. Social psychological researchers on higher education ask questions by using questionnaires, academic tests, and interviews. They observe behaviors with an objective plan and a systematic procedure. They use existing data in the forms of public documents, census and demographic information, and college or university records.

The three procedures give rise to raw data that are typically coded for analysis by transforming them into categories or numbers. Data coded into categories are called qualitative data; they describe characteristics of people or events according to nominal categories that cannot be scaled into equal intervals. Usually qualitative data are presented in the form of narratives and case studies. Data coded into numbers are called quantitative data; they describe amounts of characteristics of people or events, according to cardinal numbers that can be arranged into equal intervals. Collecting formal data distinguishes action research from reflection and problem solving. Data collection is near the center of proactive action research; it starts responsive action research. You cannot do action research in higher education without collecting and analyzing data. Data collection takes place in every step of action research. Effective action research in higher education requires planned procedures and instruments for collecting data. The primary instruments are questionnaires, interview schedules, observation categories, academic tests, public records and publications, and private documents in the form of personal journals, letters, and diaries.

Questionnaires

Sometimes known as inventories, opinionnaires, or surveys, questionnaires are printed lists of interrogative or declarative statements that individuals respond to in writing or via a computer. People normally respond to questionnaires privately and in anonymity, but groups do respond to questionnaires using discussion and polling. Questionnaires can ask for facts, feelings, thoughts, or behaviors; they can be simple or complex; they can be open-ended or have structured rating scales.

Factual Questionnaires

Factual questionnaires ask for items of information about which respondents have knowledge. Let us say that a traditional higher-education researcher hypothesizes that first-born students with siblings (not only children) are more likely than other students to seek leadership positions in student government units in colleges and universities. That researcher would want to use factual questionnaires to collect the data. For example:

    In your nuclear family, are you? (Check one)
        ____An only child
        ____A firstborn
        ____A second born
        ____A third or later born

2. Action research methods for teaching-instruction-classroom   155

How many sisters do you have? _____ (print the number)
How many brothers do you have? _____ (print the number)
What is your gender? M F (circle one)

The traditional higher-education researcher also used factual questions to measure involvement in student government: Think about the students in your college who participate in its student government.

Have you been or are you now a member of your college's student government?

YES NO (circle one)
If YES, for how many years have you been in your college's student government?
_____ less than one year
_____ one year or more, but less than two
_____ two years or more, but less than three
_____ three years or more

If YES, have you been or are you now an officer? Yes No (circle one)

If Yes, print your officer title(s) below:
_____
_____
_____

Questionnaires About Feelings

A favorite technique for measuring feelings is the structured rating scale known as the Likert scale (pronounced Lick-urt); it has five scale points: strongly agree (SA), agree (A), neutral (N), disagree (D), and strongly disagree (SD). For example:

(Circle one for each item) At this college,

I enjoy reading novels	SA A N D SD
I like the math courses	SA A N D SD
I have learned how to improve my health	SA A N D SD
I like to receive critical feedback	SA A N D SD
I like the sports that are available to me	SA A N D SD
I am able to keep up in my courses	SA A N D SD
I am developing into an adult	SA A N D SD

Questionnaires about Thoughts

One way to measure students' thoughts about a particular course or how they think about their college experience is to ask them to write open-ended responses in journals, or to have them create a reflective file folder on a personal computer. Another open-ended strategy for measuring college students' thoughts is the sentence-completion questionnaire:

In this college,

I learn best when _____
I learn least well when _____
My courses this term are _____
My teachers this year are _____

My performance on final exams has been

_____
_____

Administrators are helpful when

_____
_____

Administrators are unhelpful when

_____
_____

To assess college students' thoughts with more formal structure, use a 5-point frequency rating scale: 5=frequently, 4=often, 3=sometimes, 2=seldom, and 1=infrequently. For instance:

(circle one)

I think about my college course work	5 4 3 2 1
I think about my college teachers	5 4 3 2 1
I think about weekends	5 4 3 2 1
I think about dating	5 4 3 2 1

Questionnaires about Behaviors

To measure college students' perceptions of their own behaviors, try a 6-point frequency rating scale: 6=six or more times a week, 5=five times a week, 4=four times a week, 3=three times a week, 2=two times a week, and 1=one time or zero per week.

For example: (circle one)

I do college-course homework	6 5 4 3 2 1
I read things unrelated to my college courses	6 5 4 3 2 1
I play sports	6 5 4 3 2 1

I do course work on the computer	6 5 4 3 2 1
I use the computer for things unrelated to courses	6 5 4 3 2 1
During finals I study course work	6 5 4 3 2 1
I go out on dates	6 5 4 3 2 1
I watch TV, each viewing, for more than 30 minutes	6 5 4 3 2 1
I play table games like cards	6 5 4 3 2 1

Making your own questionnaires. As a college teacher, colleague, or administrator, who strives for continuous improvement, try to integrate the use of questionnaires naturally into your regular instructional or administrative plan. Use them in particular to enhance student involvement in learning and to increase faculty members' participation in administrative matters. With just a tiny bit of planning, you can create simple open-ended questionnaires quickly. The simplest procedure is to ask students to use a blank piece of paper, and on it to print a plus sign at the top of one side and a minus sign on the top of the other side. No names go on those pages. Have the students to list helpful or supportive things about an aspect of your teaching on the plus side, and to list unhelpful or non-supportive things about the same teaching aspect on the minus side.

As a college administrator, you can use a similar simple questionnaire by asking faculty members to list helpful and unhelpful aspects of your administrative leadership. Avoid giving long explanations for why you are using the simple questionnaire. State that you are seeking feedback so that you can improve as a college teacher or administrator. Answers to such simple open-ended questions often reveal responses that might surprise and bother you. Do not become defensive. By putting yourself into a position of openness about how you are teaching or administering, you are demonstrating strength, and decreasing the natural social distance between you and your students or you and your colleagues. Consider structuring open-ended questionnaires with specific numbers to ensure that your students or colleagues reveal enough data for analysis and discussion. For example, ask your students to write three things about the course that help them to learn and three things about the course that hinder their learning. Or ask your faculty colleagues to write three things about faculty meetings that are going well and three things about faculty meetings that are not going so well.

Assigning numbers of things, like three and three, will increase your chances of obtaining a variety of answers, a few unexpected thoughts, and some powerful quotes worth feeding back in subsequent discussions. If every student in the course is prodded to give six answers, with 20 students you could obtain 120 answers for analysis, quantitative feedback, and class discussion. Similar numbers would apply to data from your colleagues about faculty meetings. Moreover, by adding instructions to your data collection, you are stimulating your students or your colleagues to think seriously and deeply about their answers, and to help them grow beyond giving superficial clichés.

Open-ended questions also have a few disadvantages. You will find that some student responses or colleague answers are ambiguous, that different words have the same meaning, or that the same word carries different meanings for different people. And analyses of multiple answers take time. Most of the disadvantages can be eliminated by inserting structured rating scales into the open-ended items. Ask students and colleagues to put a check or an X by specific items that apply to them, as in the previous example of assessing students' birth order. Or, give your respondents the Likert scale to show whether they (SA) strongly agree, (A) agree, (N) feel neutral, (D) disagree, or (SD) strongly disagree. For example, if you have been using pairs of students to collaborate in helping each other to write better, have the students respond to:

(Circle one)
I think working collaboratively in pairs has helped me become a better writer.   SA A N D SD
or simply, (circle one)
I like how we use collaborating pairs to learn to write better.   SA A N D SD

You might also use polar opposite-meaning adjectives at the ends of a rating scale, such as the following:

Working on writing in collaborating pairs is... (Circle one number for each item below.)

1. Helpful_____Unhelpful
   +2   +1   0   -1   -2

2. Interesting _____ Not interesting
   +2   +1   0   -1   -2

3. Fun _____ Not fun
   +2   +1   0   -1   -2

You might wish to use an even-numbered scale to avoid neutral (on the fence) responses, as follows:

I think that working collaboratively in pairs has helped me become a better writer.
(Circle one number)
Agree   6   5   4   3   2   1   Disagree

or,

I like how we use collaborating pairs to learn how to write better.
(Circle one number)
Always   6   5   4   3   2   1   Never

Here is an important warning! As you create statements for your structured questionnaires with rating scales, remember to focus on a single issue in each one, such as "collaborating pairs in writing." If you were to ask students to respond, for example, to "collaborating pairs in writing and sociology", students with contrasting and divergent attitudes toward writing and sociology would probably circle "neutral" on a Likert scale or a 3 or a 4 on a 6-point scale to show how their two divergent attitudes combine. Try, too, to keep rating scales consistent throughout each questionnaire. Avoid mixing Likert scales, polar opposite adjectives, and frequency scales in the same questionnaire. Create different questionnaires for each, or at the very least, present clearly separated sections of each in the same questionnaire. Remember also to add open-ended questions to a structured questionnaire to gather richer data. For example, after items with rating scales about collaborating pairs, add, "In the open space, please write three things you want to stay the same in our collaborating pairs learning to write well together and three things you would like to change."

To summarize some key points, questionnaires are most useful for action research in higher education, when you want to: establish the startup of a responsive action research project. Quantify students' and colleagues' responses; understand your respondents' subjective states, their perceptions, ideas, and feelings. Have all respondents give their answers at the same time. Collect large amounts of data in a short time. Allow your respondents, your students, and colleagues, to be anonymous. Gather an integrated mix of scaled and open-ended data.

Interviews are oral conversations; interviewers pose questions to interviewees. The higher education participants can be interviewed as individuals, one-on-one, or as focus groups, whereby small face-to-face groups are asked to discuss particular topics. Higher education interviews vary in how informal or formal they are. Often, formal interviews are audio or video recorded. Four interview procedures are popular in higher-education action research.

One-on-One Informal Interviews

Integrate informal interviews with students or colleagues into your normal, daily college teaching and administration; do not add them to your already overly busy schedule. Just become conscious of the many opportunities you have to interview informally the individuals with whom you work. In the informal interview, have relaxed and spontaneous conversations with your students and colleagues, in order to ascertain their perceptions, thoughts, and attitudes. Do not obviously record informal conversations; instead, keep mental notes and later write summaries of the interviewees' responses in your personal journal or in a file-folder on your computer. Ask only a few targeted questions: "What do you think of how we used collaborating pairs today?" "I see." "Any other thoughts about the class today?" "Would you like to change how we are doing the pairs?" "Yes. Tell me more." Ask open-ended questions in these informal interviews. Follow broad questions with silence, wait time, and short probes to catalyze additional conversation. Remember to smile a lot and to talk very little; listen very intently with your eyes and your ears. Seek to build empathy and mutuality. Do not be defensive. Paraphrase the interviewees' answers, but only very succinctly. Try to startup informal interviews before class starts, when passing each other on campus, in the hallways of classroom buildings, in the student union, or at sporting events if appropriate. Seek to interview students and colleagues during the interstices of college and university life, during those very brief encounters between and around formal course instruction and formal campus events.

Focus Group Informal Interviews

While being casual and spontaneous, talk with a natural group of peers, either students or colleagues, about their perceptions and feelings of a class, an event, or a project. You could ask, for example, "What do you think about the collaborating pairs we used in class today?" "Anyone else feel that way?" "Any other ideas?" "How many of you agree with those perceptions?" Following a line of relaxed questioning, try to get a rough count of how many interviewees felt a particular way. Carry out informal focus group interviews standing within a group at the end of class, or when you and a group happen to be in the same place on campus, or perhaps during lunch at a cafeteria table in a dormitory or in the student union.

One-on-One Formal Interviews

Formal interviews take place as clearly planned events. In the formal interview, state at the outset that action research is underway and that you wish to collect data to improve how your college class or how your administration operates. Create a list of unambiguous and logical questions. Try them out in a small pilot inquiry before you use them with all of the students or faculty in the action research in order to polish the questions and to see how it will be best to order them. Start formal interviews with open-ended, broad questions, such as, "Tell me how you perceive our class." and develop your interview in the form of a funnel from wide-to-focused and narrow, gradually moving toward specific questions, such as, "Tell me about your reactions to the feedback I have been giving you on your papers." Follow a planned interview schedule in every interview, especially when you want to collect and compare answers of several students or colleagues. Do allow some time, however, for interviewees to talk about issues that you did not include in your interview format. Make frequent use of catalytic probes to uncover richer data, e.g., "Tell me more about that." "Please think of an example." "What specifically are you referring to?" "How do you feel about that?"

Focus Group Formal Interviews

Here, you will want to create a very formal and official atmosphere. Bring to the interview setting sheets of heavy paper to make into name tents that stand on the table in front of where each of your students or colleagues will sit. Ask the interviewees to print their name on one side of a folded tent and to place their name tent in front of them for everyone to see. If possible, use a round table. Make the interview appear serious, as though it could take place on National Public Television. Start with broad, open-ended questions. Go from one student or colleague to another, calling each by name, expecting each to answer the same question in order. In time, ask more specific questions. Seek to obtain responses from everyone on every question by calling on interviewees by name. Turn your face and body to and fro; move from one respondent to another. Accept each answer without filtering. Write answers down in front of the group on a poster board or have two participants do that on a chalk board or on a large computer screen using Power Point, if that is available. As in other forms of interviews, probe to get all students to speak and to elaborate. Be aware that focus group formal interviews can take time. Remember, however, that they can be stimulating learning opportunities for students, especially the quiet students. Seek to use focus group formal interviews as an integral and natural part of your instructional plan, particularly if you are teaching business, economics, education, English, history, or psychology and the social sciences.

To summarize, interviews can be useful to:
1. Establish rapport and empathy with your students and colleagues
2. Collect rich and personal data.
3. Probe into respondents' subjective states about a class, college, or university.
4. Obtain information from students and colleagues that do not speak up much.
5. Use students' and colleagues' remarks to stimulate contributions from other students and colleagues.

Observers carefully watch and record what they see and hear in a specific college setting. In higher education, observers make either direct observations or mediated observations. To collect direct observations, the observer must be present to see, hear, and record what takes place. In making mediated observations, observers watch videotapes or listen to audio tapes of recorded college events. Direct and mediated observations vary in their structure or absence of structure. In making structured observations, observers count how often specific behaviors occur; they zero in on a limited set of observation categories. In unstructured observations, observers do not have a set of pre-planned categories, but rather attempt to remain open to the unfolding process and flow of events. Later, they search their raw-data notes for themes and highlights. For the higher education teacher, the most efficient way to do structured observations on her or his classes is to watch videotapes or to listen to audio tapes of recorded classroom events. The college teacher can, however, skillfully carry out unstructured, direct observations by being highly sensitive to what is happening in class, by jotting down notes soon after class, and then later recording a fuller description of observed events in a personal journal or in a personal computer file.

Observant Participation

Traditional researchers, particularly ethnographers, often use the technical term, participant observation, to call attention to their favorite research method. That term has been used to label scientific observers of third-world cultures or of modern communities and organizations. Social anthropologists use participant observation when they study primitive cultures, and sociologists use it to carry out on-the-spot research in contemporary communities. In our action research in higher education, we prefer the associated label, observant participation, to refer to college teachers who observe in their own classes or to college administrators who observe in their own departments and colleges. When they do action research teachers and administrators are not acting as curious visitors; they are actually participating members. Two fundamental questions guide the research of the observant participant: 1. What should you observe? 2. How should you record what you observe? To answer the first question, list your hopes and concerns that are central to your proactive or responsive action research. In effect, your hopes represent your project goals, while your concerns are your project' possible obstacles to success. Then, focus your unstructured direct observations on participants' actions toward or away from your hopes, and on how you are dealing with or not dealing with your concerns. Three answers might be given to the second question. 1. Initially, make available for your use, notepads, cell phone devices, index cards, electronic pads, or post-it notes on which you have written symbols that stand for your hopes and concerns. You could have them numbered, color coded, or specially lettered for every one of your hopes and concerns. Use them to write down your observations while the class or the faculty meeting is unfolding or use them to jot down your observations at interstitial moments between changes during or between classes and meetings. 2. Be sure to keep a journal that you organize according to your hopes and concerns. Meditate and write in the journal at least once per week for about 30 minutes each time. 3. Report to a friend, with whom you interact often, about your observations and how you feel your action research is developing.

Structured Observations

When you carry them out well, structured observations can be more objective than unstructured observations. They typically are, however, narrower, and more focused. Many traditional researchers consider structured observations to be more valid and reliable, because narrow and focused categories of behavior are easier for most observers to use with precision. You ask very specific questions associated with your hopes and concerns, for instance, "Did female students or male students speak more?" "Did at-risk students ask as many questions as the more privileged students?" "Did at-risk students' time on task increase, decrease or stay the same?" "Did I give as much positive reinforcement to at-risk students as I did to the more privileged students?" "What were the participation rates of females versus males, or of at-risk versus privileged, in the cooperative learning groups?" "Was I more or less supportive of at-risk students today as compared with last week?" The enhanced precision in structured observations arises because it allows you to quantify the data; that is, you can obtain a count with numbers. Thus, you could say, for example, that this week you made eight (8) supportive statements to at-risk students while last week you made 4 supportive statements to at-risk students. Or, that the oral participation rates of males in cooperative groups today were 12, while two weeks ago males made only three (3) oral contributions in cooperative groups. To quantify your structured-observation data use only a limited set of observation categories, specify the units of interaction you will record and set time intervals for when entries will be recorded into the category system.

Consider using structured observations four ways in your action research:

1. Pinpoint just one or two observation categories, such as positive reinforcement and questions asked, and focus your observations on students or faculty members during a set period.
2. Train students in a class or colleagues at faculty meetings to observe specific categories of interactions during specific periods of time. By so doing, make observing a special learning experience. Integrate the process of students observing students right into your course curriculum and classroom designs for learning
3. Create ways in which college juniors and seniors, perhaps as anthropology, psychology, or sociology majors, could make structured observations of new practices you are trying with freshmen. Or enlist the more experienced students in acting both as tutors and observers of your neophyte students.
4. Collaborate with a friendly college colleague in making structured observations of each other's classes or faculty meetings.

To summarize, observations can be useful to:

1. Understand how you communicate with students or faculty with different characteristics at different times and contexts.
2. Check for both verbal and nonverbal expressions of students' feelings.
3. See which students pal around together, sit near one another, walk together between classes, and congregate together in the student union and at formal athletic events.
4. Tally how much students contribute during group discussions and cooperative projects.
5. Check on how much time students and colleagues spend on a task.

Documents relevant to action research in higher education are college records, newspaper clippings, and private journals or diaries. Colleges and universities usually have public records about students, faculty, curriculum, administrators, extracurricular events, and their governing boards. For students, colleges keep records of courses taken and grades received. They also keep student records on rates of leaving, discipline and suspension, awards, and special recognition.

Most colleges present themselves on websites; publish school newspapers, issue special news reports, and mail out special alumni reports, all of which have information about the student body and about individual students. About faculty members, colleges have catalogues, departmental newsletters, web sites, and lists of publications. Most faculty members keep up-to-date resumes or "curriculum vitas", which they make available to the public. The academic provost's office keeps detailed records of faculty achievements, including courses taught, committee memberships, and professional publications, which under certain circumstances can be made public. Academic departments and research centers have minutes of meetings and reports of special events, which include information about faculty members. About administrators and governing boards, most colleges and universities keep records (including by electronic/digital means) of administrative and board meeting agendas and of decisions about the institution's academic and student policies. Social media, Internet websites, newspaper clippings, television news reports, and personal journals or diaries can also contribute documentary data to college action research projects. Often, the college newspaper, itself, reports on school happenings, such as board meetings, students' and faculty public performances, faculty members' professional information, and students' achievements in extracurricular activities, including clubs and sports. While journals and diaries kept by students, professors, and administrators can contribute valuable data to action research, you must, of course guarantee journal authors that you will keep information confidential and that you will solicit written informed consent from the authors before using the data. Advantages of documents in higher education action research are that documentary data are not at all affected by the data collector's presence, and that historical events can be studied objectively. Disadvantages are that records might be incomplete or collected with bias, and that it is very difficult to assess the validity of the information. When working with higher education documents, you make use of a technique called content analysis or coding to uncover recurring themes and multiple meanings. Content analysis is an objective, systematic, and quantitative rendition of written products. You can use content analysis, for instance, to uncover themes and messages that are being presented to students through curriculum materials, textbooks, academic articles, and course designs, including course syllabi. You can also apply content analysis to your course lectures and discussions as well as to administrators' speeches and statements at faculty and board meetings. Ethics are ideas about moral values and correct conduct. In higher-education action research you should focus on your moral relationships to the participants, i.e., your students, colleagues, administrators, board members, and alumni. Since your action research is local (in a specific course, classroom, department, and college) and focused on whole persons who are known to one another, the requirement for you to act ethically is absolute. Your ethical bottom-line is that no student, or any other participant, is harmed by the action research, and since continuous improvement is your umbrella goal, your students ought to benefit. That sets the ethical bar of higher-education action research higher than the ethical bar for traditional research. Will your students or colleagues benefit by taking part in the action research? As you carry out action research in higher education strive to follow ten ethical principles.

Obtain data only about the local issues related to the specific project. To be ethical, collect data only on your project's educational context (e.g., descriptions of your class, department, and college), your specific target groups (e.g., numbers, ages, academic levels, sex, race, at-risk, privileged, etc.), your hopes (i.e., goals, objectives, outcomes, desired results), and your concerns (i.e., perceived pitfalls, obstacles, or what could go wrong?).

1. Discuss the action research plan with appropriate colleagues and administrators so that they provide legitimacy.
2. Obtain the informed consent of the primary participants, including their agreement to take part by summarizing for them your purposes, procedures, and hoped for outcomes.
3. Communicate with participants with care, respect, and sensitivity by treating them as whole persons rather than as research subjects. That is the HEART & SOUL of action research in higher education.
4. Keep the research data confidential on individual participants.

5. Do not disclose any data publicly without the consent of the participants.
6. Inform appropriate administrators periodically as the action research grows.
7. Integrate your action research into your everyday, primary professional work so that it supports the work rather than interfering with your regular professional duties.
8. Use the research to improve the lives of your students and your colleagues.
9. Seek ways to continue the action research with new cycles of positive action and meaningful data collection. No action without research; no research without action.

3.
PROACTIVE AND RESPONSIVE ACTION RESEARCH TEACHING-INSTRUCTION-CLASSROOM

The actions you take when using the proactive model are interdependent, circular, and ideally continuous. You start proactive action research with your own creativity by dreaming up an action plan to improve the processes and results of a particular class or by designing a different way of carrying out faculty meetings and the like. Your desire to risk doing something new frequently stems from past, preconscious, mental data collections. Those thoughts and feelings take the form of nagging frustrations, unfulfilled dreams, and unexpressed wishes. They are the psychological foundations on which your search for new and better practice stands and the bases of your proactive action research. These feelings are human, and a part of the higher education "lived" experience.

Six Steps

Your new practice should be instrumental in moving you and your class (or colleagues) from the current situation (the S) to a preferred target (the T) in the future.

1. Create a clear list of your hopes and concerns. Try to be explicit about your goals (hopes) and to be realistic about obstacles (concerns). When thinking up your list of hopes, use such verb constructions as "to achieve", "to establish," "to create", "to facilitate", "to foster", "to lead to", or "to produce".

    For example:

    to achieve more equal participation across all students
    to establish higher student self-esteem;
    to create positive student attitudes toward academic learning
    to facilitate students getting work in on time
    to foster improved student academic performance
    to lead to increased student participation in class discussions

to produce improved student test scores

When thinking about concerns, use such verb constructions as "will accept", "will be", "will feel", "will move away", will move toward", "will reject", and will not want to."

For example:

students will accept the status quo and not try to change
students will be afraid to risk new ways of doing things
students will feel insecure as I change my teaching methods
students will move from helping one another
students will move toward the more negative voices in class
students will reject the additional work I assign
students will not want to work in cooperative groups

Give special attention to concerns that could prevent your hopes from being reached and modify how you carry out your new practices accordingly.

2. Try a new practice. Reflect on practices you may want to initiate before trying them. Make sure they align with your hopes and take into consideration your concerns. Think about your values, your unfulfilled dreams, and the sort of role model you want to be. Now, design the new practice.

3. Remember this very important point! The term "new practice" applies differently from one higher educator to another. A new practice to one professor is an old practice to another. long ago given up by another, and unrecognizable or impossible to another.

4. Here are 14 ideas of "new practices":

Group investigation methods, jigsaw puzzle cooperative sharing
Cooperative learning, peer tutoring
role-playing, problem-solving fours
formal debating, helping trios
collaborating pairs, fishbowl observing
writers' workshops, journal writing and sharing
Force field analysis, S-T-P problem solving

5. Methods search and collect data. The research part begins now by collecting formal data. You can use questionnaires, interviews, observations or documents. Your hopes and concerns (listed in step 1) will guide the content of the data collection. The data help to assess whether progress is being made toward your desired goals (hopes), and whether your anticipated pitfalls (concerns) are being overcome or avoided. Before you create the data collection instruments for your study, search for methods in others' action

research. Search using terms such as action research methods, collaborative action research, college-based research, and research on college teaching. Go to search engines such as Google and Yahoo. R. Murray Thomas (2003) offered a clear discussion on data collection and instruments; he wrote about content analyses, observations, interviews, and questionnaires in helpful ways. Review the last chapter of this book again for ideas about how to create your own tailored data collection methods. Because your effort to try new practices is unique to you and your students, strive to create your own data collection instruments. The point is to use data collection techniques that make sense to you and will enhance the growth and development of your students. This is your planned change effort, no one else's.

6. Check on what the data mean. Raw data are merely numbers and words. They become useful when integrated into your reflections on your past, present, and future behaviors. They take on meaning when they help answer questions about the merit and worth of your new practices. Merit refers to intrinsic value, while worth refers to extrinsic value. For example, diamonds can be said to have merit because they are pretty; they can be said to have worth because can be exchanged for money. Thus, your new practice has merit if your students feel comfortable with it; they like what you are doing differently. It has worth if your students are learning more, achieving better, or behaving more skillfully.

7. Although fresh personal insight can be gained by silently reflecting on the data, student discussions about the data can also help with yours and theirs understanding of the project. The data of your action research will become most useful when you incorporate data results into conversations with your students about your course and your teaching practices. Other appropriate partners to communicate with about the meaning of the data include:

   - Another professor not in your college
   - A trusted colleague within your college
   - More experienced students with whom you are working
   - A small group of colleagues in your own department
   - An administrator, perhaps your department head

8. Think about alternative ways to behave. Reflect on the meanings from the data that you arrived at in Step 4. Are there some consistent themes that cut across those conversations? Now, think of the day-to-day reflections you have made on how the new practices unfolded. No information from others can substitute for your own reflections on the present about how your students are reacting. That

is one reason why writing reflections in a personal journal regularly and often can be helpful. The combination of others' understandings of the data and your own interpretations of what happened help to determine alternative ways for you to behave in the future.

9. Improve the new practice. You have now recycled to the beginning. Either fine-tune your new practices with your current students or look for another fresh start with a new student group. Either way, you have completed one cycle of proactive action research and you have continued to integrate your action research with reflection and problem solving.

Let us turn now to an illustrative case study of proactive action research in higher education.

Maxine Martin Braxton

Maxine Martin grew up in a small Appalachian coal town in West Virginia. Her father was a Baptist minister; her mother taught first grade. Maxine grew up with books and magazines all around her, and as a first-born, she was encouraged to excel in school. By the time she started senior high, she had two brothers and one youngest sister. She was the salutatorian of her high school in a graduating class of 125 students. There was no doubt in her mind or in the minds of her parents that she would attend college. Her parents, siblings and teachers were immensely proud of her. Maxine chose to attend a famous historically African American university about 100 miles away from her hometown. She would reside in a dormitory on campus for her first two years and later move into an apartment near campus with two girl friends for her junior and senior years. Her interest in books drew her to the English department for her major and to the History department for her minor. During her junior year one of her English professors strongly urged her to consider going to graduate school for a master's degree. Her parents were delighted with that idea and paved the way for her to apply to the graduate school of a major urban university in a neighboring state less than 80 miles from her home. Again, she chose English for her major and started to think seriously about becoming an English teacher. During her two years of master's studies she also took two pedagogical courses to learn about teaching methods and adult education. While she was in the last semester of her master's program one of her professors told her about a job opening at a college near her home in the Appalachian Mountains. She became enthusiastic about the idea of returning home to help her parents give guidance to her brothers and sister, and to work in a college environment which was attracting African American students with limited means and often with an inadequate high-school education. She successfully interviewed for the job and started teaching right after she received her master's degree. She was only 25 years old when she started to teach in higher education. She did not feel well prepared for the "professor" role, but she was committed to serving at-risk students in an Appalachian higher-education setting, and she felt comfortable living back home again. For the next five years Maxine Martin taught a full-time load of four or five English courses each semester, including most summer sessions. Her courses were English Proficiency Writing, a requirement for students who could not pass a special writing exam, English Composition I and II., Poetry and The Short Story, African American Literature, and a special course that she developed entitled, Southern Writers. Over those years she put herself *wholeheartedly* into her teaching, the lives of her students, the happenings in the English department, and campus life in general. In the middle of that period, Maxine met and fell in love with Steven Braxton, the college administrator in charge of student services; Steven also was a specialist for the college in service learning and had a master's degree in Developmental Education. Maxine and Steven were married in her father's church when she was 29 and he was 37. Over the next four years, they became the parents of first a boy and 30 months later a girl. Since Maxine's mother had recently retired from her teaching position, she was happily available to babysit the Braxton children with the help of Maxine's sister, while Maxine Martin continued to teach part time. During that period, the Braxtons had a house built for them just five miles away from where the Martins resided. When their children reached school age and Maxine was 36 and Steven was 44, the two of them set their minds on more advanced, graduate education. Maxine would be first because she felt a stronger need than Steven for reinvigoration and self-renewal. Furthermore, while Steven needed to be full time at their college in those days, Maxine was offered a reduced assignment of only two courses if she would agree to stay in the English department for at least two years after earning her doctorate. Her two courses, per semester, with summers off, would be English Proficiency Writing and either English Composition I or English Composition II. She enrolled again in the same urban university at which she had earned the master's degree; it was available, and convenient, and she had a close friend who entered the same doctoral program at the same time. A first-semester course in that doctoral English-Education program was *"Action-Research Based Teaching"*, a class on how to apply action research to improve the teaching of English. She was greatly impressed with the course content and process and could immediately imagine ways in which she might apply action research to her college classes. In that class she learned about professional reflection, continuous professional improvement, practical research methods, and how to carry out both proactive and responsive action research. During that first semester, Maxine and her friend attended special luncheon seminars in the Education College once every two weeks on the teaching of English. The Education dean invited visiting scholars, researchers, writers, and critics with information that she thought would help to broaden the perspectives of graduate students interested in English education. One seminar was the most impressive for Maxine. It was given by Dr. Ona Mothers, an expert in innovative methods for teaching reluctant, at-risk students how to write more effectively; she called the innovation, *"Writers' Workshop"*. For Maxine Martin, the connectedness in time between what she was learning about action research and the creative format of *"Writers' Workshop"* gave rise to a proactive action research project of her own. Maxine knew she was ready for a professional change, not a different job but rather a way of doing her job differently. After all, that is why she was going back to graduate school. She thought that she had become a bit stale, perhaps she even was in a rut; she wanted to become a different teacher. Her past self was frustrated. Too many of her students were not responding as she would like, especially the freshmen. And, then there was that college-wide interview study carried out by a graduate student from another West Virginia university in which she found that 81% of freshman students interviewed felt that English Composition I and II are the hardest first courses, while 15% felt that way about introductory math courses and 4 % felt that way about first-year freshman psychology and sociology. In applying force-field analysis to her teaching situation she could readily see that the restraining forces were overwhelming the facilitating forces.

Writers' Workshop

In writers' workshop, seats, desks, and tables are scattered around the classroom with plenty of space for movement in between. On every desk there is a yellow legal pad with a ball-point pen or, if feasible, personal laptop computers. The teacher roams about the room talking to students one-on-one, to pairs, to trios, or to small groups. The norm is that writing is always going on, both during class time and outside, between classes. Writing is a way of life; it is like constructing something or like building an object. This classroom space is a writing workshop. We come to this workshop to write. The teacher does not do upfront, direct instruction; rather the teacher is a sort of counselor or coach, who listens, encourages, inspires, reinforces, brainstorms, facilitates, and urges on. Students are expected to write, sometimes without taking their pens off the yellow pad, to read what they written, to revise, to write more, to revise, and to recycle. Another norm is for friendly helpfulness between and among students. We are in this together and we will learn more by helping one another. In pairs, trios, or fours, we each read what we have written aloud, and we offer ideas and information to one another. In the workshop space we have a large dictionary, Roget's Thesaurus, a spell checker, and a grammar checker. The course structure calls for every student to develop a "*Writing Portfolio*". The portfolio should include a variety of personal specimens, such as poems, short stories, narratives, essays, resumes, letters of job application, and research reports. The teacher specifies the kinds of specimens appropriate for the day, week, month, and semester. Students turn in their portfolios to the teacher everyone to two weeks. The teacher determines the rate with which the students turn in their portfolios, so they do not all come in at the same time. For each student, the teacher writes her reactions to their writing in the form of constructive openness (tactful, constructive, formative, critical feedback).

Hopes and Concerns

Later in that initial academic year in the doctoral program Maxine decided to try out *"Writers' Workshop"* in her two spring semester courses: English Proficiency Writing and English Composition II. Her hopes were that compared to her previous students, her writers' workshop students would:

- Spend more time writing in class
- Develop positive attitudes toward writing
- Want to become better writers
- Make fewer errors on the final papers they submit
- Write to a final standard of proficiency appropriate to the course

Her concerns were that some of her students would:

- Waste class time by being off task
- Persist in their negative attitudes toward writing
- Disbelieve that they could become better writers
- Not carefully proofread the papers they submit
- Write below a final standard of proficiency appropriate to the course

New Practices

Since Maxine was not completely comfortable with Dr. Mother's rather permissive teaching style, she decided to design writers' workshop with her own more structured style. She started the class in the traditional seating arrangement and handed to each student a standard index card on which she had printed A-1, A-2, A-3, B-1, B-2. B-3, C-1, C-2, C-3, D-1, etc. She then asked the trios to move the furniture around, and to sit together in three-person clusters around the room. The students got introduced to one another in the trios, then printed their names, mailing addresses, phone numbers, and e-mail addresses on the cards and handed them in. Before she collected the cards, she asked the students to put their ID numbers on their syllabi so that they could remember them throughout the term. Later she would use the ID numbers to regroup the class over and over again. She tried to make certain that every student in the class would, at one time or another, be grouped with every other student in a pair, a trio, or a four-person group. She would also use the ID numbers to specify which students would be working alone that day in the workshop. That small modification of Mother's plan gave her a good deal of control over group formations in the class. Maxine also decided to put some structure to the types of writing she would ask the students to do, especially in the startup of writers' workshop. She started on the first day, for example, with "writing a post card to a parent about my first week in school this semester" and moved on from there to "writing a letter to a friend back home." In subsequent class sessions she asked students to write:

- A poem about their family
- An autobiographical sketch about Who I Am
- A narrative about an event that happened over the winter holidays
- A 300-word short story about last summer
- A newspaper article about my hometown
- A 400-word essay about a famous American
- A 250-word magazine article about a favorite television program
- A 750-word research report about events in African American history

Throughout the first six weeks of the semester, Maxine sought to carry out her new role in writers' workshop. She tried to help everyone and every group. She tried to give clear and tactful feedback, and to encourage her students to help one another to become better writers.

Data Collection

After writers' workshop had been developing for one month, Maxine used three methods to assess how her new practices were affecting her students. First, she carefully observed students' reactions to the trios, to her statements about how the writers' workshop will operate, and to her first few assignments. She noted some student surprise, but high involvement in what she asked them to do. She tried to watch herself to make sure that she made many positive statements about students and that she showed support while they were writing. Maxine also decided to keep a journal of her reflections on the dynamics of the workshops. She carefully noted which students worked together and which ones worked alone. She sought to compare these classes with those she had taught the last few years. In making such comparisons, Maxine estimated the average number of minutes students in previous classes would write during class versus the average number of minutes her current writers' workshop students are writing in class. She also thought back to specific classes last year to estimate how often those students were off task compared with these current students. In both cases she was pleased that now students are writing more and off-task less. Second, Maxine informally interviewed three females and three males about the class. She asked, "How do think our writers' workshop is going?" "What do you like about writers' workshop", "What don't you like about it?" "How do you think writers' workshop could be improved?" "What ideas do you have to help students write more and better?" Third, Maxine gave a questionnaire to all students as follows:

Action Research Questionnaire

This questionnaire asks about how you feel in this class about writers' workshop. Please do not sign your name. The questionnaire is anonymous. For purposes of action research, however, please put a circle around your sex: female or male. For each statement that follows please circle whether you: Strongly Agree (SA). Agree (A), are Neutral (N), Disagree (D), or Strongly Disagree (SD). Compared to other writing classes I have had, in this writer's workshop, I am

1. spending more time in class writing   SA A N D SD
2. developing positive attitudes toward writing   SA A N D SD
3. hoping to become a better writer   SA A N D SD
4. building pride as a writer   SA A N D SD
5. writing about things important to me   SA A N D SD
6. finding enjoyment in writing   SA A N D SD

The three things I like best about writers' workshop are:
1. _____
2. _____
3. _____

The three things I like least about writers' workshop are:
1. _____
2. _____
3. _____

Meaning of the Data

Maxine used three methods to understand the meaning of the data. First, she conscientiously wrote reflections in a journal and reread them from time to time. She tried to compare the present with the past and to use those comparisons to plan for the future. She also sought to keep her original hopes and concerns in mind as she moved along. Second, Maxine fed results of the questionnaire data back to each class. She gave her own analysis and interpretation, and then checked to see if the students agreed or disagreed with her feelings. Third, Maxine met once every two weeks with her close friend, who is in the doctoral program with her, to talk about how writers' workshop was going. While they had lunch together, they both talked about their respective action research projects. Afterward, Maxine wrote in her journal any new insights that she received from her friend about how to improve writers' workshop.

Tentative Conclusions

As Maxine neared the end the spring semester, she could see clearly that her version of writers' workshop was quite successful with her students in English Composition II, but that it had been much less effective with her remedial students in English Proficiency Writing. While both classes developed more positive attitudes toward writing, and more self-confidence as writers, only students in English Composition II developed into better writers. That she proved to herself by doing "blind assessments" (she did not know the author's name) of papers of the students in the two classes. It was true that five students in the remedial proficiency course did become much better writers, but the overwhelming majority in the class did not significantly increase their writing performance.

Maxine also proved to herself that student-centered writing portfolios (collections of personal writing) could be an important component of a high quality composition course, such as the second semester of the freshman year, but that much more or a much different structure would be required in the remedial course on English Proficiency Writing. Another factor, uncovered by Maxine, might help in understanding what happened in this action research. Remember that she had collected data on the gender of her respondents. Maxine found that females and males differed in her questionnaire results (merit) and in her "blind assessments" (worth). Females enjoyed writing more than males and believed more than the males that they could write well. Even so, the females lacked pride in the quality of their written products. The males were just as proud, if not prouder than the females, of their written products. Her "blind assessments" of the students' writing portfolios led Maxine to conclude that females, for the most part, were better writers than males, at least in these two classes at this time.

Next Steps

Maxine Braxton benefited a great deal from her action research. The data, reflections, and discussions with her friend helped her to grow in perspective and to become more mature in thinking through her instructional strategies. She decided that her next attempt at action research would be to do some new things in English Proficiency Writing. She is reflecting on ways to integrate the best parts of writers' workshop with her history of direct instruction. She also intends to become more sensitive to how females and males approach the task of writing. She believes that she needs to understand more about how she might use differentiated instruction with females and males, particularly within the context of reluctant college learners.

Responsive Action Research

Kurt Lewin, one of America's most famous and versatile social psychologists, was the creator of action research. He conceived of it as alternating cycles of diagnosis and action, with the startup always entailing a data collection for diagnosis. In fact, in the Lewin tradition, it is assumed that effective "change agents", whether attorneys, consultants, physicians, psychologists, or teachers and professors, diagnose their clients' situations and problems before they take action.

Six Steps

Start by reflecting on things you would like to know about your students' or colleagues' perceptions, attitudes, thoughts, and behaviors. What sorts of data do you wish to collect from your target class or group?

Review the sorts of instruments we have already presented earlier. Do a more formal methods search, if you wish, by opening search engines on your computer. Reread the methods literature referred to in earlier chapters and referenced in our bibliography. Pinpoint a few methods to collect data that could be useful to you. Keep them short and simple. Slower to decide on an innovative practice than its proactive counterpart, the responsive model's first four steps constitute the project's initiation. The last two steps call for action and evaluation; thus, simply stated responsive action research entails diagnosis, action, and evaluation.

1. **Collect data.** On the threshold of initiating your higher-education responsive action research, you sense that your teaching or administration could be improved, and that a few classroom designs, instructional strategies, or meetings' procedures could be executed differently. While you probably are reluctant to solicit critical feedback from your students or colleagues, doing so can lead to more effectiveness in teaching and managing. Seek to collect objective data about students' or colleagues' thoughts and feelings and to start up a constructive strategy to improve your current higher education situation. The initial data collection should be short and simple. It can be as straightforward as: plus and minus signs on two-sides of a blank piece of paper (read about William Davis's action research later) pairs of students discussing strengths and shortcomings of teaching methods students freely choosing two of their class peers to collaborate with on a project an open-ended "Who am I" questionnaire a sentence completion or a paragraph completion questionnaire a colleague's observation of one your classes or faculty meetings audio taping a writers' workshop with students and later engaging them in a content analysis of what happened. The following statements are especially important for responsive action research to be effective in higher education. Make certain that you collect data from students (or colleagues) in a public, formal, and official manner so as to communicate to them the high importance of the project. It is crucial to convey to everyone that the data you are collecting will be used to facilitate improvement in the class or the faculty.

2. **Analyze data.** Analyze the data to uncover recurrent themes and patterns. The analysis can be done alone or with small, action-research committees of students or of faculty. A central feature of data analysis is searching for good ideas for action. While the themes or patterns reveal how students or colleagues think and feel about the current situation, action ideas are instrumental strategies

for moving from the current situation to a more ideal target. The combination of themes and action ideas can generate new and more creative practices. Searching for themes and action ideas may open a door to the present and indicate pathways to the future. Do not dwell on whether the data are valid in the psychometric sense, but you do want the data to be trustworthy. Remember, internal validity rather than external validity is your main concern as a local action researcher. Thus, higher-education action researchers seek data they can trust to describe accurately their own specific class, their own specific department, or their own specific college. They do not care if the data about their own situation generalizes to other similar situations. Action researchers in those other similar situations will have to collect their own local data. Strive for accuracy and precision of data with a specific student group or faculty group.

3. **Data feedback.** Select a limited number of themes and action ideas. Do not try necessarily to summarize all of the data or to cover all the possible actions you might take. The important point at this stage is to show reasonable linkages between what you have learned from the data and the changes you intend to carry out. Describe to the class or faculty group what specific changes you will try during the next few weeks or months. This presents your students or colleagues with a rational plan of future classroom or faculty interactions, emphasizes the seriousness of the changes, and offers an informal contract to which professor and students or administrator and faculty will be accountable.

4. **Hopes and concerns.** Here you should become explicit about your hopes or goals for the new actions as well as your concerns about the obstacles that might keep you hopes from being actualized.

5. **Try new practices.** Implement practices that are new to you and to the students or your colleagues. Give the new practices at least two months to take form and to have some effects. Do not make judgments too soon about success or failure. Allow for several success experiences before formal evaluations. Tune up your new practices as they unfold and develop. Reflect seriously on the present but stay the course.

6. **Collect data.** As you carry out the new practices, stay vigilant to yourself and to your students' or colleagues' reactions. This is a time to reflect on the HEART. Remain attune to the flow of classroom or meeting interaction, to expressions of feelings, to positive and negative behaviors, and to how the class or faculty group does or does not cooperate.

Check on how your participants are reacting with informal observation. Look for smiles and laughter, for heads nodding in agreement, for eye-to-eye contacts, for heads bent toward one another, and for the ease with which students or colleagues come up to you or to one another. Try some structured observation by counting rates of talking, by listening for paraphrasing, summarizing, and statements of feelings, and by tuning in to the frequency of statements that include collective words, such as "we, us, our group, and our class". Interview students or faculty members about their perceptions and feelings. Think about how to interview individuals, small focus groups, and perhaps the whole class or the entire faculty group about the new practices. Decide whether your interviews should be formal or informal. After the new practices have been in action for a month or more, there are three reasons to collect additional data:

1. To judge whether your new practices have merit. In other words, are the students or faculty colleagues satisfied with the practices? Have they developed more positive attitudes? Do they show more appreciation for one another, for the way the course is going, or for how faculty communication has improved? The best research method to assess the merits of your new practices will be a tailored questionnaire.

2. To assess whether your new practices have worth. Are the students learning the course curriculum as well as you hoped they would? Are the faculty members serving the college in more and better ways than they did before? Do the students or faculty members behave differently toward one another and toward you? Do the students perform better on academic tasks? Do the faculty members perform better in teaching, research, and service? Are there things your students or colleagues can now that will likely continue in their professional lives next year? The best research methods to assess the worth of your new practice will be interviews and observations.

3. To find new themes or action ideas that emerged as your new practices were being implemented. Were there unexpected gains from the new practices? Were there any unintended losses that resulted from using the new practices? To become fully engaged in continuous improvement, you should now look for a new focus for the next cycle of your action research in higher education. Read the following case study to get a better understanding of how responsive action research works in higher education.

William S. Davis, Jr.

William S. Davis grew up in the Deep South very close to a military base where his father was a career chef. With two older sisters, he was the only boy in the Davis household. His mother worked part time as a housekeeper. Proud to have a son, the Davis named him after his father. William did well in school and later attended a predominately Black university in New Orleans where he majored in English Education and was a four-year member of the ROTC. After a 20-year military career, he returned to his New Orleans-based university to earn a master's degree in Black Studies and American Literature. During his graduate program of studies, he minored in psychology and took courses in action research, cooperative learning, and personality. Now, at age 49, Junior, as his friends still called him, had taught Black Literature and English Proficiency Composition to undergraduates at a historically Black university in Mississippi for five years. William S. Davis Jr., still unmarried, loves to read serious Black literature. He moves easily among Mayo Angelo, Toni Morrison, Ralph Ellison, Alice Walker, Alex Haley, Richard Wright, and Ernest Gaines to name just a few. He reads the magazine, *American Legacy* from cover to cover four times a year. William also likes to write. He keeps a diary, which is especially focused on his thoughts and feelings about what he reads, and he has tried several times to compose short stories about his military career. But, after all is said and done about him, Junior lives to teach; he works hard every day to plan, design, perform, and achieve on behalf of his college students. By the middle of October in last year's fall semester, Davis became frustrated with his junior Black Literature class. What was happening with this class had happened before, but this time it was worse. This class typically is made up of some of the brightest students in the college, but many apparently were not reading the assignments. Few students were speaking up in class when William questioned them about the readings. He could not understand why these 20 and 21 year old students did not seem to gravitate toward *"Invisible Man"*, *"Roots"*, *"Color Purple"*, and *"Native Son"*. After all, most of their grandparents and parents must have had experiences like what these authors are writing about. Still, the students were coming to class without a clue about the importance of these masterpieces. Instead, many of them watched the clock and counted the minutes until lunch. They were hungry, William thought, but not for great literature. At lunch with a close colleague that semester, William experienced a poignant memory, recalling an uplifting experience he had had in his master's program. William's colleague, who had studied action research with him in graduate school, reminded him of a specific moment in class when the professor asked William to explain how responsive action research works. Back then, William answered correctly and clearly, and the professor had given him special congratulations, both at the time of William's answer as well as after the class was over. After receiving that feedback, William immediately caught up with his friend in the hallway to tell him how much he appreciated that professor. After lunch William went to his office to look up lecture notes from his action research course. He reviewed information about the responsive action research model, along with a quote from his professor: "When you teach your own college courses, remember how essential it is to listen to the voice of your students. They will not be reluctant to talk about what they think and how they feel about what happens in the college classroom." William decided then to go directly to his Black Literature students during the following class to find out what might help them become more interested in Black Literature.

Data Collection

At the start of the next class William announced that he wanted to try a process he had learned about in graduate school, a process known as action research. He asked the students to meditate silently about how his teaching was or was not helping them learn about Black Literature. Next, he told them to print a plus sign (+) on one side of a piece of blank paper and a minus sign (-) on the other side. Then, he had them list the helpful things he does on the plus side and the unhelpful things he does on the minus side. Next, William assigned each student to a female-male pair and told those pairs to agree on at least two helpful things and two unhelpful things. With 24 students in the class, 12 pairs were formed. William asked each pair to meet with another pair and to agree on three helpful things and three unhelpful things. He then brought two groups of four together to form groups of eight. Those groups agreed on four helpful and four unhelpful things. William told the students in each eight-person group to count off from 1 to 8; he assigned person number 3 in each of the three groups to act as a reporter for her or his group. The three reporters came forward to form a panel up front. In its pooling of information from the three groups, the panel decided on a total of eight helpful things and eight unhelpful things, as follows:

Helpful:
1. Gives interesting information about the authors,
2. Explains characters clearly,
3. Exudes enthusiasm for Black literature,
4. Gives extensive feedback on papers,
5. Has a clever sense of humor,
6. Grades fairly,
7. Asks challenging questions, and
8. Does not favor one gender over another

Unhelpful:
1. Covers too many authors
2. Too much lecture
3. Too much homework
4. Sometimes uses words we do not understand
5. Does not ask us how we feel
6. Asks questions that make some of us afraid to speak
7. Not enough student-to-student discussion (today is the first time we held discussions in student groups)
8. Not always clear about what he wants in our papers.

Data Analysis

During the next week, William looked at what the students came up with, and meditated on the themes he saw in their data. He thought that although his students appreciated his expertise in Black literature and were finding his information helpful, they also thought that he was talking too much and was not facilitating discussion. William saw that his questioning style often created anxiety in students, making them reluctant to speak up in class. William wondered about the large number of assignments he was giving and saw that superficial treatment of many things was not creating motivation to learn in the students. William realized that the method he created to collect the data could also be used to get the students more engaged in class discussions about what they were reading. The following week William told his students that he wanted to use the data they gave him to improve how the class would operate in the future. After summarizing the themes in the data, William asked the students to return to their groups of four and to brainstorm actions they would like to see him try. William gave each four-person group a large sheet of blank poster paper with a marker. He told each group to count off from one to four, and then assigned person two in each group to act as a recorder who would print the group's action ideas on the poster paper. Later, the recorders fastened their groups' reports to the walls, and the students milled about the room to read what the other five groups had produced. Next, William told each group to choose three action ideas from the other groups that they most liked. Then, he announced that he would study their action ideas and preferences and would give them feedback soon about the action ideas that he would actually try.

Search for New Ideas

The six groups produced a total of 18 action ideas; the whole class chose six as favorites. William put those six ideas on an overhead projector, along with comments of his own in parentheses next to each, as follows:

1. Spend more class time in student groups to learn about the readings. (Use groups of two, four, six, or eight to work on Black literature like how we worked together doing action research during the last few classes.)

2. Students generate questions to ask Mr. Davis about black authors, their ideas, and their literary themes. (Students raise questions about literature that are important to them, instead of me drilling them about the readings? My question is: Will you all read the assignments if we do that?)

3. Focus on just a few authors: spend more time on each. (Action ideas four and five seem to follow from this idea.)

4. Reread "*Invisible Man*", which we read a while ago, when our study of it was rather superficial and half-HEARTed. (Students

recognizing the importance of Ralph Ellison's classical novel wanted to understand it better and relate it to their lives.)

5. Read more of Toni Morrison's books. (Students recognizing the importance of a genuinely great black author seek to understand her difficult and challenging writing better.)

6. Students work together to report on readings to one another and to Mr. Davis. (This action idea, an extension of idea 1, could be integrated with ideas 2-5 if students were to interview me, for example, about Ralph Ellison and Toni Morrison.)

As William fed the action ideas back to the students, along with his added ideas (his information inside the parentheses), he saw many students nodding approval. He asked them if he understood how they would like him to improve the class. Virtually all students called out a resounding "Yes!" After searching his mind and his files for relevant literary knowledge William announced the following action ideas to try until the winter break:

> We will reread "*Invisible Man*" as well sections of Ellison's "Shadow and Act", an autobiographical collection of 22 essays. We will learn about Ralph Waldo Ellison in small groups I will assign you to work with different people on each book. We will start with his 1947 version of "*Invisible Man*" in groups of three. Between now and our next class, everyone should quickly review all 25 chapters of the book by skimming through the first sentences of the paragraphs. I know that it is a long book, over 500 pages, but since we have recently studied it, a quick rereading of high points should be enough for getting us started. Remembering his graduate course in cooperative learning, William then numbered off the three-person groups from 1 to 8. He went on to say: Beginning next time, groups 1 through 8 will become experts about the chapters of the same number of their group. They will prepare oral reports on the key themes, powerful events, and important lines of their group's chapter. Thus, Group 1 will cover Chapter 1, Group 2, Chapter 2, and so forth. Later on, we will discuss how the small groups are going and try to make improvements so that everyone is feeling good about what he or she is doing. Next time we will start with the reports of Groups 1 through 4 on Chapters 1-4. I will expect each group to report to the whole class, with every member involved in the presentation. Your small groups should meet outside of class at least for one hour to prepare for its

presentation. We will proceed with Chapters 5 through 8 during the next class. Then we will continue on with new assignments to cover Chapters 9-16, and Chapters 17-24, and I will be responsible for reporting on Chapter 25. Next, we will work in new small groups of four to brainstorm insights we have all gained from reading Ellison's classical novel. Then we will see where we are with "*Invisible Man*" before going on to "Shadow and Act." In that 1953 book Ellison reflects on his life experiences in 22 short essays. I will assign one essay to each person and have them collaborate in pairs to plan a brief report on each essay. But we will get to that later.

Hopes and Concerns

William's hopes were that his students would:
- Participate actively with involvement in the small groups and in whole-class presentations.
- Develop favorable attitudes toward the class.
- Learn more about literature.
- Develop improved oral and writing skills.

William's concerns were that some of the students would:
- Hitchhike during small-group discussions and whole-class presentations, depending on others to carry the workload.
- Develop uncomfortable feelings toward the class.
- Avoid doing homework reading and small group planning.

New Practices

William carried out the rereading of "*Invisible Man*" as planned. He was pleased with how involved most students were with the group work and in making reports to the whole class. William observed that those students who had not spoken up in class were speaking in the small groups and to the whole class. He was impressed, too, with the accuracy and the structure of the group reports about the Ellison chapters. For the study of Ellison's "Shadow and Act", he observed that the pairs worked well in class as well as spending considerable time out of class to help each other make reports. Running out of class time for 22 oral reports, he asked the students to write down their oral comments about their essay in the form of a radio script, as though public radio were doing a weekly series on Ralph Ellison 40 years after his "Shadow and Act" essays were published by The New American Library. Next semester, those students who register for Mr. Davis's second course on Black Literature will be treated to an in-depth investigation of Toni Morrison.

Data Collection

William Davis used three methods to collect research data on his students' reactions to the new practices. First, he observed participation and active involvement in the small groups and during whole-class presentations. He was particularly tuned in to observing students whose participation had been relatively low, compared to others before the action research began. He had taken care, moreover, to give those previously reticent students extra encouragement. William moved from group to group during small-group work to observe and to encourage, or to answer questions about Ellison and about language Ellison used. Second, William used part of every third class during the Ellison series to interview students about the new practices. He would divide the class into new groups of two or three so that all had an opportunity to speak. He would at times combine groups to engage students in whole-class discussions. As a result of those debriefings, William was able to fine-tune the small-group work as it developed. He was also able to give tips on how to make small-group presentations to the whole class more interesting and livelier. Third, at the end of the semester William converted his list of helpful and unhelpful teaching techniques into a structured questionnaire. With that questionnaire, William assessed the merit of his new practices. He sought to assess if his students thought that he had continued to do the helpful things and had discontinued the unhelpful things. The questionnaire was similar to the following:

Student Perceptions of Mr. Davis' Class After the Action Research Began

Below are 18 things that could happen in Mr. Davis's class. Please circle one answer next to each item to show whether you strongly agree, agree, feel neutral, disagree, or strongly disagree (SA, A, N, D, SD). Since the action research began,

Mr. Davis
1. Gave information not in the books about the authors.   SA A N D SD
2. Lectured too much   SA A N D SD

3. Explained characters well	SA A N D SD
4. Covered too many authors	SA A N D SD
5. Was fair in grading	SA A N D SD
6. Assigned too much homework	SA A N D SD
7. Showed enthusiasm for literature	SA A N D SD
8. Seldom asked us about what we think and feel	SA A N D SD
9. Gave extensive feedback on papers	SA A N D SD
10. Drilled us on what authors are trying to get across	SA A N D SD
11. Had a good sense of humor	SA A N D SD
12. Questioned us to make us feel afraid to make a mistake	SA A N D SD
13. Did not favor one gender more than the other	SA A N D SD
14. Did not spend enough time on difficult assignments	SA A N D SD
15. Asked challenging questions	SA A N D SD
16. Did not have enough student-to-student discussion	SA A N D SD
17. Was unclear about what he wanted in our papers	SA A N D SD
18. Used words we did not understand	SA A N D SD

To assess the worth of his practices, William prepared an essay examination to judge how well this class in Black or African American Literature compared to others. His data showed significant improvement in students' attitudes about the class since the action research began. Also, he found improvements in what the students felt they were learning and in their skills in writing. He was also mostly pleased with the students' performances on the final essay exam, but there still were a few problems that he would work on during the next semester. Perhaps his highest moment came with the information that 22 of the 24 students had decided to take Black Literature II from Mr. Davis.

4.
COOPERATIVE AND COLLABORATIVE WORK-GROUP PROCESSES FOR TEACHING-INSTRUCTION-CLASSROOM

College and university participants with common concerns and goals can use cooperative action research to inquire about, and to improve upon educational issues and problems. We use the word, cooperative, to refer to joint work to reach the same hope or goal; we use the word, collaborative, to refer to joint work to promote individual hopes or goals. Thus, case studies of action research forthcoming in this chapter are cooperative and collaborative. Two very different social processes characterize effective cooperative action research in higher education: supportive communication and collegial fellowship.

Supportive Communication

Supportive communication calls for team members to exchange mutual esteem, obligation, and respect with one another. Supportive communication includes:

- Understanding others' ideas and feelings
- Acknowledging others' beliefs and values
- Showing concern for others' happiness and welfare
- Expressing empathy and positive regard
- Giving assistance and expressing admiration
- Demonstrating acceptance and warmth

Supportive communication enhances the ability of team members to feel included, secure, and to perform competently. Traditional research has shown, for instance, that soldiers perform dangerous duties more effectively when interpersonal relations in their platoons are friendly and supportive. Industrial work groups perform more competently when interdependent workers communicate mutual respect. College students' ideas in student-problem-solving groups are accepted and used more when they are friendly with one another. Some students achieve better academically when they feel accepted and respected by their classmates. For more examples, read Schmuck and Schmuck (2001, Chapter Two).

When new students or faculty are expected to cooperate in college groups, they frequently feel anxiety about how they will perform. They think, "Will I be competent here?" "Will I be able to contribute to this group's success?" "Will anyone appreciate me in this group" Will others think I am carrying my load?" "Will other students or faculty colleagues listen to my ideas?" "What might I do to be influential in a positive way?" Such mental questions reveal college students' and faculty members' personal thoughts about competence, acceptance, and influence, and how important their personal emotions are to their success in fitting into the college culture. Three psychological motives need to be actualized within the context of supportive communication: 1. achievement, 2. affiliation, 3. power. The motive for achievement can be actualized by joining with others to solve important challenges together. The affiliation motive can be actualized by mutual expressions of positive feelings, help, and responsibility to one another. The motive for power can be actualized by accepting the importance and relevance of one another's ideas and feelings as group members work together. Within colleges and universities, a strong foundation of supportive communication is required for cooperative action research to work well.

Collegial Fellowship

As Maxine Martin demonstrated in her version of Writers' Workshop, constructive criticism exchanged between student friends can convert anxiety and fear into positive energy for learning and development. Since college students in traditional settings carry out many of their learning activities one-on-one with college teachers, they need to learn how to exchange constructive criticism and how to act as critical friends with other students. A similar statement can be made about many college teachers. They too carry out many of their daily routines without much formal interaction with colleagues, except for the occasional faculty meeting. Thus, they too need to acquire the ability to exchange constructive criticism with colleagues. Perhaps the most difficult challenge in the highly charged higher education culture is delivering effective constructive criticism. Think of William Davis's Black Literature class, a group of fairly seasoned college juniors and seniors, many of whom felt academically insecure and doubtful of their ability to succeed in an advanced literature course. Mr. Davis found that through pairing students in a context where he had emphasized supportive communication, he was able to build in exchanges of constructive criticism. Moreover, he realized that collegial fellowship pairs did best after he had done some team building and cooperative learning with the whole class. Let us explain three psychological assumptions that under gird the collegial fellowship procedure:

> Supportive communication by itself will not necessarily facilitate development, learning, or problem solving. Critical friendship about shortcomings should accompany supportive communication, allowing the student or faculty recipient to correct mistakes, reduce errors, and arrive at an enhanced understanding. 2. College students or faculty will accept and use criticism more readily when it is given by empathic peers or colleagues than when it comes from a hierarchical or impersonal source. 3. Supportive communication and constructive criticism enhance learning when they are implemented within a social environment of an egalitarian and a reciprocally helping relationship. Those are psychological conditions that both Maxine Martin and William Davis were working toward with their students. We now describe a collaborative critical friendship model that we, the authors, have used in our own doctoral seminars, both in the education of superintendents of public schools and in the education of administrators in higher education. Since doctoral education places a premium on competent writing for course papers, theses, comprehensive examinations, and dissertations, we have found that many of our doctoral students approach the task of writing with hesitation, and insecurity. They need help in overcoming writers' block, and fears of failure. Pairing students often helps them cope with their fear of failure in writing and propels them on to enhanced confidence with their comps and dissertation. In the style of two-way, collaborative peer tutoring, we ask our students to work through the following steps with each other:

1. Each student writes a 500 draft about an educational issue about which she or he would like to do action research.
2. The student partners (the pairs) exchange their drafts with each for an initial reading.
3. Without referring to the draft, each student writer explains to her or his partner the main points that are being set forth in the draft. In other words, each summarizes the primary points in his or her draft.
4. Each tutor (listener) gives feedback to the writer about any gaps between the draft and the oral summary. This can help each writer to see how her or his draft could be written more clearly.
5. The partners tell each other how they will rewrite their drafts.
6. Each partner reads the other's draft, circling anything that is unclear, inaccurate, grammatically incorrect, and so forth. This can help each writer to become more precise in his or her prose.
7. Each student spends time alone to rewrite the draft.
8. The students turn in their papers to us, the professors, for our constructive feedback.

Group Processes

Successful cooperative action research requires college teachers to be competent in reflection, problem solving, research methods, and group processes. What follows are group-process standards that are necessary to strive toward if a college faculty group is to carry out effective cooperative action research. When doing cooperative action research in higher education:

1. Establish member feelings of inclusion, membership, and trust
2. Foster member shared influence and dispersed leadership
3. Emphasize member friendliness and team cohesiveness
4. Reduce social status differences among diverse members
5. Practice sound meeting skills, i.e., convener, recorder, agenda, and time frame
6. Use formal communication skills, e.g., paraphrasing and summarizing
7. Make appropriate formal group agreements
8. Learn to use consensus decision-making
9. Debrief the team's group processes, i.e., the group talks about how it is doing in meeting the first eight standards
10. Take care to judge whether the team follows through after the meeting on decisions made at the meeting

Collaborative Action Research

In the earlier work by Schmuck in *Practical Action Research for Change* (2006), cooperative action research is defined as a democratic means to implement positive change, and as remarked earlier in the book, we suggest that, "democratic participation and equalitarian collaboration are essential ingredients to carry out action research". The term "cooperative" is typically used in K-12 settings. The term "collaborative" is more common to higher education and is being considered more often these days in our era of transdisciplinary relationships on university and college campuses. Collaborative relationship building can occur horizontally across disciplines or vertically between levels of academic disciplines or departmental ladders within the institutional infrastructure. Academic administrators who are preparing for accreditation or other quality improvement measures can use vertical decision-making teams to collect data and make changes to meet academic standards. This can occur between a provost and a dean, a dean and a department chair, or a chair and a faculty member. Horizontally, faculty who teach at the same classification level in the same or in different disciplines, can form collaborative teams to collect data and change curriculum based on needs or demands within that classification level. Put simply, collaborative synergies can occur North and South, East and West, and at the crossroads of collegial networks. State systems or regional clusters of colleges and universities are strongly encouraged to consider action research teaming and networking for positive change on larger scales, units of analyses or loci of control. Good resources for garnering collaboration is this regard is *Collaborative Learning Techniques: A Handbook for College Faculty* (2005) by Barkley, Cross and Major and *Group Processes in the Classroom* (2001) by Schmuck and Schmuck. In our present era of global transdisciplinary, transnational and transcultural synergies, action research teaming through collaboration provides the institution, and its principal stakeholders, with timely opportunities to strengthen academic infrastructures for promoting student learning with tangible outcomes.

A resource for creating frameworks for supplementing this section of the book is *Disciplines as Frameworks for Student Learning* edited by

Riordan and Roth (2005). This work contextualizes several disciplines (history, mathematics, philosophy, economics, literature, and chemistry) for improving student learner outcomes that could be helpful in transdisciplinary faculty collaboration. Another good source is *Decoding the Disciplines: Helping Students Learn Disciplinary Ways of Thinking* (2004) by Pace and Middendorf. Like cooperative action research, collaborative action research can be carried out at the horizontal or vertical campus levels, from one- on-one academic alliance to campus-wide networks of communities of practice. For purposes of clarification, community of practice is defined as "a group or network of individuals who share concern, a set of problems, or a passion about a topic, and who deepen their knowledge and expertise in this area by interacting with each other on an on-going basis" (Allee, 2003). Another term that has been defined by Allee and used in this book is "generative learning". This term is defined as "value-driven learning that seeks what is alive, compelling, and energizing and that expresses a willingness to see radical possibilities beyond the boundaries of current thinking" (Allee, 2003). Action research can energize movement from stagnate standardization to radical transformation. While community of practice describes how networks should operate on the modern campus, generative learning should be embraced as the framework for discussing the instructional process beyond ordinary, conventional, and traditional teaching. Faculty, in collaboration with their students and other faculty members, are principle stakeholders in the teaching and learning processes. Following are various ways collaborative action research can be conducted under different circumstances and case studies of faculty conducting action research through collaborative relationship building.

One-On-One Collaboration

One-on-one collaboration or academic alliance building through partnership occurs when one person advises, guides, or mentors another person. Such examples of this type of synergy were presented in earlier chapters. One-on-one collaboration can also occur when two faculty work together on a synergistic action research project. The figure below highlights the myriad of potential collaborative partnerships.

Figure 5. Potential One-on-One Collaborations

1. A faculty member and another faculty member

a. A faculty member in a remedial class and a colleague perform action research to matriculate students from a remedial math class to a math class in the major.
b. A faculty member with a colleague conduct research in a transdisciplinary core course in liberal arts.
c. Two or three science faculty members focus on making a core course in chemistry more interesting to their students by infusing some type of innovation.
d. A journalism faculty member pairs with a colleague in the English department to conduct research on the differences between journalistic writing and writing for composition.

2. A faculty member and a student:

a. A faculty member in the required liberal arts curriculum core and a student athlete use action research to improve the student's reading and writing skills.
b. A faculty member in biology and a student who is failing in a required biology course explore outdoor and environmental activities that will help the student understand theory from practice.
c. A faculty advisor and a student explore alternative settings and circumstances for conducting library research.
d. A faculty member in health and physical education and a student athlete examine balances between athletic performance and academic productivity.

3. A faculty counselor and a student:

a. A faculty counselor and a foreign student apply action research to help each other understand differences between their cultures.
b. A faculty counselor and a student who is experiencing behavioral challenges uses action research to determine preventive and proactive measures for mitigating against disruptive conduct.
c. A faculty counselor and a resident hall student find ways to deal with the students' inability to get along with a roommate from a different cultural background.
d. A faculty counselor and a female ethnic minority student determine typical signs of racial intolerance and needs for racial reconciliation at extracurricular college activities in the student center.

4. A dean or chair and a faculty member:

a. A department chair and a faculty colleague might study alternative ways to engage and pair younger and older students for service-learning experiences.
b. A college or school dean and a faculty colleague explore alternative ways to engage science and liberal arts students in training or teaching at the high school level.
c. A college or school dean and a faculty colleague look for ways to integrate leadership development in senior capstone classes.
d. A department chair and a faculty advisor study methods to help students persist and matriculate from the lower to the upper divisions in the undergraduate curriculum.

Face-to-Face Collaborative Workgroups:

When formulating horizontal or vertical collaborative teams on the college campus, often workgroups are created to forge relationships and implement tasks that require interdependent and routine face-to-face meetings. In *Knowledge Management in Modern Academe: The Work in Progress at Jackson State University* by Maddirala and Stevenson (2004), these workgroups were characterized as decision-making units. These decision-making units (DMUs) were organized for and with faculty to apply knowledge management and action research across the entire campus. Maddirala and Stevenson wrote "policy issues were entrusted in formalized faculty groups as DMUs". The role of the DMUs is in collectively solving various academic issues. DMUs are commissioned to recommend policy decisions on any given academic issue. For developing recommendations for the provost, all DMU deliberations, discourse and decisions must be guided by the rubric of mission centrality, budget constraints and limitations, adherence to policy, parallel practices, meeting accreditation standards, following legal and ethical standards, and connection to university strategic planning. The result or results of DMU work should be an outcome or outcome that is either demonstrable or deliverable.

As mentioned in Schmuck's work, to be effective in implementing action research, members within the group must clearly communicate with one another to bridge the mutual understanding for the proposed purposes of the research. These groups must practice efficiency during discourse, resolve conflict together, make decisions about continued and future steps that are acceptable to the stakeholder within the group, and maintain the highest regard for value differences within the work group. Given the wide range of international diversity dimensions in higher education relative to gender, race, age, culture, ethnicity, sexual orientation and physical challenge, the element of value difference must be engaged or balanced and with the highest standards of collegial openness. These diversity characteristics are further compounded within the professoriate and are also divided by diverse disciplines and different academic subject matters that undergird and guide faculty delivery of instruction. The below figure highlights some typical face-to-face workgroup scenarios and compositions:

Figure 6. Typical Face-to-Face Workgroups:

1. A college or university administrator with a new group of students drawn from different academic disciplines and classification levels:
   a. An upper division department chair in business collaborates with a small group of graduate students to study how students in business or economics can effectively serve in a newly formalized community economic center for urban renewal in the neighborhood.
   b. A lower division faculty advisor/counselor and a selected group of student representatives in student government examine strategies for mediating and managing conflict between two different fraternities in the same residence hall.
   c. A college or university dean and a small group of upper-division engineering students examine ways to strengthen the required calculus course for students who have trouble.
   d. A dean of students and a small group of freshman students determine strategies for making the required freshman orientation more user friendly to promote a welcoming environment.
2. Collaborative workgroup teams of faculty from different disciplines and student classification levels:
   a. A sophomore and junior faculty member conduct research on establishing matriculation guidelines from the lower to the upper division majors within liberal arts.

b. Upper division faculty members in public health with expertise in communicative disorders conduct research on students who seek improvement in diction and annunciation prior to a required oral capstone, senior project.
c. A group of faculty members who teach core courses in social work conduct research to determine if students are learning from their extracurricular field-based activities relative to alcohol intervention.
d. A group of faculty members who teach statistics from three separate disciplines find ways to create a core syllabus on mathematical understanding leading to understanding quantitative research.

3. Trans-disciplinary faculty groups from the arts, sciences, and the professions charged with responsibility for representing the disciplines and colleagues:
    a. Two faculty members, one from the school of education and the other from the school of technology research ways to integrate inter-technology for on-line classes required by certified teachers.
    b. A department chair, two faculty members, a faculty advisor, and two staff members from the division of student life find alternative methods for integrating ethics into required service-learning courses.
    c. A group of faculty members, one from the school of agriculture and the other from the school of environmental science, explore ways to provide real-life activities to students who are required to work on global-climate projects.
    d. A group of administrators and deans from different disciplines discover ways to improve constructive discourse at faculty meetings related to shared governance.

4. College or school advisory groups or governing boards with faculty, staff members, and elected student government officials:
    a. The advisory council or board for the school of arts and humanities conducts collaborative research to establish understanding and maintaining channels of communication on academic matters within the school.
    b. A group of faculty and school staff members research alternative strategies for addressing cultural diversity in the classroom.
    c. An advisory school group finds ways to identify internships in the local community for cooperative learning within the business and technology sectors.

4. Cooperative and collaborative work-group processes
For teaching-instruction-classroom

      d. An internal advisory group for the school of taxation examines ways to implement a new course that translates tax codes into plain language for accounting majors.
5. Internal or external advisory groups with diverse ethnic groups and other people from varying cultures:
      a. A predominately non-minority advisory group of men from local commerce conducts research on whether public communications concerning gender are sensitive to the diverse workplace.
      b. An external or internal advisory group, in an era of local economic decline, studies how to look for ways for supplementing the internal budget with external/extramural funding sources.
      c. An academic advisory group of faculty in literature studies strategies for making classes in poetry more relevant and user friendly to English majors to improve enrollment in poetry classes.
      d. An advisory group composed of faculty and graduate students in fine and performing arts examines ways to integrate aesthetic appreciation of those arts for students who major in graphic design and visual arts.

Campus-Wide Stakeholders'
Committees OR Groups

Compared to small face-to-face work groups of faculty, staff and students with no more than two levels of hierarchy, campus-wide stakeholder work groups can have three or more levels of line authority to promote shared decision-making and academic governance in higher education. Vertically, those could encompass the: (1) department or program level; (2) the school or college level; and (3) the vice presidential or provostial level. Horizontally, typically, could range across disciplines, programs, schools, colleges, etc. These large groups are representative of the three primary and principal stake holder groups on campus: students, staff, and faculty. This group can serve as a catalyst for campus-wide action research by engaging the principal stakeholders in examining current practices on an academic matter and developing new strategies to improve a practice. The goal is to promote the dimensions of the community of practice and promote positive change for fostering a conducive environment and academic climate for mutually beneficial learning. Often, as mentioned earlier, this can be done at the "crossroads".

Proactive Projects

Campus-wide committees engage in collaborative, proactive research when they actively participate in campus-wide initiatives or programs that have wide-ranging impact to the campus. This could include in-service workshops for sexual harassment, teamwork workshops, diversity workshops, staff, and faculty development for on-line technology, improving campus morale, or other areas to promote a collegiate environment. After the interventions, the group collects data to plan the next cycle of steps for proactive action research. See later figures for topics in this regard.

Responsive Projects

Campus-wide committees engage in collaborative, responsive research when they complete needs assessments, surveys or questionnaires, focus groups, or other observations concerning a compelling area to the group. Once data are collected and analyzed, the information gained can give the impetus and new insight for new practices, and the next cycle of steps in responsive action research unfold. See Figure 7 for ways stakeholders may launch responsive action research.

Campus and Community-Wide Networking

Very often, college and university campuses forge "town and gown" relationships and strategic alliances within the local community, the immediate region, on a state-wide basis, or beyond – and increasingly abroad. These groups are frequently identified as external advisory groups to the campus, a college or school, or a department. See Figure 8 for reasons these broader groups could establish initiatives to carry out action research within their service delivery area.

CASE SCENARIO

Collaborative action research can be implemented in various ways, as illustrated by eight different case scenarios below – four are proactive and four are responsive. They do not exhaust all possibilities, nor do they incorporate all variables that are typical to higher education. However, they can serve as a prototype for workgroups to consider when developing their own case studies to meet the specific needs, demands, and distinctions that are specific to the college or university culture.

Figure 7. Campus-Wide Stakeholder Action Research

Proactive Research

Campus-wide stakeholder committees might engage in proactive research to:

1. Increase student learning in a course-content area
2. Improve faculty-staff relations to promote a conducive climate
3. Increase communication channels between staff and students
4. Enhance inclusiveness of female students in male dominated majors
5. Enhance inclusiveness of male students in female dominated majors
6. Improve the quality and efficiency of stakeholder meetings and personnel development
7. Enhance students' willingness and skills in facilitating their peers' academic productivity
8. Increase abilities of faculty and students to participate in community service learning

Responsive Action Research

Campus-wide stakeholder committees (or groups) might engage in responsive action research to:

1. Evaluate staff members' thoughts and feelings about their own adult learning needs
2. Check feelings of gender inclusion or alienation among faculty, staff, or students
3. Examine the faculty's perception and attitude toward college administration leadership
4. Check staff or faculty members' reaction to conflict resolution at stakeholder meetings
5. Diagnose students' attitude toward different learning styles and teaching methods
6. Assess faculty's attitudes or perceptions toward campus budget procedures
7. Check staff or faculty reaction to how campus chairs and deans are implementing tenure and promotion policies
8. Diagnose students' views, attitudes, and perceptions about local international students

Figure 8. Faculty-Staff-Student-Stakeholder Taskforces

In the current economic climate within higher education and beyond college administrators and governing boards are examining ways to reduce cost, generate revenues, seek external/extramural funding support, avoid duplication of services, enhance efficiency through technology, down-size programs to appropriate capacity and other areas related to improving efficiency of operations and effectiveness of instructional delivery to enhance student outcomes. Some campuses will form stakeholder task forces to advise the governing structure or board to implement measures of efficiency and effectiveness. These stakeholder groups might engage in action research to:

A. Enhance the campus' capacity and capability to use modern technology effectively
B. Improve the campus' standing in the competitive/academic marketplace
C. Increase older adults' participation in adult or continuing education programs
D. Assess local citizens' perceptions of campus alliances and areas of improvement
E. Check the perception of local business and industry concerning curriculum relevance and skill-set employability
F. Diagnose why most local citizens voted against constructing a new annex to the medical school

One-On-One Collaboration

Samantha Green and Jorge Smith decide to implement a tutoring program at the college for sophomore students enrolled in remedial math classes and senior students who major in accounting. Samantha and Jorge learned about this innovation at another college with higher matriculation rates of students from remedial math to majors in math, economics, and accounting. Samantha's students will be trained by Jorge's students in mathematics for about an hour, three times a week. Samantha and Jorge collaborate in proactive research to prepare the tutorial training programs for the students.

Identify Hopes and Concerns

Samantha and Jorge agree on the following hopes for the tutoring:
a. Increase students' knowledge and skill sets in mathematics

b. Enhance students' motivation and enthusiasm for mathematics
c. Foster student-to-student relationship building during instruction
d. Encourage senior students to mentor and guide remedial math students concerning focus, dedication, and personal discipline

Samantha and Jorge also brainstorm their concerns for what could go wrong:
a. The remedial math students are not responsive to senior student guidance
b. The remedial math students consider the tutoring to be worthless and not worthwhile
c. Some senior students may not provide accurate mathematical information to the remedial students
d. A few faculty members from the mathematics department complain that the student-to-student tutorial is ineffective

Try a New Practice

Samantha and Jorge take a few days to prepare their perspective students for the tutoring project. They pair the remedial math and senior level students according to their perceived inter-personal compatibility and implement the initial tutoring sessions twice a week. Samantha and Jorge spend an hour with their students on opposite days to brief them on the progress of the tutoring and strategies for improving the project.

Collect Data

After the tutoring takes place for several weeks, Samantha and Jorge separately collect data from one another's students. Given the training Samantha and Jorge received in graduate school on focus-group interviews, Samantha interviews remedial math students as an entire class. Jorge, on the other hand, conducts single interviews with the senior students. Samantha and Jorge inform students they want to identify and determine what is going well and what needs to be improved in the tutoring project. They ask the students to sit comfortably in a circular configuration and speak one after the other around the circle. Each student explains an attribute about the tutoring and another area that could be improved. At the end of each group interview, Samantha and Jorge ask students individually to complete the following sentence:
1. My tutoring colleague's name is ...

2. Compared with other ways to learn math, working with a peer student is...
3. For me, mathematics is ...
4. About mathematics, my tutoring peer colleague feels...

On the following week, Samantha and Jorge give their own students a mathematics test.

Check What the Data Mean

Samantha and Jorge analyze the group interviews and the sentence completion items. They discuss together their data analysis and the mathematics testing scores and results. From the interviews, Samantha and Jorge compile a list of what is effective and what needs to be improved in the tutoring process. For the sentence completion items, Samantha and Jorge used a five-point Likert scale to gauge how many responses are highly positive, positive, neutral, negative, or highly negative. They also score the mathematics tests for exact accuracy then they brainstorm together ideas about what the data mean. They decide together to bring the two groups together again to discuss how to improve the tutoring project and its implementation based on the data gathered.

Reflect on Alternative Ways

Samantha and Jorge bring their two groups to the library media center to participate in a power-point presentation about the results. They explain that the data reveals most students feel positively about the tutoring project with a few students recommending some changes. Samantha and Jorge take turns stating what is effective in the tutoring and asks students to pair up and generate additional ideas for improvement. A week later, Samantha and Jorge bring their groups together again. This time they discuss several problems that need to be resolved to improve the tutoring project:
1. One hour may not be enough time for effective and efficient tutoring
2. Some remedial math students do not complete the assigned homework as a follow up by their senior student colleagues
3. Some senior students lack the patience and tolerance for understanding remedial math student issues
4. Some of the tutorial pairing of the students lack personal compatibility to foster mutual learning

Samantha and Jorge ask the student pairs to brainstorm ways to solve the above problems. Many of the remedies for the problems incorporated on-line interactions between sessions. Samantha and Jorge together print the list of student ideas on poster paper for public review and collective assessment.

Fine-Tune the New Practice

Samantha and Jorge inform their students that the tutoring project will be postponed for a week so that the improvements can be strategically planned for future progress and success. They explained that while the tutoring project has been generally successful, it could be improved in a few targeted ways. They each work separately with their own groups. Samantha has the senior students' role-play tutorial relationship building in pairs. She teaches the students the different ways and strategies for positive reinforcement and academic support. She also asks the students to role-play the coaching process and identifies several mathematical complications that can be coached on-line between class sessions. Jorge uses student pairs as part of his instruction as well. He asks the pairs to practice the mathematical complications that commonly come up as an issue during the tutorial process. He has the pairs discuss how homework assignments can be improved and urges them to spend more disciplined time to complete the assignment. Jorge also provides examples for positive reinforcement and learning collaboration in class and on-line. Samantha and Jorge convene their combined groups again for a meeting. They ask the students to sit together in tutorial pairs. Samantha summarizes what she did with the remedial math students and Jorge summarizes what he did with the senior students. Then they ask the tutoring pairs to brainstorm ways on how to be more focused, dedicated, and disciplined during the tutorial process in class *and* on-line. On the following week, the tutorial project resumed, and the tutorial process was improved based on the modifications implemented by Samantha and Jorge and the involvement of the two student groups with their strategic input incorporated in the improvement process.

Small Face-to-Face Workgroups (One Faculty Member with Students)

For the past decade, he has been a faculty member in the department of health, physical education, and wellness at Charleston College. Rashid Brooks has been impressed with many of the student athletes who come to him for help with academic and social problems. He decides to ask a group of alumni who were athletes at Charleston from past years (three female alums from the eighties, three male alums from the eighties, three female alums from the nineties, three male alums from the nineties, and four more recent alums from the last two years – two female and two males – all ranging from the varying sports of football, basketball, volleyball, soccer, track and field) to collaborate with him on an action research project to help Brooks' student athletes feel more comfortable about their academic performance and interactions in the classroom with other non-athlete students. Rashid invites the student alums to come to the campus, tour the new facilities and have lunch with him in the new cafeteria. Rashid tells the alums about his experiences with the current student athletes and his desire to do action research on the problems. Then Rashid leads the alums through collaborative team building exercises to empower them with strategies of action research and get them acquainted with the methodology and design. Rashid tells the alums about how responsive action research works and he teaches them how to conduct interviews successfully.

Collect Data

Rashid and the alums conduct one-on-one interviews with about 80 of the 100 student athletes at Charleston College. Each member of the action research team, including Rashid, agrees to interview the student athletes randomly selected from class lists that represent four different majors. Each interview is scheduled for about thirty minutes during the school day before athletic practice. The interviews take place over three weeks. Prior to the interviews, Rashid, the professor, and the alum action researchers meet with the student athletes in the new gymnasium. Rashid talks briefly about the value of academic performance and student interaction on the college campus by all student athletes. Rashid introduces the idea of the collaborative research project and the teams of alums who will work with him. Rashid explains the first step – the one-on-one interviews – and the importance of every student athlete participating in the research for future athletes coming to Charleston. He explains that participation in the interviews is voluntary.

Analyze the Data

After the interviews, Rashid and the alums agree on a strategy to analyze the data. They decide to construct lists of concrete examples from answers to questions 1, 2, and 6. (See Figure 9 for the questions for the one-on-one interview). (For question 3, they tally the number of items that better, about the same, or occur less for each. For question 4, they give each interviewee a number and construct lists of all interviewee's academic challenges and classroom interactions. For question 5, they give each interviewee a simple yes or no choice and try to discern reasons for no responses. Figure 10 lists the themes in the data that the action research team found.

Distribute the Data and Announce Changes

Rashid asks the faculty of his student athletes if the research team can use forty-five minutes of class time to feed data back to the student athletes. Rashid gets approval from the respective chairs and deans to visit several classes on one day, giving the action researchers an opportunity to speak to all one hundred student athletes. At the feedback sessions, the action researchers summarized data from step two and described changes that will be tried (See Figure 11 List of Changes). During the last fifteen minutes of each feedback session, the researchers divide the student athletes into trios to obtain reactions to their ideas for positive change and to brainstorm additional innovations or ideas for improving student athlete life at Charleston College.

Figure 9. Questions for One-On-One Interviews

A. Tell me what you like most about being an athlete at Charleston?
B. Tell me what you do not like as an athlete at Charleston?
C. What is your academic major? Why did you choose this major and what have been your experiences in the classroom? Please explain your answer.

D. Outside your classes and athlete practices, are you participating in other academic or social activities with non-athletic students? If so, which activities?
   E. Do your best friends attend Charleston or another institution?
   F. What changes at Charleston would help you with improving your academic performance and enhance your interactions with non-athletic students?

Figure 10. Themes in the Data

High points of the data reveal the following themes:
   A. Things liked most about Charleston College.
   B. Things liked least about Charleston College.
   C. Majors of students and chosen programs of study and experiences in the classroom.
   D. Percentage of student athlete involvement in extracurricular activities with non-student athletes
   E. Percentage of friends' school and percentage of friends attending Charleston
   F. The changes that would make the student athletes improve academic performance and enhance student interactions in and out of the classroom

Identify Hopes and Concerns

Rashid and the alum action research team hope to:
- Increase academic performance and student interaction at Charleston College.
- Help student athletes appreciate academics and diverse student interaction at Charleston College.

Figure 11. Changes for Charleston College
- Rashid, the academic dean and athletic director lead a series of academic improvement assemblies for athletes and others in the library. The student athletes and the alums attend the academic assembly. The topic of the meetings is how to increase academic performance and student interactions between athletes and non-athletes.
- The health, physical education and wellness department launches a new compelling program of intramural sports followed by social academic activities at Charleston. Each team and social group is composed of equal numbers of athletes from certain sports and equal number of non-athletes from various majors.

- Rashid discusses other on-line activities as a possibility to bridge interactions and communications between student athletes and non-athletes in the same major.
- Professor Brooks leads fellow faculty in problem solving, conflict resolution, and classroom remedies for greater academic performance and student interactions in the classroom.

Their Concerns Are That
- Student athletes from certain majors do not work well with others.
- Intramural sports and subsequent social activities may cause student distractions.

Try a New Practice:

Rashid, the academic dean, Jessica, and the athletic director, Joshua, launch the academic assemblies in the library. They hold one a week for ten weeks to address the students. On the eighth week, Rashid leads an assembly, during which he announces different strategies for improving academic performance and student interactions. Rashid works with his fellow faculty to facilitate the intramural games. Each of the teams during the intramurals represents different majors and sports. The alums agreed to referee the games. Students and alums also initiate discussions with the local, competing college to create similar competitions with athletes from various sports and disciplines. Rashid convenes faculty and students to discuss the improvement of academic performance and student interaction garnered from the data.

Check Others' Reaction

Rashid and the alums continue to meet as an action research team for an hour one a week over lunch. Between those meetings, they collect data as follows: After dividing the 100 students by sport and discipline, each member of the team, including Rashid, informally observes and interviews his or her group of students. The observation focuses on participation in academic activities, extracurricular activities, and other social events with students. They look for indications that the student athletes are interacting with non-athletes. The informal interviews focus on student athletes' perceptions and attitudes about the new actions. When the researchers discuss their observations and interviews and their meanings, they seek strategies to refine and fine-tune the new action instituted.

Figure 12: Special Survey of Charleston College Student Athletes

Please circle one answer next to each item to identify whether you strongly agree, agree, feel neutral, disagree, or strongly disagree. (SA, A, N, D, or SD)

    A. Professor Brooks' assemblies with student athletes have helped me with academic performance and student interactions.
       SA   A   N   D   SD

    B. The new intramural program helps student athletes and non-athletes get to know each other to discuss mutual challenges.
       SA   A   N   D   SD

    C. My academic performance could improve by interacting more with others in my major.
       SA   A   N   D   SD

    D. My student interactions with other students could improve by interacting more with others in social and academic activities.
       SA   A   N   D   SD

    E. I believe constructive, academic competition between athletes and non-athletes would improve both performance and classroom interactions.
       SA   A   N   D   SD

    F. Other changes I would like to see at Charleston College are:
       _____
       _____

Collect Data

After new actions resulting from this action research project have been carried out for a semester, professor Brooks and the alums construct a questionnaire to administer to all student athletes. The questionnaire has six items, each to be answered with a Likert scale. (See Figure 12).

Small Face-to-Face Collaborative Groups (Collegial Faculty Teams)

Madison's Law School dean joins five of her faculty at a statewide conference on critical thinking and reasoning across the curriculum. Since Xenia Poindexter (torts) and Gus Blackburn (contracts) were already cooperating on their case study assignments for first year law school students, the two of them asked Federico Cotton (criminal law), Raymond Sinclair (legal research), and Ashley Gilbert (legal writing) to go to a law school conference with them and the dean. At the conference, the collaborative group decided to try proactive research with critical thinking and reasoning across the curriculum for first-year law students.

Identify Hopes and Concerns

The collaborative team, consisting of the dean and the five faculty members, agree on the following hopes and concerns for the critical thinking and reasoning across the curriculum project:

1. Help students see how appropriate legal reasoning and critical thinking is paramount to all subjects.
2. Impress upon first-year law students the importance of critical thinking and reasoning.
3. Upgrade students' critical thinking and reasoning skills through multiple feedback channels.

The team also discusses its concerns for what might go wrong:

- Some students might find it difficult to think differently from their previous undergraduate experiences.
- Faculty might not use enough critical thinking and reasoning exercises in case studies for students to comprehend.
- Faculty might shortchange other required skills concerning legal doctrine and black letter law because so much attention is given to legal critical thinking and reasoning.

Try a New Practice

The collaborative team decides that each faculty member will assign critical thinking and reasoning exercises to the first year law students. Ashley chooses Monday, Raymond Tuesday, Federico Wednesday, and Gus and Xenia Thursday and Friday respectively. The team of six meet once a week to discuss its' new practice. To cope with the possibility that their concerns might come true, the team also decides the following:

- Each faculty member tells students at least once a week about the importance of critical thinking and reasoning to understand legal principles.
- Only Xenia and Gus assign critical thinking and reasoning exercises for homework and they will alternate from week to week.

- Once every three weeks, the team discusses how well students seem to be learning the critical thinking and reasoning examples each faculty member offers.

Collect Data

After six weeks, the team collects data on effects of its collaborative efforts. Ashley and Federico prepare a questionnaire to assess first year law students' attitudes toward critical thinking and reasoning. Raymond gives a test in legal research in which students must complete a case study analysis based on the application of critical thinking and reasoning. Xenia and Gus score samples of the students' work for their legal writing quality. All five ask the first-year law students to write a paragraph on their feelings about critical thinking and reasoning in each class.

Check What the Data Mean

Each faculty member analyses the data he or she has collected. Raymond creates a spreadsheet with student names and scores on attitudes and tests. Gus and Xenia do a content analysis of most common weaknesses in students' critical thinking and reasoning. The team meets several times during the semester to discuss what the data mean.

Reflect on Alternative Ways

Raymond's spreadsheet shows that female students have more positive attitudes toward critical thinking and reasoning than males. In legal research, females' test scores are higher than those of males. The team urges Raymond to have the males work in critical – collaborative partnerships or in collaborative trios to get them more involved in embracing and understanding critical thinking and reasoning of legal principles. Xenia and Gus find that quite a few of the students write better in torts than they do in contracts. Xenia, Gus, and Federico decide to exchange critical thinking and reasoning samples from their classes with one another during the next three weeks. Ashley and Federico find that students feel negative about applying critical thinking and reasoning in criminal law and legal writing. The team decides to focus on critical thinking and reasoning assignments for the next six weeks in torts, contracts, and legal research. Ashley primarily emphasizes the legal writing skills needed for understanding legal principles.

Fine Tune the New Practice

The team presents the results of the action research to students and other faculty in the law school. The dean convenes the panel, emphasizes the centrality of effective critical thinking and reasoning for student success in law school and later in the practice of law once students graduate and prepare for the state's bar examination. Each faculty member from the team presents information, data, and results from the action research. They end by describing the changes they will make to improve legal education in the first year and by reaffirming their collegial and common commitment to critical thinking and reasoning. The dean leads faculty and students in questions and answers about the first year law school curriculum at Madison Law School of Jackson University.

Small Face-to-Face Collaborative Groups (Diverse Faculty Team)

Michael Chong (academic advisor) and Samuel Caruthers (literature) chat one day about their growing mutual concerns for negative interpersonal relations among Greater Good College students. Both have heard college students talking about one another, their professors, and several academic administrators. Jessica Pierce (sociology) joins Michael and Samuel to say that she has heard quite a few anti-Muslim statements from students lately. Michael tells Samuel and Jessica about a few disruptive arguments between Hispanic and Muslim students. Michael adds that Ernesto Strasburg (biology and chemistry) told him about anti-Muslim sentiments he overheard among students in the science labs. Ernesto sees the other three in conversation. He confirms what Michael said. The four faculty members decide to talk about their shared concerns with Eugene Dupree (college provost). When Eugene HEARTs the concerns of the faculty members, who represented disciplines at the college, he tells them he shares their concerns. He invites them to join him to reduce anti-Muslim prejudice at Greater Good College and to improve the academic climate, culture, and appreciation of ethnic diversity.

Michael tells the group about responsive action research from a professorial development institute he participated in at Urbana-International University. All agree to collaborate for the rest of the academic year in research to improve Greater Good' academic culture and climate and, in particular, reduce anti-Muslim prejudice. Eugene announces the action research at a faculty assembly, inviting others to communicate their perceptions to Michael Chong who serves as chair at the responsive action research team.

Collect Data

The research team agrees with Michael's idea to collect data via questionnaire, interviews, and observations. Drawing information from a college course, Michael introduces a questionnaire titled Student Questionnaire on Cultural Engagement, which assesses students' perceptions of conflict, communication, decision-making, and mutual respect between faculty and students, among the students, and among the faculty. The team tailors the questionnaire to Greater Good by modifying its language and by adding a few questions about prejudices and discrimination. Eugene suggests collecting in English classes since all Greater Good students are required to take English each semester. Michael and Samuel agree to work together in Samuel's literature class to train students in interview samples of students and staff instances of racism and prejudice at Greater Good College. Eugene, Michael, and Ernesto agree to create a form for structured observations in common areas of the college, during lunch, student assemblies, and athletic events. All five team members volunteer to act as observant participants in those different behavior settings during the semester.

Analyze the Data

Data from questionnaires, summarized by Richard on spreadsheets, show that students perceive high conflict within the student body. What surprises the team is the high number of students who do not think the provost or faculty care about student conflicts. In fact, almost half of the students do not believe the provost will listen to them or that faculty really wants to help students with their campus-cultural problems.

Results of student interviews from some classes highlight intergroup-conflict and cross-cultural tensions. One concerned open conflict between male athletes and Muslim-Americans. The interviewers point out, from observations during the interviews that few male Muslim-Americans are on sports teams and that male Muslim-Americans typically are better academic students than male athletes. A second tension shows up between socially oriented female students who hang around male athletes and academically oriented females who tend to run the colleges' performing and fine arts projects. Faculty's observations agree with the findings of the students in certain classes.

Distribute the Data and Announce Changes

The collaborative research team believes that the most important target for data feedback and change is the Greater Good faculty. Team members think that the faculty must change its relationships with students if students are to change their relationships with one another. The team forms a panel to feedback data at a faculty assembly meeting. Faculty members agree that they are part of the problem and would like that to change for the betterment of Greater Good College, and its mission which clearly promulgates the importance of embracing cultural difference and diversity. Eugene tells the faculty that he has the president's approval and the college board's permission to cancel classes on the Wednesday before Thanksgiving so faculty can go retreat together. He describes a comfortable facility in the countryside near Greater Good where the faculty will go on Tuesday after classes and have time to work together until Wednesday afternoon. The main issues for the academic retreat are to determine how to turn around negative and conflicting energy at Greater Good, and how to demonstrate to students that the faculty is genuinely concerned about students as human beings, life-long learners, and global leaders. Eugene ends the session by telling faculty that the action research team will hire a neutral and credible facilitator to run the retreat.

Identify Hopes and Concerns

The Greater Good research team hopes to:
- Reduce intergroup conflict and cultural tension among students

- Increase collegiality, respect, and friendliness among students
- Help students realize that campus administrators and faculty want to reduce conflict and tensions, and increase collegiality, respect, and friendliness among students

Figure 13: Greater Good' Problems

The facilitator defines Greater Good' problems as the following:

A. The situation is that certain male students and male Muslim-Americans are engaged in unproductive and disruptive conflict; the target is for male Muslim-Americans to feel friendly towards one another with respect and collegiality.
B. The situation is that some socially oriented females and some academically oriented females are engaged in unproductive and disruptive conflict; the target is for both groups to feel friendly toward one another with respect and collegiality
C. The situation is that many students think that college administration does not care about student conflicts and cultural tensions at Greater Good College; the target is for students to believe that campus administrators are sensitive to their concerns and are trying to reduce student conflict and cultural tension at Greater Good
D. The situation is that students think that most faculty do not care about reducing student conflict and student tension at Greater Good; the target is for students to believe that most teachers do care about their concerns and are trying to reduce student conflicts and tensions at Greater Good
E. The situation is that Greater Good faculty has no procedure, process, policy, or protocol to access students' concerns; the target is for Greater Good' faculty members to institutionalize procedures and processes for both assessing and acting on student concerns

The team is concerned that:

A. Bringing conflict and underlying tensions into the open will backfire and increase conflicts
B. The retreat will not allow enough time for effective faculty problem solving
C. Some faculty members will not participate with genuine interest and enthusiasm

Try a Practice

Eugene, Michael, and Olivia summarize the teams' data for the facilitator, who uses an official working paradigm. The idea is that a problem is a gap between an unsatisfactory current situation and a more desirable goal or target. The problem is solved or reduced when a path or plan is found from situation to target. See above figure for the facilitator's assessment of Greater Good' problems. The facilitator commences the retreat with a few warm-up activities and a group exercise to demonstrate how to collaborate in problem-solving groups. Next, the facilitator leads the five problem-solving groups (each with ten members and a facilitator from the action research team) through the first five steps of the problem solving sequence:

1. Specify the problem
2. List helping and hindering forces
3. Specify multiple alternative solutions
4. Plan for action
5. Anticipate obstacle

By Wednesday afternoon, each small group presents its action plan at a faculty assembly. After the action plans are presented, the facilitator asks each group to nominate one person to work on the action research team to coordinate the follow-through of its action plan. The new group and coordinators meet with the facilitator to discuss next steps. Figure 8 outlines the action ideas.

Figure 14. Action Ideas at Greater Good

A few ideas from each problem-solving group are as follows:

Group 1: Get key leaders of the male athletes and male Muslim-Americans to run a cross-cultural activity, with both athletic and social interaction to raise funds for the colleges' new center for community of practice. Have Michael and Olivia run a constructive confrontation with a sample of male students and a sample of male Muslim-Americans.

Group 2: Get key leaders of socially oriented females and academically oriented females to do the paradigm problem solving together on the target of a supportive social-cultural climate for everyone. Have Olivia and Samuel run a series of brief get-better-acquainted activities with female students who are members of different informal groups?

Group 3: Have Eugene visit every team, social club or organization, fraternity or sorority, athletic event, or other extracurricular group during the next semester to listen to student concerns. Eugene should bring deans and chairs with him. The administrative team runs an annual questionnaire survey of students on aspects of college climate and culture.

Group 4: Assign every faculty member a "preceptorial advisee group" of students to counsel, guide, and mentor 35 to 45 minutes, once a week.

All literature and sociology faculty should present instructional modules on racism and prejudice several times during the semester.

Group 5: This group also came up with ideas for an annual survey of students and how advisee groups for each faculty. It suggests, too, that the outside facilitator who led the Greater Good College at the retreat should carry-out the paradigm problem-solving with heterogeneous groups of males and females on reducing racism, cultural conflict, cultural tension, and prejudice among students.

Check Others' Reaction

The newly formed team of coordinators (two from each problem-solving group) decides to track faculty reaction to the retreat. Another coordinator interviews three or four colleagues about their attitudes toward the retreat and what, if anything, they are doing differently. Samuel and Olivia ask students in their classes to write stories about the retreat and its aftermath for the college newspaper "The Tribunal". Ernesto lectures on leadership, character, culture, and social responsibility at his meetings with his male athlete students. Michael and Eugene interview a sample of Muslim-American students.

Collect Data

Toward the end of the semester, the team of coordinators replicates data collection of the preceding semester. Results show a better climate and a more conducive culture at Greater Good, but improvements should still be made for sustainability. Greater Good forms a college climate and culture committee to continue the project for future years.

Small Face-To-Face Groups (Institute Board of Trustees)

Margaret Walker Institute, a small liberal arts college with 36 faculty members is organized into four teams; freshmen, with seven faculty and three counselors/advisors; sophomores, with six faculty and three counselors/advisors; juniors, with seven faculty and two counselors/advisors; and seniors, with seven faculty and one counselor/advisor. Walker is governed by an advisory board with nine members – four faculty members (one from each team), one counselor/advisor (from each classification level), one academic support staff (a librarian), two academic chairs, and the institute's president. After three training sessions in collegial communication and meeting skills, the board feels it is ready to communicate with Welty's stakeholders.

Identify Hopes and Concerns

The board agrees to the following hopes for itself:
- Make decisions and take actions that enhance student learning outcomes
- Solve problems collaboratively and conduct shared decision-making
- Maintain clear communication channels with stakeholders
- Lead in making Walker a healthy environment for students and staff
- Establish strong ties with off campus stakeholders and citizens in the Walker community

Later, the board spends an entire meeting brainstorming what members believe could go wrong:
- Reaching consensus might be difficult
- Losing sight of students as we become engaged with one another is a possibility
- Maintaining two-way communication with stakeholders might be difficult
- Getting ample off-campus stakeholders involved in the institute might be challenging

Try a New Practice

Acting on advice from the board chair, the president asks each advisory board member to serve as a communication link between the board and Welty's stakeholders. The president links with the provost, support staff members and other chairs and deans from student life and academics. The counselors help each faculty member link with other counselors on each team. The librarian links with the reference librarian, periodical, journal, government document librarian, archivist, and other support staff who work in the library's computer lab. The academic chairs take on the formidable task of linking to the Walker community leaders. The president pledges to help the academic chairs find effective ways to communicate with off-campus, community leaders. The new practice at Walker is an organizational structure for effective communication and shared decision-making to support academic governance. Walker is to be a representative collegiate democracy in which the board, as the primary advisory body, strives to maintain effective communication channels between itself and its principle stakeholders on campus and in the community.

Collect Data

After functioning in a collegial spirit for a semester, the board divides itself into three sub-groups with three members each to collect different sorts of data. Sub-group one (two faculty and a counselor/advisor) collects data from students. Sub-group two (two faculty and the librarian) collects data from staff. Sub-group three (two academic chairs and the president) collects data from community leaders. Sub-group one uses questionnaires to collect attitudinal data from students. It also asks each faculty member to rate his or her students on academic achievement/performance scales. Sub-group two decides to interview a sample of staff members about its perceptions and attitudes toward the advisory board. Each member of the sub-group interviews six of the Walker staff members. The entire sample of 20 is made up of 14 faculty (four from each team), the provost, and five staff members. Sub-group three mails a simple one-page questionnaire or survey to all community leaders to assess their awareness of, knowledge of, and attitudes toward the advisory board of trustees.

Check What the Data Means

The advisory board meets a month later to discuss the data. Sub-group one finds that Walker students are happy with the institute and that faculty rate 85 percent of Walker students as "doing well enough" in their academic learning and social development. Two issues emerge from the data that impress sub-group members. One, as students move from sophomore, junior, and senior class levels, they tend to become increasing negative toward the institute; and two, most of the lowest 25 percent of students who faculty rate as underperforming in academic learning and social development are male students in the sophomore and junior class levels. Sub-group two finds that 16 of the 20 interviewees perceived the advisory board as too separated and set-off from the rest of internal campus stakeholders. Eight of the 16 used the term arrogant to describe the advisory board. 12 of the 16 refer directly to lack of communication between board members and themselves. The lack of communication is pronounced between the board and both sub-groups in the class levels of the junior and senior teams and support staff personnel. Interviewees happiest with the board are the freshman students and the sub-groups two and three teams. Sub-group three receives only 25 percent of the community questionnaires. The data indicates that most of the 25 percent are aware of the advisory board, and their attitudes toward it vary from neutral to positive. Members of sub-group three decide that 25 percent return rate is too low and that probably those community leaders know very little about the advisory board.

Reflect on Alternative Ways

The Walker advisory board of trustees invites an expert on board governance from a national association of governing boards to help find alternative ways to build communication channels with effectiveness to its principal stakeholders. The consultant leads the nine-member board through problem-solving, brainstorming, conflict resolution, consensus building and action planning. See Figure 15 for results of the advisory board's work with the expert consultant.

Fine Tune the New Practice

Over the rest of the school year, the advisory board puts ideas from the working paradigm into action. By the year's end, the advisory board has opened communication channels between itself and its principle stakeholders, and many more community leaders are taking part in Walker activities and programs. But more needs to be done, and the project continues for subsequent years during an economic period when the institute seeks extramural, outside, and external financial support.

Figure 15. Results from the Walker Advisory Board Working with the Expert

The following ideas emerged from the advisory board working with the consulting expert:

A. Seven of the board members will divide each of their stakeholder groups in a new way. Instead of using former criteria of membership to teams or to official roles of the institute, the board members will each choose six to eight colleagues with whom they have frequent contact.
B. Two community leaders and the president will invite other community leaders who returned the questionnaire to a special "town and gown" meeting for problem solving. The goal of that meeting will be to establish effective communication channels on campus, on-line electronically, and in the community.
C. The nine-member board will communicate with complete transparency in a circular format to promote circular communication and engagement with principle stakeholders. The agenda for the board meetings will be set after input and involvement of principle stakeholders.
D. The Walker board will recommend that staff, faculty, and students reorganize itself into modern learning communities of practice, showing matrix relationships across political, academic, and bureaucratic channels of communications. The challenge will be to develop horizontal and vertical decision-making units or collaborative teams to secure and sustain effective communication. Such units and groups might focus on problems that prevent student persistence and institutional retention of students as well as outreach efforts to the community.

Small Face-To-Face Groups (University Board)

In the rural region of the Delta-Heartland State, the university's seven-member board discuss their concerns about the lack of service-learning activities faculty assign to students. In this university of 32,000 students, the service-learning issue goes back to the former president, who moved Delta-Heartland State to a policy of no service learning as extra curricula activity. That president felt all learning should occur on campus. Now that a new president has been hired, the Delta-Heartland board decided to address the service-learning policy again. The new president tells the board that a service-learning policy could be an appropriate topic for responsive action research, which he learned about recently at a convention of the Global Rural-Remote-Regional Higher Education Association.

Collect Data

Board members and the president arrange to collect three sets of data about service learning: questionnaire data from community stakeholders, interview data from presidents of rural/regional universities, and document data on what research says about service learning and community engagement. The questionnaire, one mailed to each community organization with some affiliation to the university, is titled "Service Learning and Community Engagement Attitudes". After a brief introductory paragraph about service learning, the questionnaire starts with the following question:

About service learning and student engagement in the community, we would like the faculty to assign (Please answer one)
1. Much more than now
2. More than now
3. The same
4. Less than now
5. Much less than now

The respondents are asked to elaborate on their answers to the questions in order to help board members and the president understand respondents' reasoning. Each board member talks by telephone with presidents of five rural/regional universities about their service-learning policies. Each interview lasts about 15 minutes. After the interviewer introduces herself or himself as a Delta-Heartland State board member and comments of the board's interest in service learning policies, "do you have a service learning policy at your university?" If yes; "please describe your policy" and "please send me a copy". If no, "please tell me whether faculty assigns service-learning activities". And finally, the interviewer uses a few probes such as "can you give me an example" or "please tell me more about that". A Delta-Heartland vice president volunteers to do research on the internet about service learning and community engagement.

Analyze the Data

The university board gets an 80 percent return on the questionnaire. The rate is high because each board member called many community organizations, encouraging them to respond. The results showed that 77 percent of the community organizations want more students from the university involved in service learning, 19 percent want the same amount, and four percent want less. Of the 35 regional presidents, 22 discuss their service-learning policy. Thirteen presidents say that their universities leave service learning up to the faculty and their respective disciplines, with no formal service-learning policy; at those universities, faculty assign service-learning activities to their students. The vice president's report on internet research concerning service learning and community engagement concludes that service learning can enhance student learning outcomes when it provides opportunities for students to translate the theories that they learn in the classroom into actual practices in the community. That means service learning facilitates student learning when students see that it fits logically into what they learn in the classroom when faculty use it to reinforce theory into practice. After several discussions about the data, board members decide to hold several community meetings to advocate the new service-learning policy intended to enhance the overall college experience of students.

Distribute the Data and Announce Changes

Board members make another round of phone calls to community organizations inviting community leaders to attend upcoming community meetings on service learning. At the meetings, the president presents data from the paradigm, and each board member states his/her advocacy for service learning. The board chairperson leads the audience through a question-and-answer discussion. Finally, the board members elicit ideas from community leaders about the quality of service learning being provided. Both meetings end with the board announcing it will decide on a service-learning policy for Delta-Heartland at its next regular meeting.

Identify Hopes and Concerns

The Delta-Heartland board hopes to:
- Enhance student learning outcomes and community engagement through service learning
- Motivate faculty to assign service-learning activities
- Convince community organizations that service learning can be an important facilitator of campus-community relationship building

The Delta-Heartland board is concerned that:
- Some faculty might resist assigning service learning because they believe all leaning should occur in the classroom
- Some community leaders will not see the importance of service learning
- Some faculty will give too many service-learning assignments

Try A New Practice

The Delta-Heartland board passes a policy specifying that faculty should assign service-learning activities to students regularly to enhance students' engagement in the community. The Delta-Heartland board announces its support for three professional development workshops for faculty to work out the details of the service-learning policy.

Check Others' Reactions

During the professional development workshops, the vice president documents how faculty members feel about service learning for students. Virtually, all faculty members agree that students should be able to apply the theories that they learned in class to community settings. After considerable discussion, the president and the faculty decide that at least one day a week, students should be involved in some type of service-learning activity. For freshman and sophomore students, they decide students should spend less time in the community and more time in class to refine their academic performance. Later, at another community meeting, the vice president presents details of the service-learning policy to community leaders.

Collect Data

The following semester, after the new policy is in full swing, the Delta-Heartland board launches data collections to assess how the service-learning policy is working. It asks the president and vice president to write a questionnaire with a tailored matrix for each faculty member, to measure faculty's perceptions and attitudes toward the service-learning policy. The matrix lists students' names vertically on the left and service-learning activities across the top. To complete the cells in the matrix, each faculty member uses a five-point scale:
1. Very high level of achievement

2. High level of achievement
3. Medium level of achievement
4. Low level of achievement
5. Very low level of achievement

To gather community leaders' views, each board member conducts telephone interviews with 10 community leaders, drawn at random, making a total of 58 community interviews. During each 20-minute interview, community leaders are asked about strengths and weaknesses of the service-learning policy, how it might be improved, and whether they want more, less, or the same amounts of service-learning activities and community engagements of students within the community. In general, the data reveal that the service-learning policy is working well and faculty as well as students sees the benefits of the service-learning experience.

Faculty Senate

To engage an entire faculty in action research is logistically challenging. Focusing on a faculty senate might serve an institution best in this regard. Some College-wide innovations offer excellent opportunities for whole faculties to carryout self-study and collaborative reflection. Such an ideal opportunity arises at Monterey Bayou University, when college administrators announce that the university will offer half of its classes on-line. These on-line courses will be provided after faculty members have identified which courses are best for on-line and electronic synergy. The mandated curriculum change presents Monterey Bayou faculty with an opportunity for college-wide proactive action research.

Try a New Practice

With only a semester to prepare for the changes, the Monterey Bayou faculty set aside one full day and five half-days for professional development in on-line instruction. The provost and the department chairs hire on-line learning consultants from a local technology company. The consultants divide the 30-member faculty into 10 critical collegiality teams. They use probing dialog to help faculty members plan how to transform in-class instruction to electronic learning delivery. As the dialog unfolds, it becomes apparent that many faculty members wish to use more collaborative strategies and on-line group projects in their teaching. Thus, the provost and the department chairs decide to focus two of the five half-days on on-line group processes.

Incorporate Hopes and Concerns

During the full day of the professional development training, the provost and department chairs lead faculty in a discussion about hopes and concerns. One prominent hope is to devote more time to a Technology Enhancement Instrument (TEI) created by the local technology company. The technology company's instrument calls for seven steps to enhance on-line learning:

1. Create a pedagogical paradigm for new student learning,
2. Inform students what they will learn and why it is important to learn the paradigm,
3. Use diverse on-line activities to provide information about the paradigm,
4. Demonstrate concrete examples of skills, competencies, and concepts to be learned,
5. Confirm that students are grasping and understanding what is being demonstrated,
6. Give assignments for practice, either in class or on-line for individualized learning, and
7. Summarize what has been presented in the paradigm.

In subsequent professional development sessions, the Monterey Bayou faculty conducts group problem solving on concerns and observations (See Figure 16 complete identification of hope and concerns by Monterey Bayou faculty).

Collect Data

The provost and the department chairs collect data from faculty during professional development training and from faculty and students during the first semester of on-line course offerings. During professional development training, the provost and the department heads collect data to track the faculty's reactions and instructional changes. Figure 17 explains the ways data are collected from faculty. The provost and the department chairs meet during the semester to make constructive changes in the professional development sessions.

Figure 16: Hopes and Concerns of the Monterey Bayou Faculty

Hopes:

- Students will learn more about the discipline and perform better on end of semester tests conducted on-line
- Faculty will give more time to each of the elements in the technology enhancement instrument, with more concentrated time to teach
- The students will experience a greater variety of teaching and learning methods and will become more engaged in on-line research in collaboration with other students
- There will be more opportunities to give students feedback, anytime and from anywhere, as they practice what they have been taught on-line

Concerns:

- We will need help in how best to integrate in-class and on-line synergies
- More time could be wasted on-line because the professor is physically not in the classroom with the students
- Some students may not learn well on-line versus in-class instruction
- Some students may not have access to computer technology

Figure 17. Ways Data are Collected from Monterey Bayou Faculty

- The provost and department chairs ask faculty to fill out post-meeting reaction questionnaires about on-line learning. The post-meeting forms ask for constructive and non-productive things about each session and for suggestions on how to improve future sessions.
- The provost and the department chairs interview five to six colleagues once every two weeks about the transition from in-class instruction to on-line delivery.
- The provost and the department chairs observe faculty members' active involvement in the professional development training. They discern whether faculties can apply the Technology Enhancement Instrument to instruction.

During the school year, while on-line classes are underway, the provost and department heads form the 10 pairs of faculty members into five groups of four each to get everyone to collect data from Monterey Bayou's new on-line curriculum.

4. Cooperative and collaborative work-group processes 233
For teaching-instruction-classroom

One group of four presents a questionnaire on the steps of the Technology Enhancement Instrument for its colleagues to complete every two weeks. With the first data set, the initiators want to remind their colleagues of the faculty's commitment to on-line learning design. The second group of four creates interview statements to ask its colleagues how on-line instruction does or does not improve student learning outcomes. The third group administers a questionnaire to assess students' attitudes toward on-line classes. The fourth group prepares interview questions to measure students' reactions to on-line classes and chooses 20 students at random to interview during the semester about how to improve the new instruction delivery. The fifth group observes classes by focusing on faculty's use of pedagogical strategies to improve on-line learning. Finally, the provost and department chairs give achievement tests to all students at the end of the semester. They compare those scores with students' achievement test scores from a year ago when the current on-line class material was delivered in class.

Check What Data Mean

The Monterey Bayou faculty retreats for a week during the summer to check what the data mean. Each of the four person data collection teams presents its findings and interpretations to the faculty. The provost and department heads discuss the meaning they each derived from the data.

Reflect on Alternative Ways

During the third day of the retreat, the faculty reflects on next steps to refine on-line instruction and student learning. Figure 18 defines the key points.

Fine Tune the Practice

During the summer, the provost prepares a new curriculum catalogue that identifies all on-line classes across the disciplines in the arts, sciences, and professions. Later in the summer, the Monterey Bayou faculty spends a few days reflecting on the Technology Enhancement Instrument and planning details for its orientation day with students. The new on-line course offerings have boosted enrollment at Monterey Bayou and enhanced technological proficiency of the faculty.

Figure 18. Key Points to Refine On-line Instruction at Monterey Bayou

The faculty should receive more training in the administration of the Technology Enhancement Instrument and in alternative ways to implement collaborative learning on-line.

- Pairs of faculty members will design more on-line classes together.
- Some revision will be made in the curriculum so that on-line classes are offered to supplement in-class subject matter within the discipline and student majors.
- The faculty will spend the first day of the academic semester orientating students to on-line teaching and learning. The orientation will include information about the discipline, information about the faculty's enthusiasm for on-line learning and information on the pros and cons of on-line teaching and learning.

Face-to-Face Task Force

The provost and the faculty senate want to determine how students view the mission integration of faith based education at Mercy Catholic Academy. Mercy Catholic Academy is a residential liberal arts institution. They appoint a fifteen-member task force of faculty, staff, and students to execute the study. The provost asks the dean of arts and sciences to chair the task force. To form it, the provost and the dean nominate seven faculty members, and seven other stake holders who are staff, students, or board members. The provost and several members of the task force gather information to access students' views about the Mercy's success with mission integration. The academic dean and several faculty members tell the task force about collaborative, responsive action research. They use the term needs assessment, to describe the research, defining needs as current conditions at Mercy that should be improved.

Collect Data

The task force decides to use formal interviews to collect data. Two faculty members draw a random sample of one hundred fifty students. Each task force member agrees to interview ten students. Figure 19 lists the three open-ended interview questions. For more data, the task

force uses content from interviews to prepare a structured questionnaire. The questionnaire has four sections:
1. A list of ten strengths (academic, student, financial, development, administration), each accompanied by a Likert scale
2. A list of eight shortcomings (academic, student, financial, development, administration), each accompanied by a Likert scale
3. A list of eight conditions that should be improved, each accompanied by a three-point scale
4. A list of demographic questions, including inquiries about race, gender, and religion

For ease of analysis, the questionnaire is printed so that the answers can be electronically scanned. It is mailed to all the residents' halls at Mercy.

Analyze the Data

Results reveal that Mercy students agree on the schools' strengths, but they agree less on its shortcomings. Of the shortcomings that call for improvement, the four that are most frequently mentioned are:
1. Cultural diversity integration
2. Conflict resolution integration
3. Integration of other religious beliefs
4. Integration of globalization issues

Figure 19. Three Open-Ended Interview Questions

A. What do you see as the mission integration strengths at Mercy?
B. What do you see as the mission integration shortcomings at Mercy?
C. What conditions would you like to see improved at Mercy?

The task force finds that 78% of the returned questionnaires were filled out by Catholic students. Many students who were Christian but were not Catholic did not return the questionnaire.

Distribute the Data and Announce Hopes

The taskforce holds campus community meetings to feedback data and collect more reactions from students. Since thirty-five students attended the first meeting at the Mercy student union, task force members decide to hold subsequent meetings in residence halls. They divide into pairs, one faculty member and one staff or student in each pair, to run seven meetings throughout the resident halls at Mercy. Discussion in the residence halls bring out two more needs for change: provide an outline of the mission integration on the Mercy website and conduct workshops for students, staff, and faculty on how the mission integration could be improved. The taskforce announces that it hopes to respond effectively to campus concerns and that it will make policy recommendations to the provost and the faculty senate next semester.

Try a New Practice

The taskforce makes four recommendations to the faculty senate. Figure 20 outlines the taskforce's recommendations. The faculty senate acts on recommendations one and four by posting a new mission integration framework on the website, Mercy students will be surveyed for their perceptions of need for mission improvement. The faculty senate also asks the provost to organize strategies to work on recommendations two and three. In turn, the provost engages the academic deans' council and presidential cabinet in its own action research about the mission integration framework. The presidential cabinet appoints a five-person committee of staff and faculty to meet about mission integration across the campus. For the strategic framework concept, the staff, students, and faculty agreed to develop this for the website. The president and provost also announce the establishment of four workshops per year to the entire campus on mission integration. The president and provost, in conjunction with the faculty senate, also announce the implementation of mission integration assessment as an annual process in conjunction with accreditation standards.

Figure 20. Taskforce Recommendations

The taskforce makes four recommendations to the faculty senate:
1. Initiate a strategic plan to integrate cultural diversity, conflict resolution, various religious beliefs, and related globalization issues across the curriculum
2. Develop a strategic outline and framework of mission integration on the Mercy website
3. Sponsor workshops across campus to refine and fine-tune mission integration on an on-going basis
4. Make mission integration assessment of needs a routine part of the institution's annual evaluation process

Check Others' Reactions

Each faculty-senate member makes ten to fifteen phone calls to check students' reaction to the new mission integration framework. With those data, the faculty-senate makes a few changes in the framework. The deans' council and the presidential cabinet studies students' perceptions and participation in mission integration activities. The academic dean, along with department heads, collects data on other concerns and observations from staff, students, faculty, and board members at Mercy.

Collect Data

The faculty senate holds a campus-wide meeting at the end of the school year to elicit students', faculty, and staffs' reactions to the taskforce recommendations. At the meeting, faculty-senate members listen to all concerns, record key points, and ask all participants to complete a post-meeting reaction form on effectiveness of meeting procedures to support shared governance. At its next meeting the faculty-senate, in conjunction with the Mercy board of trustees announce that every two years it will sponsor a survey on students' perceptions, attitudes, reactions, and observations on Mercy's' mission integration strengths, short comings, and needs for improvement.

Reflections

Reflect on earlier sections by creatively answering the following questions:
1. For your academic department school or college, create a plausible scenario for action research with a one-on-one collaborative, one faculty member with students, one faculty team member from another discipline, a mixed faculty transdisciplinary team, the faculty senate, or the whole faculty
2. For your college or university, create a plausible scenario for action research with the board of trustees or a campus-community taskforce
3. Pick three that you think are realistic possibilities. Explain.

5.
FINAL COMMENTS AND CAUTIONS FOR HEART

We have introduced the concepts in **HEART:** *Desk Guide for Administrative and Academic Decision Making with Higher Education Action Research* to equip and empower administrators and academicians with the leadership tools to make effective and expeditious decisions. The H, E, A, and R in our title stood for "higher education action research" and the word "now" stands for "net outcome work" which represents the sense of yielding results, urgency, relevance, responsiveness, and expeditiousness that is too often needed by administrators in higher education to collect data, collectively analyze the data and collectively decide on new direction. "NOW" in our book title also captures the both the essence and essentials of the collaborative and collegial group work completed by "decision-making units" or "DMUs." This desktop guide introduced the concepts of diagnostic, prognostic or prescriptive action research for data-driven decision-making by college and university administrators who are constantly trying to make daily decisions to advance their campuses in a marketplace that has become penetrating with competitiveness and unprecedented with growing global demands and accelerating societal needs. We recommend two additional books for the readers that should serve as complementary and companion information resources to this desk guide. They are:

- ❖ Creswell, J. W. (2012). *Educational Research: Planning, Conducting, and Evaluating Quantitative and Qualitative Research (4th ed.).* Boston: Pearson Education, Inc.
- ❖ Schumck, R.A., Bell, S.E., and Bell, W.E. 2012. *Handbook of Organizational Development in Schools and Colleges: Building Regenerative Capacity.* 5th edition. Santa Cruz: Exchange Pointe International

Given the perplexing, perpetuating and persistent challenges that are often specific to American minority serving colleges and universities, we are strongly encouraging that these institutions examine these above books. The first half of HEART dealt with institutional-action decision-making in the workplace from an ***administrative*** perspective and the second half dealt more with academic decision-making in the classroom-action from a ***faculty*** perspective. All universities and colleges can leverage with and profit from this convenient desktop guide for day-to-day leadership challenges in the today's administrative office or the instructional classroom. Given the perplexing, perpetuating and persistent challenges that are often specific to HBCUs and other minority serving institutions of higher learning, we can't over emphasize enough that these institutions, in particular, should examine our action research concepts for increasing student persistence toward degree completion and graduation; improving alumni and constituent relations; fundraising and external relationship building; fine-tuning and refining financial stewardship; enhancing media relations, improving athletic administration and academic compliance; implementing support services and infrastructure for student life; diversifying the campus culture and climate; and developing new academic program innovations on campus, online and in their targeted community market share.

The general concepts from this desktop guide grew out of the successful implementation of knowledge management and action research at a historically Black research-intensive university in the Deep South where Stevenson (2003) describes the administrative office as the "locus of control" and the instructional classroom as the "unit of analysis" for making decisions, leveraging intellectual capital and building learning communities of practice in modern higher education. We believe our recognition for bold new paradigms, paragons and dimensions for higher education administrators and faculty, along with action research, can improve the internal operations, academic prowess, and administrative practices on the modern campus -- particularly given the wealth, breadth, and plethora of available technological resources and social media algorithms. We believe that, as proved at an institution of higher learning where we have worked, many administrative decisions can be made more instantaneously, promptly, speedily, directly, effectively, efficiently, and forthwith in the context of *"tout de suite"*. Indeed, quite often, dealing with administrative problem in higher education is like playing the game of "whackamole"; as soon as you solve one problem that pops up, another one pops up, then another. As discussed in chapter III, action research can also be used for self-reflection about one's own administrative leadership style and delivery. Although our methodology is conceptualized for execution with thirteen steps over a three-day period, it should be noted that conventional action research is a continuous process that requires cyclical practice in higher education administration. We recognize that the action research methodologies for classroom application in the second half chapters of VI, VII, VII, and IX does take more time beyond the three-day prototype in the first half of the desktop guide. Our methodology should be integrated into daily administrative practice and institutionalized on campus as part of an infrastructural system for tacit and explicit knowledge management.

We believe action or "applied-translational" research provides the opportunity for higher education administrators, both new and seasoned, to upgrade and advance their skills in leadership development. Given the participatory and democratic nature of our methodology, we suggest that our process provides the academic avenues for knowledge exchange of learning experiences for sustaining a collegial community of practice and leverage human capital on the college or university campus. As mentioned by our publisher, Given the recent media coverage about controversial and debatable decision-making at institutions of higher learning in Pennsylvania, New Jersey, Florida, Alabama and others, this book can serve as a resource for meeting institutional challenges, approaching them with sequential structure, getting key stakeholders involved in *analytics*, and formulating recommendations for future arbitration. The action research process, for making these tough decisions HEART, provide a collaborative convergence to move the process expeditiously and strategically from a collegial examination of facts and issues. This process certainly supports the widespread advocacy--in higher education and other business and governmental venues--for fostering organizational learning, leveraging human capital, institutionalizing human empowerment, and growing learning communities of practice for success. By designating, distributing, and dividing HEART responsibilities vertically and horizontally – from the small unit level to the larger department level --- HBCUs can forge ahead with a new bold agenda for the African American community and the United States. With the intellectual capital and cerebral currency at HBCUs, administrators can leverage collective strengths for future progress. With past and present generations of administrators consistently and constantly focusing on the future based on DDDM and HEART, the HBCU is manifested from intergenerational loop learning and the sector becomes permanently engaged, cyclical, and everlasting. HBCUs as a sector can do more together than apart in this fierce academic marketplace where more minority students of color, including those who are higher risk and lower income, now have choices to attend non-HBCU institutions despite the recent Supreme Court rulings on affirmative action in higher education. HBCUs must build on their historical foundations to position with future fundamentals for progress.

HBCUs must maintain our mission not only by just looking backward in reflection. HBCUs must also modernize our mission from always looking forward with continuous retrospection in the revolving, evolutionary, and revolutionary African dimensions of *Sankofa*. As long our public K-12 is remains in its current condition and higher education access continues to be legally threatened for those who are impoverished, underserved, underprivileged, underutilized, underrepresented and marginalized -- HBCUs will always be needed and in demand for the greater good of advancing the global human condition.

BIBLIOGRAPHY

Albert, L., Moore, M. and Mincey, K. 2004. "Learning Along the Way: An Ongoing Journey". *Progress: Supporting the Scholarships of Teaching and Learning.* American Association for Higher Education. Washington, D.C.

Allee, V. (2003). *"The Future of Knowledge: Increasing Prosperity Through Value Networks".* Butterworth-Heinermann: Amsterdam.

Barkley, E. F., Cross, P.K., and Major, C.H. 2005. *Collaborative Learning Techniques: A Handbook for College Faculty.* Jossey-Bass: San Francisco.

Bolman, L. G. & Deal, T. E. (1984). Modem approaches to understanding and managing Organizations. San Francisco, CA: Jossey-Bass Publishers

Brighton, C. and Moon. 2007. *Action Research Step-by-Step: A Tool for Educators to change Their Worlds.* The H.W. Wilson Company/WilsonWeb.

Burton, C. 2008. *On Higher Education: Selected Writings, 1995 – 2006.* Johns Hopkins: Baltimore, MA.

Cambridge, B. 2004. *Progress: Supporting the Scholarships of Teaching and Learning.* American Association for Higher Education. Washington, D.C.

Cox, M. and Richlin, L. 2004. *Building Faculty Learning Communities.* Number 97, Spring. *New Directions for Teaching and Learning.* Jossey-Bass: San Francisco.

Creswell, J. W. 2012. Educational Research: Planning, Conducting, and Evaluating Quantitative and Qualitative research (4th ed.). Boston: Pearson Education, Inc.

Crookes, G. 2005. *Resources for Incorporating Action Research as Critique into Applied Linguistics Graduate Education.* The H.W. Wilson Company/WilsonWeb.

Dewey, J. 1916. *Democracy and Education.* New York: Free Press.

Dezune, D. 2000. *Learning from Change. American Association for Higher Education.* Stylus: Sterling, Virginia.

Esposito, J. and Smith, S. 2006. *From Reluctant Teacher to Empowered Teacher-Researcher: One Educator's Journey toward Action Research.* The H.W. Wilson Company/WilsonWeb.

Follet, Mary P. 1940. *Dynamic Administration.* New York: Harper & Brothers.

Freire, P. 1970. *Pedagogy of the Oppressed.* New York: Herder & Herder.

Goldys, P., Kruft, C., Subrizi, P. 2007. *Action Research: Do It Yourself.* The H.W. Wilson Company/WilsonWeb.

Hansen, S., Kalish, A., Hali, W. Gynn, C. Molly, M. L., and Madigan, D. 2004. *"Developing a Statewide Faculty Learning Community Program"* in *Building Faculty Learning communities.* Number 97. Spring. New Directions for Teaching and Learning. Jossey-Bass: San Francisco.

Harris, P. and Moran, R. T. 1983. *Managing Cultural Differences.* Gulf Publishing Company. Houston

Harris, P. 1985. *Management in Transition.* Jossey Bass. San Francisco

Heidegger, M. 1962. *Being and Time.* New York: Harpers.

Jarvis, P. 1999. *The Practitioner-Researcher: Developing Theory from Practice.* Jossey-Bass Publishers: San Francisco.

Kotter, J.P. 1990. *A Force for Change: How Leaders Differ from Management.* Free Press. New York.

Lewin, K. 1948. *Resolving Social Conflicts.* New York: Harpers.

Lippitt, R., J.E. Watson, and B. Westley. 1958. *The Dynamics of Planned Change.* New York: Harcourt Brace.

Livingston, J. (1980) *Class Notes on Action Verbs* from Professor John Livingston's Class Taken by Joseph Martin Stevenson in 1980 for master's degree in social science education, California State University at Sacramento. Sacramento, California.

Lomax, P. 1991. "Managing Better School and Colleges: An Action Research Way" in *Bera Dialogues.* Number 5. Multilingual Matters Ltd. Cleveland, England.

Marrow, A.J. 1969. *The Practical Theorist: Life and Work of Kurt Lewin.* New York: Basic Miles, M. B. 1981. *Learning to Work in Groups.* 2nd ed. New York: Teachers College Press.

Maddirala, J. and Stevenson, J. 2003. *Knowledge Management in Modern Academe: The Work in progress at Jackson State University.* The Executive, A Business Journal.

Marshall, C. and Rossman, G. 2006. *Designing Qualitative Research.* 4th Edition. Sage Publications: Thousand Oaks, London, New Delhi.

Mata-Segreda, A. 2006. *Action Research for the Change in Education.* The H.W. Wilson Company/WilsonWeb.

Merriam, S. 1998. *Qualitative Research and Case Study Applications in Education.* Jossey-Bass Publication: San Francisco.

Miller, Y., and Jameson, J. 2003 *Empowering Researchers in Further Education.* Trentham Books: London, England

Moffett, D., Reid, B., Zhou, Y., and Brewton-Parker College. 2008. *Student Teacher Candidates' Effect on Student Learning as Measured Through Action Research Projects.*

Pace, D. and Middendorf, J. 2004. *Decoding the Disciplines: Helping Students Learn Disciplinary Ways of Thinking.* Number 98. Summer. New Directions for Teaching and Learning.

Questia. 2013. *Higher Education Administration.* http://www.questia.com/library/education/higher-and -adult/higher-education/administration

Riordan, T. and Roth, J. 2005. *Disciplines and Frameworks for Student Learning: Teaching the Practice of the Disciplines.* Stylus: Sterling, Virginia.

Ross-Fisher, R. 2008. *Action Research to Improve Teaching and Learning.* The H.W. Wilson Company/WilsonWeb.

Rubin, G. and Jones, M. 2007. *Student Action Research: Reaping-the Benefits for Students and School Leaders*. The H.W. Wilson Company/WilsonWeb.

Sagor, R. 1993. *How to Conduct Collaborative Action Research*. Association for Supervision and Curriculum Development. Alexandria, Virginia.

Schmuck, R. A. 2006. *Practical Action Research for Change*. 2nd ed. Thousand Oaks, CA: Corwin Press

_____ 2009. *Practical Action Research: A Collection of Articles*. 2nd ed. Thousand Oaks, CA: Corwin Press

_____ 2008. *Lewinian Lessons for Action Researchers: The Polish Psychological Forum*. Bydgoszcz, Poland.

Schmuck, R.A. and P. Runkel. 1994. *Handbook of Organization Development in School and Colleges*. 4th ed. Long Grove, IL.: Waveland.

Schmuck, R.A. and P. Schmuck. 2001. *Group Processes in the Classroom*. 8th ed. New York: McGraw-Hill.

Schumck, R.A., Bell, S.E., and Bell, W.E. 2012. Handbook of Organizational Development in Schools and Colleges: Building Regenerative Capacity. 7th edition. Santa Cruz, CA Exchange Pointe International

Schoen, S. 2007. *Action Research: A Developmental Model of professional Socialization*. The H.W. Wilson Company/WilsonWeb.

Schon, D. 1983. *The Reflective Practitioner*. New York: Basic Books.

Schon, D. 2000. "The New Scholarship Requires a New Epistemology: Knowing in Action" in Learning from Change D. DeZure. American Association of Higher Education. Stylus: Sterling, Virginia.

Scriven, M. 1980. The Logic of Evaluation. Inverness, CA: Edge Press.

Thomas, R. M. 2003. Blending Qualitative and Quantitative Research Methods in Theses and Dissertations. Thousand Oakes, CA: Corwin Press.

Stevenson, J. M. 2000. "The Modern Provost" in *Education,* Volume 121, Issue 2, p347.

Stevenson, J.M. 2001. "Provost's Proposed Metro Centers for Jackson State University: Targeting New Revenue Streams from Multicultural Enrollment Markets. Cabinet Presentation: Office for the President, Jackson State University. Jackson, Mississippi.

Stevenson, J.M. 2003. "Vision 2020: Modernizing the Academy with Preservation of Past Prospicience and Foresight for the Future at a Research-Intensive University" in Education, Volume 123, Issue 3.

Stevenson, J. M., Buchanan, D., and Sharp, A. 2007. *"Commentary: The Pivotal Role of the Faculty in Propelling Student Persistence and Progress Toward Degree Completion"*. *Journal of College Student Retention,* Vol. 8, Number 2, pp 141 – 147.

Thomas, L., Cooper, M., and Quinn. 2003. *Improving Completion Rates Among Disadvantaged Students. Trentham: England.*

Valli, L., vanZee, E., Rennert-Ariev, P., Mikeska, J., Catlett-Muhammad, S., and Roy, P. 2006. Initiating and Sustaining a culture of Inquiry in a Teacher Leadership Program. The H.W. Wilson Company/WilsonWeb.

Walker, R. 1985. Doing Research: A Handbook for Teachers. London: Methuen.

Warren, S., Doorn, D., and Green, J. 2008. Changes in Vision: Teachers Engaging in Action Research. . The H.W. Wilson Company/WilsonWeb.

Wenger, E., McDermott, R., and Snyder, W. (2002). *Cultivating Communities of Practice: A Guide to Managing Knowledge.* Cambridge: Harvard Business Press.

Wikipedia, (2013) Definition of Sankofa. http://www.uis.edu/africanmericanstudies.students/sankofa/

Wisker, G. 2008. The Postgraduate Research Handbook. 2nd Edition. Palgrave Macmillan: Great Britain.

Wyner, J., Bridgeland, J., Diulio, Jr., J. (2008) Achievement Trap: How America Is Failing Millions of High-Achieving Students from Lower-Income Families. Jack Kent Cooke Foundation & civic Enterprises with Original Research by Westat.

Zambo, D and Zambo, R. 2006. Action Research in an Undergraduate Teacher Education Program: What Promises Does It Hold? The H.W. Wilson Company/WilsonWeb.

Zuber-Skerritt, O. 1992. Action Research in Higher Education: Examples and Reflections. Kogan Page Limited: London.

Selected Databases and Websites for Education Research

ABI/INFORM Complete (ProQuest)
With a focus that is scholarly and international, this database indexes, and provides abstracts to over 6,500 major business journals. Full text content is available for 4,000 of these journals.

ACM Digital Library
Provides bibliographic records and full-text content in the fields of computing and information technology. In addition to all of the ACM publications, coverage also extends to conference proceedings, newsletters, multimedia titles and newsletters.

Academic Search Premier (EBSCO)
A multi-disciplinary database developed for the academic community. It consists of a wide collection of peer-reviewed, full-text articles from more than 4,700 scholarly publications. Indexing is provided for an additional 8,000 publications.

Almanac of Higher Education
Published by the Chronicle of Higher Education, the Almanac provides statistics and an analysis of trends in higher education. http://chronicle.com/section/Almanac-of-Higher-Education/615/ (Some content on this site is available only with a subscription)

Business Source Complete (EBSCO)
A comprehensive database for peer-reviewed, full text journals that cover all aspects of business. Indexing and abstracts to major business journals, some dating back to 1886, are also provided.

Dissertations and Theses (ProQuest)
Provides citations and abstracts to over 3 million dissertations and theses from around the world. Over one million full-text dissertations are available for download.

EdITLib Digital Library
(Association for the Advancement of Computing in Education) is an online resource that provides peer-reviewed research in educational technology and E-learning. International in scope, this resource includes published articles, conference papers, multimedia, and e-books.

Education Full Text (Wilson through EBSCO)

Broad in scope, this database provides indexing, abstracts and full-text content to hundreds of journals and books in the discipline of education.

Education Research Complete (EBSCO)

Provides access to one of the largest and most comprehensive collections for education research. Covering all aspects and levels of education, the database includes full-text articles for more than 750 journals, and full text for nearly one hundred monographs, books, and education conference papers.

Education Full Text (Wilson/EBSCO)

Covering a wide spectrum of subjects that relate to education, this database provides full text, as well as indexing and abstracts for several hundred periodicals, books, and yearbooks. Education Full Text brings important resources to education professionals and policy makers.

ERIC (Education Resources Information Center)

Sponsored by the Institute of Education Sciences, a part of the U.S. Department of Education, ERIC is an online database of over 1.4 million records. Dating back to 1966, ERIC covers all areas of educational research and information, and among the items indexed are journal articles, research reports, and position papers, teaching guides, instructional materials, and books. http://www.eric.ed.gov/

Google Scholar

Google Scholar provides access to many types of scholarly research. A single search across multiple disciplines locates and identifies scholarly output from academic publishers, professional societies, online repositories, universities, and websites.

JSTOR

A multidisciplinary, full-text, retrospective database, that provides access to digital, scholarly publications. At present, over 1,700 journals are represented in JSTOR.

LexisNexis Academic

Provides access to thousands of full text business, legal, medical, and general news publications. Legal research is supported by access to Shepard's Citation Service and full text content of federal and state cases and statutes, and articles in over 1500 legal journals, reviews, and newspapers. Full-text coverage of business and news journals and newspapers is available. LexisNexis Academic also provides access to transcripts from major radio and television networks, and congressional hearings.

Library Literature and Information Science (Wilson/EBSCO)

Reporting the latest trends in librarianship, this database provides full text to selected publications in the field and indexing and abstract to those publications. Conference proceedings and books are also detailed. Library Literature also addresses topics that deal with automation, censorship, and government aid.

National Center for Education Statistics (NCES) (U.S. Department of Education, Institute of Education Sciences)

The primary federal agency charged with collecting, collating, analyzing, and disseminating education data. The NCES collects domestic as well as international data. Among its publications are *The Condition of Education* and *Digest of Education Statistics.* http://nces.ed.gov/

Professional Development Collection (EBSCO)

Designed for professional educators, this database has full text to over 500 education journals. Of this number, over 350 titles are peer reviewed. Additionally, there is access to more than 200 education reports.

PsycARTICLES (American Psychological Association [APA])

A full-text database that covers all areas of psychological science, including the field of education. All of the journals published by the APA, the Canadian Psychological Association as well as English language journals from the Hogrefe Publishing Group and in the database.

PsycInfo (American Psychological Association [APA])

With over 3 million records, PsycInfo provides indexing and abstracting to research in the behavioral sciences and mental health. The publications cited are peer-reviewed and include journals, books, and dissertations.

ScienceDirect (Elsevier)

A major full-text database for peer-reviewed journals in the sciences, technology, medicine, and the social sciences. The database also provides full text chapters from more than 11,000 books.

Social Sciences Citation Index (Thomson Reuters)

A multidisciplinary database to the literature of the social sciences. Part of the *Web* of Science®, Social Sciences Citation Index provides access to over 3,000 major journals in the social sciences.

Indexes journal articles, dissertations and books that deal with aspects of sports, including sports medicine, exercise, physiology, and nutrition. The database indexes back to 1985. A full-text edition is available.

Statistical Abstract of the United States (U.S. Census)

Provides authoritative and comprehensive social, political, and economic statistical summaries of the United States from federal agencies and private organizations. In addition to statistical data, The Statistical Abstract also serves as a guide to additional sources of information. http://www.census.gov

Teacher Reference Center (EBSCO)

An index and abstracting service to approximately 280 of the most popular journals for teachers and administrators.

U.S. Department of Education

All federal assistance to education is initiated and administered by this Department. It also assists the president in implementing educational policies and laws. The Department's website provides information relative to news, data, research, best practices, grants, policies, and legislation. A searchable website is available at, http://www.ed.gov/

United States Education Dashboard

The President has set a goal that by 2020 the United States will have the highest percentage of college graduates in the world. The Dashboard, through four indicators, tracks the progress of this goal. http://dashboard.ed.gov/

APPENDICES

Appendix A: Action Verbs for Accomplishing Objectives

THE FOLLOWING VERBS ARE OFTEN FOUND IN PROPOSAL DEVELOPMENT AND ARE USED TO HELP EXPLAIN THE NATURE OF THE PROPOSED PROJECTS (Livingston, 1981)

abort	cement	desert	energize	internalize	reform
absorb	centralize	desist	engage	involve	regress
abuse	change	detain	engrave	iterate	reiterate
accent	circumvent	detect	enjoy	justify	release
acclaim	collaborate	deter	enlarge	lecture	rely
acclimate	combat	detract	enlighten	lend	render
accommodate	commemorate	deviate	enrich	lose	renew
accomplish	commence	devise	entice	magnetize	replicate
achieve	comment	devote	erode	make	represent
administer	communicate	differ	escalate	meet	retrieve
advance	compact	dig	evolve	model	sacrifice
affirm	compel	digest	exceed	moderate	seek
aid	compromise	dignity	excel	modernize	segregate
allot	conceal	dim	except	monitor	seize
allude	concentrate	dip	excerpt	motivate	sell
ameliorate	conceptualize	disable	exclaim	narrate	sensitize
animate	concoct	disagree	exclude	normalize	serialize
annex	concur	disarm	execute	nourish	simplify
annihilate	condone	discharge	exemplify	nurture	solidify
appease	confer	disclose	exempt	obfuscate	solve
appraise	confide	discount	exercise	object	soothe
approach	confirm	discourage	exert	obscure	specialize
ascend	conform	discuss	expedite	obstruct	speculate
aspire	confront	dispatch	experience	offer	stimulate
assert	congest	dispel	experiment	officiate	suggest
attain	congregate	disperse	explore	oppose	supplement
attempt	constrain	dispose	express	optimize	surpass

attest	construe	disprove	extend	pacify	surrender
attribute	consummate	dispute	extrapolate	pad	suspend
attune	contaminate	dissipate	filter	perceive	synthesize
avoid	contend	dissociate	find	perform	systematize
ban	contest	distill	force	perpetuate	take
banish	cooperate	distinguish	formulate	persist	teach
bargain	coordinate	diverge	freeze	persuade	think
barter	correlate	diversify	freshen	peruse	thrust
behave	corroborate	dominate	gauge	polarize	tolerate
benefit	counter	doubt	humanize	popularize	transcend
besiege	cultivate	dramatize	idealize	populate	transpire
bleed	cushion	drive	ignite	portray	travel
bless	cycle	dwell	imitate	proceed	trust
blot	debate	dwindle	impact	proffer	try
blur	debrief	economize	impart	program	urge
bore	decipher	educate	impede	progress	utilize
bowl	declare	elevate	impel	propagate	visualize
bridle	decontrol	elicit	implant	propel	
budge	deduce	elude	imply	quit	
buffer	defeat	embark	imprint	radiate	
bump	defend	embrace	inactivate	ratify	
burst	defer	emit	inaugurate	react	
camouflage	delegate	emphasize	incubate	reason	
campaign	deliberate	empower	infer	recap	
cannibalize	delimit	emulate	inhibit	recede	
capitulate	delineate	enable	insist	reclaim	
capsize	denote	encompass	inspire	recount	
careen	depart	encourage	install	recreate	
caress	depend	encumber	instill	rectify	
cast	depict	endeavor	institute	recur	
castigate	deplete	endorse	instruct	recycle	
cater	depreciate	endow	insure	redeem	
cause	derive	endure	integrate	refine	

Appendix B: Action Verbs for Explaining Nature of Projects

THE FOLLOWING LIST OF VERBS ARE USEFUL IN SPECIFYING WHAT IS TO BE DONE WHEN ACCOMPLISHING OBJECTIVES. WHILE THIS IS NOT AN EXHAUSTIVE LIST OF THE VERBS ONE MIGHT USE, IT INCLUDES MANY OF THOSE THAT ARE OFTEN USED, (Livingston, 1981).

abandon	certify	define	fabricate	produce
abolish	charge	deflect	facilitate	prohibit
abridge	chart	delete	fasten	project
abstain	choose	deliver	forfeit	propose
abstract	cite	demand	forgive	publish
accelerate	classify	demonstrate	fragment	qualify
accept	clean	depress	fuse	quantify
account	clear	descend	generate	question
accredit	cleave	describe	give	quote
accrue	clip	design	hold	raise
accumulate	cluster	destroy	identify	rank
acquire	codify	detach	illustrate	read
activate	collate	detail	implement	recall
adopt	collect	develop	improve	receive
adjourn	color	diagnose	increase	record
adjust	combine	diagram	inculcate	recruit
admit	come	dilute	individualize	refer
adopt	commend	diminish	inform	regulate
advise	commit	direct	initiate	reject
agree	compare	disburse	innovate	remove
align	compensate	discard	inquire	repair
alter	compete	disconnect	insert	replace
amend	compile	discover	institutionalize	reply
analyze	complete	display	introduce	report
anchor	comply	disseminate	invade	require
annotate	compose	dissolve	itemize	resign
answer	compress	distribute	keep	restore
apply	compute	divert	label	restrict
appoint	conceive	divide	leave	retain
apprise	conclude	donate	lubricate	return
approve	condemn	draw	magnify	review
arrest	condense	duplicate	manage	search

assess	confine	eliminate	map	select
assimilate	connect	employ	measure	send
assure	conserve	empty	memorize	separate
attach	consign	enact	modify	simulate
attack	constrict	enclose	nominate	specify
attract	construct	encode	notify	spend
augment	consult	enforce	obligate	submit
award	consume	enlist	observe	summarize
bend	contact	enquire	obtain	supervise
bestow	contain	enter	occupy	supply
bid	contract	equalize	organize	support
blow	copy	equip	omit	survey
break	correct	eradicate	operate	tabulate
bring	counsel	erase	originate	testify
budget	count	erect	participate	transcribe
build	cover	escape	pay	transfer
burn	create	establish	penetrate	transmit
buy	cure	estimate	permit	transplant
calculate	cut	evaluate	place	transport
cancel	decrease	examine	play	unity
capitalize	decide	exchange	point	validate
capture	decode	excuse	practice	verify
carry	decorate	expand	preclude	
care	decrease	expend	predict	
catalog	dedicate	explain	present	
catch	deduct	expose	preserve	
censure	deescalate	extract	prioritize	

Appendix C: Action Verbs that are Specific and Non-Specific

CLEAR TERMINOLOGY IS EXTREMELY IMPORTANT WHEN WRITING OBJECTIVES. SOME VERBS ARE QUITE SPECIFIC AND INDICATE WHAT IS TO BE DONE, WHILE OTHERS ARE VAGUE AND CAN BE INTERPRETED IN VARIOUS WAYS (LIVINGSTON, 1981).

EXAMPLES:

VERBS THAT ARE SPECIFIC & INDICATE WHAT WILL BE DONE	VERBS THAT ARE NON-SPECIFIC MUST BE DEFINED
ACCUMULATE	APPRECIATE
ADVISE	BELIEVE
BEND	ENJOY
CONTRAST	FEEL
COMPARE	GRASP
IDENTIFY	KNOW
MANDATE	THINK
SELECT	UNDERSTAND

Appendix D: Leadership Influences of Presidents/ Executive Administrators

President Paul Patricks, the Preservationist

Past Influenced Presidents focus on the historical foundations of the institution and the deep heritage of the African American access to higher education from the post-slavery era to the post-civil rights era. They hold strong racial-sensitive views and they remain emotionally connected to the past, specifically for African Americans, and personally appreciative to those (social, political, historical, artistic, and religious, etc.) in the past who contributed to the founding of HBCUs. To this end, they feel the need to put resources in the institution's infrastructure that anchor these historical foundations. They want to keep enrollments and employment levels based on past capacities and present capabilities; and they want the curriculum to primarily celebrate the culture and contributions of African American academicians and "Black" scholars. They get along very, very well with older alums and use traditional ways to fundraise, based on historical compassion and philanthropic sympathy. One of the Reverends on Dr. Patricks' search committee summed up the general sentiment of the committee when he stated, *"Dr. Patricks, we need you to anchor our institution's deep history and profound past. Our people gave come too far and we have worked too hard to lose what we have as part of our treasured heritage."*

President Cathy Carpenter, the Contemporarian

Present Influenced Presidents emphasize their efforts on the current state of affairs at the institution and keeping up with status quo existence. While they appreciate institutional history and heritage, they are more concerned about keeping the doors open, primarily for African Americans, in order to exist in the post desegregation era. They live in the present and deploy resources to those areas that maintain present enrollment and employment levels with little concern about immediate growth. They believe the curriculum should be responsive to the job market and faculty should teach career-ready topics so that students can graduate, get jobs, and contribute back the institution. They support enrollment and employment with other race integration but only to a certain extent. They tend to be more data-driven; management oriented and focuses on effective performance and efficient productivity with emphasis on benchmarking, processes, structures, budgets, finance, ethics, and legal issues. They are strong advocates of maintaining enrollments based on alumni and family relations at a time when more students are choosing non HBCUs over their parent's HBCU experiences. One of the faculty members on Dr. Carpenter's search committee, who was an economist, captured the essence of the committee's feelings when she stated, *"Dr. Carpenter, we need you to help us keep the doors open, the budget balanced, the students focus on learning, and get our faculty and staff paid up to the market levels that they deserve."*

President Thomas Taylor, the Transitionist

Near Future Influenced Presidents believe in moving the institution from its past and present status to the next level with an emphasis on opening the campus to other populations beyond African Americans and capturing the new cultural diversity market. They tend to be more cosmopolitan and set on increasing the enrollment, partnering with other institutions, going after external funding, creating more online classes, and working with the younger alums. Although an advocate of the arts, they particularly encourage more emphasis on science, technology, engineering, and mathematics. They believe the future of the institution is based on its ability to be well positioned in the current competitive marketplace. They also think students must graduate with the skills sets, dispositions, attitudes, knowledge bases and behaviors to be productive in the new global marketplace. They are people-oriented with accountability; believe in taking calculated risks and thinking outside the box. They think at least 5-7 years out, which they believe will be the length of their presidential tenure. They believe enrollment growth will only occur of the institution reaches out to non-African Americans and collaboration with non HBCU institutions. One of the students on Dr. Taylor's search committee commented, *"Dr. Taylor, we need you to take us to the next level for the coming decade and we want you to stay with us for next ten years to make it happen with responsible accountability."*

President Angela Anderson, the Avant-gardist

Far Future Influenced Presidents are entrepreneurial, innovative, and creative but only to the extent these areas can be benchmarked, measured, and provide evidence of effectiveness. They are strong advocates of global diversity and internationalizing the entire institution. They think 20-25 years out and recognize that they may not be around to see the benefits of their leadership. They tend not focus on the past and only the present as related to setting the foundation for the next 20-25 years. They believe in extending the campus's offerings through online classes and extended campus arrangements beyond the campus' local existence and location. They are futuristic in how they deploy resources to areas that support far-reaching, stretch goals. They believe the curriculum should focus on technology, global languages, futurism, transdisciplinary diversity, and globalization. They tend to be cutting-edge and state-of the art in thought. They believe future growth is based on global coalitions, collaborations, and strategic alliances with international partners through online, onsite, and abroad confluences of mutual benefit. They are not deemed popular given their far-reaching visions because campus stakeholders want more immediate manifestations during their stay on campus. A member of Dr. Anderson's search committee, who represented the business community warned, *"Dr Anderson, you are too late for today and too early for tomorrow. Where are we going to get the resources to carry out this vision that you have for the next 20-25 years?"*

Annotated Bibliography of Suggested Readings on Action Research for Low-Income-High Risk Students in Higher Education

(Special thanks to Paula Wingard for this compilation)

Borman, Geoffery D., et al. "Academic Success Among Poor and Minority Students." *Center for Research on the Education of Students Placed at Risk (CRESPAR).* 52 (2001): 25. Results taken from a study by CRESPAR suggest that minority students from low socio-economic status (SES) backgrounds were exposed to greater risks and fewer resilience-promoting conditions than otherwise similar low-SES White students.

Campbell, France A., and Craig T. Ramey. "Cognitive and School Outcomes for High-Risk African-American Students at Middle Adolescence: Positive Effects of Early Intervention." *American Educational Research Journal.* 32.4 (1995): 743-72. *Google Scholar Beta.* 2008. Google. 8 May 2008. Long-term intellectual and academic benefits related to early childhood educational intervention were found in a sample of students from low-income families (98% African American). <http://www.scholar.goggle.com>. Path: High-Risk African American students.

Croninger, Robert G. and Valerie E. Lee. "Social Capital and Dropping Out of High School: Benefits to At-Risk Students of Teachers' Support and Guidance." *The Teachers College Record.* 103.4 (2001): 548-81. *Google Scholar Beta.* 2008. Google. 8 May 2008. <http://www.scholar.goggle.com>. Path: Social Capital; Dropping Out of High School. Croninger and Lee find that students who come from socially disadvantaged backgrounds and who have had academic difficulties in the past find guidance and assistance from teachers especially helpful. They discuss the implications of these findings for investigations of dropping out, risk, and social capital.

"David Baker: Universities are Failing Low-Income Students." *Google.* 2008. Google. 8 May 2008. <http://www.goggle.com>. Path: David Baker; Failing Universities. Baker explains that an initiative is needed because some universities have failed to overcome the educational, cultural, social, and financial barriers that make higher education an unattractive or unconsidered option for many students.

"Do Universities Have a Role in Managing Public Schools: Lessons from the Penn Partnership Schools?" *Penn GSE Perspectives on Urban Education.*4: 6 Apr 2008 <http://www.urbanedjournal.org/>. This article asserts that schools must fundamentally rethink the ways in which they organize instructional practices; there is a need of creating accountability for learning outcomes and support to achieve them.

Downey, Douglas B., and Shana Pribesh. "When Race Matters: Teachers' Evaluations of Students' Classroom Behavior." *Sociology of Education.*

77.4 (2004): 267-82. In this article, Downey and Pribesh reveal the results of their study in "white teacher bias," and its effects on black student performance in the classroom.

Duffy, Jennifer O. "Invisibly at Risk: Low-income Students in a Middle and Upper-Class World." *Google*. 2008. Google.8 May 2008. <http://www.goggle.com>. Path: Invisibly at Risk; Low-income Students. *Wiley Interscience*. <http://www3.interscience.wiley.com/ journal/>. Women's studies programs, multicultural centers, and organizations to support gay, lesbian, bisexual, and transgender students are campus fixtures. Duffy asserts few now question diversity's contribution to the education of all students. Jennifer Duffy suggests that it is time to acknowledge, support, and celebrate one more form of diversity that is mostly hidden: *social class*.

Flores, Margaret M. and Maria Kaylor. "The Effects of a Direct Instruction Program on the Fraction Performance of Middle School Students At-Risk for Failure in Mathematics." *High Beam*. 2007. Encyclopedia. 28 May 2008 <http://www.encyclopedia.com/doc/1G-166050229.html.> This article investigated the effects of a Direct Instruction program implemented with middle school students identified as at-risk for failure in mathematics.

Green, Susan K., et al. "Peer Tutoring, Individualized Intervention, and Progress Monitoring with At-Risk Second-Grade Readers." *Preventing School Failure*. Green and others examine the effect on at-risk second graders of twice weekly peer-tutoring sessions with repeated readings combined with once per week tutoring by a college student.

Henderson-Sparks, Joan, et al. "Student Teacher Preparation: A Collaborative Model to Assist At-Risk Students." *Preventing School Failure*. 46.2 (2002):80-5. Henderson-Sparks and other scholars evaluate the various types of at-risk students, in addition to providing statistics and other studies; a collaborative method is given in student teacher preparation in dealing with at-risk students.

Jones, Dionne J. and Betty Collier Watson. "High Risk Students and Higher Education: Future Trends. ERIC Digest." *ERIC*. 1990. ED325033. <*http://*www.eric.ed.gov/>. *Google Scholar Beta*. 2008. Google. 8 May 2008. <http://www.scholar.goggle.com>. Path: High Risk Students, Higher Education. Jones and Watson examine the increasing enrollment of high-risk students-minorities, females, low-income, and disabled individuals that is expected to continue into the 21st century.

"Keeping Low Income Students Out of College." Online Posting. 18 Oct. 2007. College Scholarships Blog. 8 May 2008. <http://www.collegescholarships.org/blog/2007/10/18/keeping-low-income-students-out-of-college/>.*Google Scholar Beta*. 2008. Google. 8 May 2008. <http://www.scholar.goggle.com>. Path: Keeping Low Income Students Out of College. This article examines a popular theory: more and more free money will put more disadvantaged and minority students into college and solve the problem of low college attendance rates among high poverty students; higher education continues to throw at low-income students, the numbers actually attending college and staying in college remain low.

Khattri, Nidhi, et al. "Students at Risk in Poor, Rural Areas: A Review of the Research." *National Institute on the Education of At-Risk Students.* (1997): 2-44. Khattri and others review the research on rural education and at-risk students to determine the relative influence on student outcomes of poverty and community location.

Kulik, Chen-Lin C., et al. "College Programs for High Risk and Disadvantaged Students: A Meta-Analysis of Findings." *Review of Educational Research.* 53.5 (1983): 397-414. *Google Scholar Beta.* 2008. Google. 8 May 2008. <http://www.scholar.goggle.com>. Path: High Risk, Low-Income Students. This meta-analytic synthesis of findings from 60 evaluation studies showed that special college programs for high-risk students have had basically positive effects on students. High-risk students who enrolled in such programs stayed in college somewhat longer than control students did, and they received somewhat better grades in regular college work

Laffey, James M, et al. "Supporting Learning and Behavior of At-Risk Young Children: Computers in Urban Education." *Journal of Research on Technology in Education.* 35.4 (2003):423-40. Laffey and other scholars examine implementing technology as part of urban school reform effort. The article examines the potential of Interactive Computer Technology (ICT) to contribute to learning and behavior problems.

Legum, Harry L. "Impact of a Career Intervention on At-Risk Middle School Students' Career Maturity Levels, Academic Achievement, and Self-Esteem." *Professional School Counseling* (2004):11. 9 May 2008 <http://findarticles.com/>. Legum assesses the effects of a 9-week career intervention program on at-risk middle school students' career maturity levels, self-esteem, and academic achievement.

Manlove, Jennifer. "The Influence of High School Dropout and School Disengagement on the Risk of School-Age Pregnancy." *Journal of Research on Adolescence.*8.2 (1998): 187-220. *Google Scholar Beta.* 2008. Google. 8 May 2008. <http://www.scholar.goggle.com>. Path: Influence of High School Dropout. Using data from a recent longitudinal cohort of 8th graders, Manlove found that factors relevant to teens' school experiences—including characteristics of their school and classroom, their family background, and individual engagement—were associated with the risk of school-age pregnancy leading to a live birth.

Ornelles, Cecily. "Providing Classroom-Based Intervention to At-Risk Students to Support Their Academic Engagement and Interactions with Peers." *Preventing School Failure.* 51.4 (2007): 3-11. Ornelles uses a multiple baseline design to evaluate the effects of a structured intervention on the engagement and initiations of 3 children identified as at-risk for school difficulty.

Podoll, Sue, and Darcy Randle. "Building a Virtual High School...Click by Click." *T.H.E. Journal.* 33.2 (2005): 4. *EBSCOHOST.* Jackson State U Lib. 7 May 2008 <http://www.ebscohost.com>. To provide quality education, South Dakota's Rapid City Academy provides smaller student-teacher ratios, individualized learning plans, strategy-based learning, flexible schedules, and independent and group-led classed.

"Reauthorization of the Higher Education Act." *Google.* 2008. Google. 8 May 2008. <http://www.scholar.goggle.com>. Path: Reauthorization of the Higher Education Act. Office of Post-Secondary Education. <http://www.ed.gov/offices/OPE/PPI/Reauthor/index.html>. General listing of archived information on priorities of previous administrations.

Reyes, Olga and Leonard A. Jason. "Pilot Study Examining Factors Associated with Academic Success for Hispanic High School Students." *Journal of Youth and Adolescence.* 22.1 (1993): 157-71. *Google Scholar Beta.* 2008. Google. 8 May 2008. <http://www.scholar.goggle.com>. Path: Academic Success for Hispanic High School Students. This study examines characteristics that distinguish succeeding and failing Hispanic students at an inner-city high school. While research on this topic has historically focused on dropouts, this study seeks to better understand successful high school students.

Reynolds, Arthur J., et al. "Long-Term Effects of an Early Childhood Intervention on Educational Achievement and Juvenile Arrest: A 15-Year Follow-up of Low-Income Children in Public Schools." *Journal of the American Medical Association.* 285.18 (2001). *Google Scholar Beta.* 2008. Google. 8 May 2008. <http://www.scholar.goggle.com>. Path: Low Income, High Risk students. Reynolds determines the long-term effectiveness of a federal center-based preschool and school–based intervention program for urban low-income children.

Rumberger, Russell W. and Katherine A. Larson. "Student Mobility and the Increased Risk of High School Dropout." *American Journal of Education.*107 (1998). *Google Scholar Beta.* 2008. Google. 8 May 2008. <http://www.scholar.goggle.com>. Path: African American Students; High Risk Students.

Sledge, J.R., and P. Morehead. "Tolerated Failure or Missed Opportunities and Potentials for Teacher Leadership in Urban Schools?" *Current Issues in Education.* 9.3 (2006): 1-14. Sledge and Moorhead examine the existing role of teacher leaders while addressing many of the missed opportunities for teacher leaders to impact student achievement.

St. John, Edward P. "What Really Influences Minority Attendance? Sequential Analyses of the High School and Beyond Sophomore Cohort." *Research in Higher Education.* 32.2 (1991): 141-158.*Google Scholar Beta.* 2008. Google. 8 May 2008. <http://www.scholar.goggle.com>. Path: African American Students; High Risk Students. St. John examines three factors that are identified that can potentially improve college attendance by minority students: improved academic preparation in elementary and high school, increased aspirations for higher levels of educational attainment, and increased levels of financial aid.

Suh, Suhyun, et al. "Predictors of Categorical At-Risk High School Dropouts." *Journal of Counseling and Development*.85 (2007): 196-203. Scholars provide key contributing factors to school dropout among 3 categories of at-risk students: low grade point averages, suspension, and low socioeconomic backgrounds.

The Education Trust. 2007. 8 May 2008. <http://www2.edtrust.org/edtrust/>.
Google Scholar Beta. 2008. Google. 8 May 2008. <http://www.scholar.goggle.com>. Path: Teaching High-Risk students, Low Income; Higher Education.

INDEX

A

Action Research, 28, 30, 149, 154, 178, 190, 197, 205, 243, 244, 245, 246, 258
actionable knowledge, 27
administration, 149, 160, 161, 181, 205, 220, 234, 235
African-American Literature, 173
Allee, V., 198, 243
American Association for Higher Education, 31
analyze data, 181

B

Barkley, E.F., 197, 243
Black Literature, 184, 185, 190, 191, 195
Blackburn, Gus, 214
brainstorming, 30, 144, 145, 146, 223, 225
Bridgeland, J., 26, 246
Brighton, C., 28, 243
Brooks, Rashid, 210, 213, 214
Brown, Nakeesha. *See* Pickens, Nakeesha (Brown)
Burton, Clark, 24, 29, 243

C

Cambridge, B., 31, 243, 246
campus-wide stakeholder, 203
Caruthers, Samuel, 217
Catholic, 234, 235
Cheyenne State, 226, 227
Chong, Michael, 217, 218
Christian, 235
Clark, Burton, 24
collaborative, 25, 28, 30, 31, 32, 171, 193, 195, 197, 198, 200, 202, 204, 210, 211, 215, 216, 219, 226, 230, 231, 234, 237, 259
collect data, 153, 181, 182
Color Purple, 184
Cooper, M., 26, 245
cooperative, 148, 151, 164, 165, 170, 184, 188, 193, 194, 195, 196, 197, 202
cooperative learning, 170
cooperative sharing, 170
Cotton, Federico, 215
Cox, M., 243
critical thinking, 144, 145, 214, 215, 216, 217
Crookes, G., 243
Cross, P.K., 197, 243
curriculum, 25, 30, 149, 150, 165, 166, 167, 183, 197, 199, 200, 206, 214, 215, 217, 230, 232, 233, 234, 236

D

data collection, 154, 177, 185, 190
data feedback, 182
dean, 150, 174, 197, 200, 201, 212, 213, 214, 215, 217, 234, 237
democratic, 25, 151, 197
department chair, 197, 200, 201, 202
Diulio, J. Jr., 26
DMU (decision making units), 200
documents, 165

E

Education, 26, 30, 226, 243, 244, 245, 246, 258, 259, 260, 261, 262, 267
elementary school, 26, 262
Ellison, Ralph, 184, 188, 189, 190
English Composition, 173, 174, 175, 176, 179
English Proficiency Writing, 173, 174, 176, 179, 180
Esposito, J., 29, 243
ethics, 167
Eudora Welty Institute, 222
faculty counselor, 199
focus group formal interviews, 162
focus group informal interviews, 161

F

Follet, Mary P., 243
force field analysis, 144, 146

G

Galileo's Law School, 214
Gilbert, Ashley, 215
Google, 171, 258, 259, 260, 261, 262
graduate school, 26, 172, 174, 185, 207
Green, Samantha, 28, 206, 246, 259
group processes, 197, 245
group work, 150, 189, 190

H

high school, 26, 172, 200, 261, 262
Hiller, 29
Hispanic, 217, 261
Hopson, Dr. Roberta, 174, 176, 177
Horne, Walter, 181, 184, 187, 188, 190, 191, 193, 195

I

interviews, 160, 211
inventories, 154
Invisible Man, 184, 187, 188, 189

J

Jackson State University, 25, 200, 244, 267
Jameson, J., 29, 244
Jeremiah College, 210, 211, 212, 214

K

K-12, 25, 29, 30, 197, 267
knowledge management, 23, 26, 28, 200

L

Lewin, Kurt, vi, 180, 244
Likert scale, 155, 158, 159, 208, 214, 235

M

Maddirala, 200, 244
Major, C.H., 197, 243
mature higher educator, 144
Mercy Catholic Academy, 234
Middendorf, J., 198, 244
Mississippi Valley State University, 25
Morrison, Toni, 184, 188, 190
Muslim, 217, 219, 220, 221, 222
Muslim-American, 219, 220, 221

N

Native Son, 184

O

Observant Participation, 163

observations, 162, 163, 164, 165, 170, 183, 204, 213, 218, 219, 231, 237
One-on-One Collaboration, 199
one-on-one informal interviews, 160
open-ended questions, 158
opinionnaires, 154
organizational learning, 23, 25

P

Pace, D., 198, 244
Pembroke University, 217
Pickens, Nakeesha (Brown), 172, 173, 174, 176, 177, 193
Pierce, Jessica, 217
Poindexter, Xenia, 214
postsecondary education, 26
Proactive Action Research, 28, 152, 169
problem solving, 146, 147, 148, 150, 151, 154, 170, 172, 195, 196, 213, 220, 221, 226, 231
psychological, 142, 147, 153, 169, 194, 195

Q

qualitative data, 28, 32, 153, 154
quantitative data, 28, 154
questionnaires, 154, 155, 156

R

reflection, 141, 142, 146, 150
Responsive Action Research, 28, 152, 180
Riordan, T., 198, 244
Roots, 184
ROTC, 184
Roth, J., 198, 244

S

Sagor, 30, 245
Schmuck, Richard, 267

Schon, 29, 245
self confrontation, 144
Self-Knowledge, 142
Shadow and Act, 188, 189
Sinclair, Raymond, 215
situation-target-path (STP) concepts, 144, 145
Smith, Jorge, 29, 206, 243
Southeastern State University, 230
Strasburg, Ernesto, 217
Structured Observations, 164
supportive communication, 193, 195

T

Technology Enhancement Instrument (TEI), 231
Tesch, 28
Thomas, R. Murray, 171, 245
Tobias College, 217, 218, 219, 220, 222
town and gown, 204, 226
traditional research, 147, 193
transcultural, 197
transdisciplinary, 197, 199, 237
transnational, 197

U

University of Queensland, 30

W

Wisker, 29, 32, 246
writers' workshop, 170, 175, 176, 177, 178, 179, 180, 181
Writers' Workshop, 174, 175, 176, 194
Wyner, J., 26, 246

Y

Yahoo, 171

Z

Zuber-Skerritt, O., 30, 246

ABOUT THE AUTHORS

Joseph Martin Stevenson and **Richard A. Schmuck** are teaching and research professors in the world's first Executive Ph.D. program in urban higher education, Jackson State University (JSU), Jackson, Mississippi. Richard has been a visiting professor and executive in residence. Joseph is the founder, professor, and executive director. Richard is Professor Emeritus, University of Oregon, after serving on the faculties of Michigan, California at Santa Barbara, Temple, and Leuven in Belgium. Before Jackson State University, he was a visiting scholar at Arizona State University West. Richard is a social psychologist, expert in action research, group processes, and organization development, all applied both to K-12 and higher education. Richard has been a true friend, colleague, and mentor for HBCUs. Richard was a "freedom rider" in the Deep South and is the recipient of the *2010 Lifetime Achievement Award* of the International Association for the Study of Cooperation in Education. Richard represents the best of humanitarian-scholarship, transcending from the HEART, to the head, to the hand. Joseph has both K-12 and higher education leadership experiences in both public and private sectors. Joseph was born at Meharry Medical College and was raised on the campus of Fisk University, only a few blocks from Tennessee State University. He has served as a university provost at Jackson State and Mississippi Valley State Universities and on the faculty of Tougaloo College. He has lectured on strategic leadership and knowledge management at Tuskegee University, consulted for Alabama State University and Morgan State University, and has written commentaries on HBCUs for *Diverse Education* and the *Chronicle of Higher Education*. As a Kellogg Leadership Fellow, he served in the Office of the President at Howard University and as a Visiting Provost in Residence for the National Association for Equal Opportunity in Higher Education (NAFEO) in Washington, D.C. He was given the "Outstanding Leadership Award" by the Thurgood Marshall Fund. As a Subject Matter Expert, he surveyed scientific research capacity for the Department of Defense and the Technology Management Training Group at Chicago State University, Dillard University, North Carolina A &T State University, and other minority-serving institutions of higher learning in Florida, California, and Texas. He has completed postdoctoral and executive education at Carnegie Mellon, Vanderbilt, Harvard, Stanford, Yale, and Tulane.

Debra A. Buchanan is a 30-year higher education administrator. She is a native of the Mississippi Delta, a graduate of Charleston High School and Mississippi Valley State University. She has earned graduate degrees in counseling and higher education. Debra wan an employee of Jackson State University from 1995 to 2014. While at JSU, she served in various administrative roles including associate dean of students and housing director, assistant to the vice president of student life and director of the Ronald E. McNair Post-baccalaureate Achievement Program, vice provost of student life, executive director of academic and student life assessment and program accreditation, facilitator of university strategic planning, executive director of the writing center, and the executive director of the Center for Distance Learning and Instructional Technology. As a member of the graduate faculty, Dr. Buchanan has taught statistics and the history of higher education to community educators pursing degrees in Jackson State's graduate teaching programs in the College of Education and Human Development. By virtue of her leadership and success in these various positions, she has established an outstanding reputation for professional and successful performance.

Melissa L. Druckrey was appointed the dean of libraries at Jackson State University by Joseph Martin Stevenson during his tenure as provost at the institution. She has assisted him on several research initiatives concerning higher education futures, HBCUs, dissertation quality and advancement in science, technology, engineering, and mathematics. Melissa attended Jackson State College with an interest in liberal arts. She later received her MLS, with a concentration in academic libraries, from the University of Southern Mississippi and the PhD in urban higher education from the College of Education and Human Development at Jackson State University. Melissa has particular expertise in locating academic data bases, information resources, and knowledge management repositories for higher education decision-making by administrators, doctoral students, and faculty.

Jeton McClinton has more than 15 years of experience in instructional technology, distance education delivery and development with extensive experience in e-learning systems and methodologies. Her research background has focused on creating effective change in graduate education with particular attention to effectiveness and efficiency with technology integration. Her research interest includes qualitative research methods and design, faculty professional development, student learning styles in electronic environments, the utility of non-traditional students in a knowledge driven society and patterns of social interaction, discourse, and cognitive processing in electronic environments. Dr. McClinton She also holds significant academic scholarship credentials with research experience in both educational technology, leadership development and distance education fields. The synergy of these two areas help profile Dr. McClinton as an innovator, highly-driven and committed to quality and growth in her workplace.

Karen Wilson-Stevenson, CFRE, EMBA is a higher education and nonprofit executive with more than 40 years of experience in advising academic and other leadership on developing analyses, strategies, policies, resources, and initiatives to improve equity and effectiveness in education. Within that time Ms. Wilson-Stevenson has also raised more than $300 million to support a variety of institutions and causes with which she has been affiliated. Karen is a graduate of

Case Western Reserve University where she earned her baccalaureate in Paleopathology. She received an Executive MBA from the University of Maryland University College and a diploma from the Universiteit Antwerpen in Business/European Emphasis. Karen is currently completing her Executive PhD in Urban Higher Education at Jackson State University and is the author of THEORRY for undergraduate students, as well as a co-author of HEART & SOUL, Neurodiversity Within A Divided Nation, and several other publications.

www.ingramcontent.com/pod-product-compliance
Lightning Source LLC
Chambersburg PA
CBHW052104230426
43671CB00011B/1933